Management for Professionals

The Springer series *Management for Professionals* comprises high-level business and management books for executives. The authors are experienced business professionals and renowned professors who combine scientific background, best practice, and entrepreneurial vision to provide powerful insights into how to achieve business excellence.

More information about this series at http://www.springer.com/series/10101

Nick Shannon • Bruno Frischherz

Metathinking

The Art and Practice of Transformational Thinking

Springer

Nick Shannon
Management Psychology Ltd.
London, England

Bruno Frischherz
Didanet GmbH
Luzern, Switzerland

ISSN 2192-8096 ISSN 2192-810X (electronic)
Management for Professionals
ISBN 978-3-030-41063-6 ISBN 978-3-030-41064-3 (eBook)
https://doi.org/10.1007/978-3-030-41064-3

This Springer imprint is published by the registered company Springer Nature Switzerland AG
The registered company address is: Gewerbestrasse 11, 6330 Cham, Switzerland

Foreword

I greet with great appreciation, inspiration and optimism this powerful work that you are about to read. It seems to me that the core commitment of the authors is to "Studying Thinking in Action". By bringing this commitment together with a huge amount of hard work, Shannon and Frischherz have made a great leap forward in the integration of the theory and practice of dialectical thinking in a world that, as they make clear in their introduction, desperately needs it.

First, they provide an accessible summary of the complementarity of what they differentiate as logical versus dialectical thinking. Whilst accessible, it reflects well their immersion in the complex history of efforts to conceptualise dialectical thinking as both a philosophical and a psychological phenomenon. Then, they put front and centre the tension that the book addresses: on the one hand, the vast majority of the world's educational traditions have put much greater emphasis on the logical, which focuses on organising an assumed-to-be-fixed reality, than on the dialectical, which focuses on the processes by which transformations occur, and the potential roles of the human thought and action in such transformations. At the same time, the increased pace of transformation in natural, technological and social structures and processes make increasingly intense the need for humans to think dialectically to understand and deal with such transformation.

Whilst adult development as an area of psychology has continued to grow rapidly since I published *Dialectical Thinking and Adult Development* in 1984, the development of thinking in adulthood, to my mind, remains of vital importance but under-researched. So I am pleased that the conception of dialectical thinking as (1) a level and form of organisation of thought and (2) identifiable by patterned moves-in-thought, that I advanced and explored in my own research and publications has been built upon and taken forward some thirty years later to form the basis of a book that aims to stimulate thinking about thinking. Dialectical thought has been present in Western philosophy since pre-Socratic times and in Eastern philosophy for even longer and is also clearly represented in the intellectual histories of almost every academic discipline. Shannon and Frischherz show us how dialectical thinking can be used as a tool to help adults come to terms with, and find solutions to, problems in which increasing numbers of people are experiencing increasing complexity. Although I first came to recognise dialectical thinking as a set of "family resemblances" that were noticeable among world outlooks across philosophy and specific disciplines, Shannon and Frischherz take a huge step forward in differentiating and integrating "a set of thinking modes" that people can apply alongside the tools of logical thinking. This conception is central to their filling an important gap between the abstract nature and the practical application of models of dialectic.

Central to this work is the concept of *Metathinking*. The concept itself suggests the possibility of people being able to choose among thinking approaches. We can first ask what modes of thinking are most useful for framing the problem at hand, and then explore to what extent those modes facilitate solutions to the problem. In introducing Metathinking, the authors lay out in a systematic, and again accessible way, a menu of various modes of thinking we can choose among and ultimately integrate in framing and addressing problems. This menu is not only useful as a reminder of our options, but the menu is equally valuable from an educational/developmental/consulting perspective in detecting "what is missing?" If a mode of framing a problem is absent from the repertoire of an individual, an organisation, or a policy-maker or policy-making body, this will inevitably pose a limitation on the problem-solving process. One primary audience for this book is those who see themselves as facilitators of more practically effective problem-solving, and the authors have provided a technique for such would-be facilitators to discover the growing edges to which they must pay attention to succeed in their aspirations.

The practical intent of this book is didactic—to provide the reader with the means to become a more complete thinker. The authors' efforts to immerse themselves in a history of abstract writings and to present what they have studied in a systematic way that makes its usefulness in practice clear constitutes an essential first step. But central to their great leap forward is their use of case studies. Looking at four very different levels of human socio-cognitive process, they draw on the same framework and the same methods of analysis for facilitators and participants alike to discover pathways to progress. They further put at our disposal a set of what they call "mind-opening questions". Having demonstrated several practical examples of the application of modes of dialectical thinking, the final part of this book provides a broad set of exercises designed to stimulate a kind of thinking in readers that might enable them to integrate different perspectives and to see reality in a manner that transcends some of the limitations of more formalistic logic. The authors have laid it all out there and now it is up to us—researchers and facilitators, to build on their work by studying, teaching, facilitating and practising dialectical thinking with different groups of people addressing the most salient problems in their lives and work.

I envision a wide range of audiences who will find this work as exciting and clarifying as I did. I hope we will all make direct use, in various areas of our lives, of the tools Shannon and Frischherz provide. But if you are not sure if you're ready to embark on this effort, you might want to start by looking over Chap. 13. It provides the authors' summary of their rich case studies and the lessons that they believe can be learned from this case analysis method and process. I applaud my colleagues taking on this challenge and successfully linking the theory and practice of dialectical thinking, as well as providing us such a broad suite of tools for carrying forward this work. Enjoy!!!

Boston, MA, USA Prof. Michael Basseches

Preface

We are very happy to present our book about *Metathinking* to the readers. We have been working on this book for three years. The collaboration between a psychologist from England and a linguist and philosopher from Switzerland was a dialectical process in which we both learned a lot about each other's way of thinking, language and culture. We hope that the synthesis has been successful.

We would like to take this opportunity to thank various people:

- Michael Basseches and Otto Laske for their fundamental ideas about dialectical thinking passed on to us in books and workshops;
- Iva Vurdelja, Brendan Cartmel, Thomas Jordan and Oliver Robinson for their valuable comments on previous versions of the text;
- Nitza Jones-Sepulveda for the positive cooperation with Springer;
- our wives Lorna and Barbara, who have always supported us in this three-year writing process with encouragement and help.

And now we wish you, our readers, an inspiring and enjoyable read.

London, England — Nick Shannon
Luzern, Switzerland — Bruno Frischherz

Contents

List of Figures

List of Tables

1 Introduction

How can you become a better thinker? This is the question that this book seeks to answer. You may already have the view that there is not much that people can do to change the quality of their thinking and that it's just something that is fixed. But we invite you to look back over your life and to consider how your thinking might have changed since you were younger. Do you see the world today just as you did several years ago? We suspect not. You may also consider that you have already learned how to be a "good enough" thinker. That would have been, after all, the purpose of those years that you put in studying at school and perhaps at university. And yet, we all know what it is like to be faced with an intractable problem or difficult choice. We are all prone to making mistakes and finding ourselves changing our minds. It is said commonly that we are today living in a "VUCA" world, where "VUCA" stands for volatile, uncertain, complex and ambiguous, and it is argued that the pace of change is accelerating. Whilst it is hard to prove the claim that our generation is experiencing more change in our lifetimes than previous generations, certainly the combined forces of rapid technological development, business globalisation and the instant communication of information provided by the Internet have created an environment where the social structures and systems that we once saw as very stable are being overturned and becoming increasingly complex.

Thinking is an activity in which we are continually engaged from morning to night and perhaps even whilst we are sleeping. It is central to human existence. In his book, "Thinking, fast and slow" the Nobel prize winner, Daniel Kahneman, distinguishes what he calls "System 1 and System 2" thinking.[1] System 1 "quick" thinking is largely automatic and unconscious, for example, when we know

[1] Kahneman (2011).

N. Shannon and B. Frischherz, *Metathinking*, Management for Professionals,
https://doi.org/10.1007/978-3-030-41064-3_1

instantly the answer to a problem without knowing how we know it. Some people describe this as intuition. By contrast System 2 "slow" thinking is what we commonly describe as thinking. It takes the form of a conscious, deliberative process. Typically, we find ourselves engaged in some form of internal dialogue, exploring, analysing, structuring and transforming information in order to make a decision, to communicate with someone else or to come to a conclusion. Kahneman argues plausibly that whilst we might like to consider ourselves as rational System 2 thinkers, we are, in fact, beholden to System 1. Operating our System 2 thinking is slow, hard work, and many of us do not have the appetite to pursue it, especially when the answers we seek are hard to find. System 2 is also vulnerable to error because most of the information that comes to it is filtered by System 1 and is therefore inaccurate and incomplete. Our perceptions become our reality, and our perceptions are generated in the moment by System 1. Kahneman hypothesises that System 1 has been designed from evolutionary necessity to take short cuts and to come to quick conclusions, using what he calls "heuristics" or rules of thumb. These heuristics introduce many biases into our thinking, leading to decision-making processes that are far from perfect rationality.

In this book, we want to advance the idea that, despite its flaws, the human mind has a very important trick up its sleeve, one that Kahneman underplays. That trick is the process of *reflective thinking*. We have the capacity to examine our own thoughts and from there to "rethink" them. For example, you might say to yourself as you read this. "I am thirsty". With a moment to reflect on that statement, you might add more accurately perhaps "I have the feeling that I am thirsty". And with further reflection, you might even go so far as to say "I have noticed that I am having the feeling that I am thirsty". At each subsequent stage, you have built on your original thought, transforming it in the process from a simple statement of thirst to one that is about the process of becoming aware of your feeling of thirstiness. It is this process of reflecting on your own thought processes to which we draw your attention throughout this book, because by noticing your thinking you have the capacity to change your thinking. We call this process "Metathinking". Using Kahneman's terminology, it might also be called "System 3" thinking. More specifically, this book is designed to help you recognise what is missing from your thinking currently and, from there, to become a stronger, deeper thinker. We don't pretend that this is necessarily an instantaneous or easy project on which to embark. As Kahneman notes, overcoming System 1 thinking is difficult. And yet, an awareness of how one is thinking and how else one might think creates the possibility not only of correcting for any bias or missing ideas, but also for opening one's mind to alternative possibilities.

This book, then, is an attempt to redress the balance by helping readers identify the patterns in their thinking and expand their thought processes by choosing alternatives. It is intended for the general reader with an interest in developing a broader toolkit of thinking skills with which to deal with the increasing complexity of today's world. In it, we will introduce you to a framework of thinking tools that we loosely label "dialectical thinking" to distinguish them from the "logical thinking" that is the hallmark of what psychologists call the "Formal Operational

Stage" of cognitive development. This stage, first recognised by the Swiss psychologist Jean Piaget, is characterised by the systematic use of rules of deduction using abstract concepts.[2] For example, a manager of a sales team in an organisation might reason that in order to improve the performance of the team, he needs to set goals and reward people for the attainment of such goals. He would assume, logically, that he would get more of the behaviour that he rewarded. However, he might not necessarily anticipate that there might also be some unintended consequences, such as the extent to which some people take short cuts to achieve their targets and do so in a way that fails to achieve the objective of the targets. In the case of a sales team, this might take the form of price discounting to a level that resulted in more sales but less overall profit. By applying the framework of dialectical thinking modes and thought patterns when considering problems, you will become able to "open your mind" to such unintended consequences and to develop more sophisticated solutions to such problems. Whilst Piaget's investigations into cognitive development stopped at the formal operational stage, we believe that you will discover in yourself a more advanced and complete stage of thinking.

At the same time, we have to admit that the mind's capacity to operate on itself creates something of a paradox. How, for example, can we use a tool to investigate how the tool itself operates? How can the tool stand apart from itself and how, if the tool is subject to error, can we be confident that whatever the tool reveals about itself is correct? We don't pretend that we have the answer to this conundrum, but there are perhaps two ways forward. Firstly, you can read what follows for yourself and see if it makes sense and is useful to you in some way. Secondly, you can engage in some of the exercises with another person, entering into dialogue and exploring each other's thinking. We guarantee you will be fascinated by what you can discover about the way your different minds operate.

The book is structured into three parts, which we consider loosely as theory (the why), application (the what) and practice (the how). Our aim is to give you the practical tools you need to become a deeper, more complete thinker. In the first part, we set out a theoretical framework for more developed thinking. To begin with, we describe a conversation between two executives who think differently about the subject of data privacy. We then illustrate the distinction between two types of thinking, logical and dialectical thinking, with examples. We argue that awareness of the type of thinking that a person is using and an understanding of different ways to think can lead a person to a more complete, satisfying and powerful view of the reality that surrounds them. Drawing on scholarly work by Michael Basseches, Otto Laske and Roy Bhaskar, we outline four dialectical thinking "modes" and twelve thought patterns that comprise a framework of ways to view reality in a way that can help people to understand their world and the problems they face. We show how the conscious use of such a framework provides people with tools for thinking that transcend the perspective that logical thinking alone can confer.

The second part of the book—application—is devoted to a set of case studies from a variety of professional disciplines where we set out how the use of the

[2] Piaget (1936).

complete set of thought patterns can transform people's thinking about a particular complex problem. This part will show you the benefits of applying what you can learn by becoming an accomplished "Metathinker". We have chosen studies at four different levels of analysis, individual, team, organisation and society, in order to demonstrate that Metathinking can be applied in a whole variety of different contexts. If you are a coach, you may be interested in the individual case study on Sonja, a product development engineer in a pharmaceutical company in transition to being a manager. The case identifies how her thinking developed over the course of four years. If you are a manager, you may be interested in the case study on a senior management team as they set about exploring the sources of their resilience over a two-day workshop. If you are leading an organisation or consulting to one that is contemplating some form of transformation, you should find it interesting to read the organisational case study that looks at several perspectives on enacting a digital transformation. And if you are a policy-maker and interested in health care, you may want to read the final case study about the differences in thinking about national healthcare systems.

In the final part of the book, we present a broad variety of Metathinking exercises to help you to develop and practice transforming your thinking. These exercises are organised along two dimensions, breadth and depth. The breadth axis will take you from learning to identify new thought patterns in the written or spoken words of other people, to reflecting on your use of the thought patterns and then finally to applying them in novel ways. The depth axis will take you from learning four modes of dialectical thinking, to learning a set of twelve thought patterns (three for each mode). You are welcome to dip in and out of the exercises as you think fit or to work through them systematically. Depending on your situation, you may find some exercises more relevant than others. In order to simplify your choice, we have set out three different sets of exercises for organisational leaders and policy-makers, coaches and mentors, and researchers and teachers. You will be able to find answers to some of the exercises in the appendix.

We conclude by linking Metathinking with leadership. Here, we consider that the first act of leaders is to transform their thinking about reality and create a new vision. They then act on their environment to bring that vision into reality. The Metathinking process enables you to develop your vision and to see how it might be brought about. Finally, we discuss how the Metathinking Framework itself might be developed. Ours is not the last work on Metathinking, nor should it be. But if we have somehow enabled you to gain more insight, or solve a particular problem that was troubling you, or even avoid making some kind of error, we will consider that this book has done its job.

References

Kahneman, D. (2011). *Thinking, fast and slow*. New York: Farrar, Straus and Giroux.
Piaget, J. (1936). *Origins of intelligence in the child*. London: Routledge & Kegan Paul.

Part I
What is Metathinking?

Types of Thinking

2

A Discussion Between Two People

Imagine for a moment a conversation between two executives in a large multi-national insurance company. They are talking about future strategy and the possibilities for their business emerging as the result of new technologies. Their company offers insurance to private clients for their homes, vehicles, travel and health. Gerry is an American based in Atlanta in the USA, while Jean is Belgian and works from Brussels. Gerry has an exciting vision which he starts to outline as follows:

> "Jean, a whole new realm of possibilities is opening up for our business. We now have the capability to know more about our clients than ever before. Think of it! Supposing we were to gather data from a customer by accessing their medical records, exercise routines, dietary preferences, credit history, car journeys, and leisure interests we could predict with much better accuracy the likelihood of them having an accident, falling ill, or making a claim for a travel related problem. We could know everything about their physical fitness, maybe even their genetic susceptibility to certain diseases."
>
> Jean is more cautious, "Yes, I see what you are saying. That's much better than relying on the demographic profiles we depend on currently, but how would we ever get all that information and integrate it?"
>
> "Jean, the data is there already!" exclaims Gerry. "We just have to grab it and collate it. Our clients have phones that track their movements, watches that monitor their health, and they post their travel plans on Facebook and Instagram, and make their bookings through Expedia. Not to mention all the data collected by their use of store loyalty cards and shopping records on Amazon. We can make inferences about the kind of personality they have from their posts on social media and the posts from other people that

N. Shannon and B. Frischherz, *Metathinking*, Management for Professionals,
https://doi.org/10.1007/978-3-030-41064-3_2

they like. We can even draw up a profile of them from their social networks and use that to sell them all sorts of add on products."

"Well, I acknowledge all of what you say Gerry" replies Jean. "But here in Europe we have data protection laws that complicate matters somewhat. The EU recently brought into force a new regulation called the GDPR (General Data Protection Regulations). Companies are banned from collecting data for one reason and then using it for another. You can get fined heavily if you do that over here, isn't it the same in the USA?"

"Not exactly. Overall, companies are not allowed to use deceptive acts and practices. In fact, the Federal Trade Commission has managed to fine Google and Facebook for doing just that in recent years. But providing companies are careful they can get round the rules and, in any case, the fines are minimal compared to the potential profits. Facebook seems to have escaped serious sanctions when it passed on its users' data to political parties both here in the USA and, closer to you, over in Britain where it transferred data to a company called Cambridge Analytica which was then used to influence voters in a referendum. But that's not what we are trying to do. My research hasn't shown up any legal reason across all fifty states in the USA why we could not do as I am suggesting." responded Gerry.

"Goodness" says Jean "I had no idea of the differences between the EU and the USA in this respect. But let's think this through for a moment, doesn't personal data belong to the person which it identifies? Shouldn't they have rights over how it is used?"

"Well, you could argue that but on the other hand, isn't it simpler to think of it like this? You own what you create or what you pay for that someone else has created. When someone uses an 'app' or puts data on-line through a commercial website, the business that owns the app or the website has, in effect, collected the data in exchange for providing a service to the person, often at no cost to the individual themselves, so they should be able to benefit. Doesn't it seem reasonable that they should have the right to use the data that people put in the public realm anyway? Essentially they have paid for it, so they should own it."

"Ah, in Europe we see a somewhat bigger picture" responded Jean. "When people submit their data through such technology, they do so under the assumption that they are communicating information either for their enjoyment or, for example, to make their shopping easier. They don't see it as a sale of their personal data for the commercial gain of another party, and they expect an element of protection against their data being used for purposes that they do not know about or have not approved. They also anticipate that they might want to have their data deleted at some point in the future. If their personal data is treated in effect as belonging to another organisation, then they lose that element of control. More importantly still, they are at risk of losing information that comprises their identity. And that could cause them no end of time and trouble, not to mention money, to restore."

"Hmm" says Gerry "that's a bit extreme. But in any case, if that is a concern, they don't have to use such technologies. The fact is that people want to benefit from the online systems that companies like ours create, but they don't want to pay for them. We have invested hundreds of hours of work to create such systems and to manage our databases, and we put them to good use so that we can offer competitive prices for our insurance products. So our clients benefit. Isn't that a fair exchange? And, anyway a lot of the data we have stored didn't just come from our clients, we bought it legitimately from third parties."

"Look Gerry, that may be the case now, but technologies are changing very fast these days. It's hard for ordinary people to keep up. The public are only just waking up to the fact that they are being presented with advertisements on lots of websites that they visit because of the data that they have already parted with. And who knows where all this might go in the future? What if it turns out that we decide to decline clients health insurance based on the fact that they once went shopping for certain drugs, even though they were actually doing that on behalf of an elderly relative. Would that be fair?"

"Oh, that's something I had not considered, Jean. Yes, I guess that is possible, but then there will always be some anomalies in any system that is created. Hopefully exceptions such that you mention will be few and far in between. We are talking about what brings the greatest good for the greatest number here."

"No, I'm sorry Gerry. It's not that simple. Here in Europe we see a relationship between people's rights over their data and their rights as human beings. For example, the right to privacy is taken very seriously here as a basic human right. When Google's "Streetview" cameras come down a person's street photographing where they live and what they have in the front gardens, people are inclined to think that their privacy is being invaded. So the GDPR is designed to enshrine that right by setting standards for data use and privacy across the entire EU. Basically any data that is identifiable as belonging to a particular person is protected. The individual has the right to ensure their data is not passed on or used in any way that they did not give their consent, and even to have it deleted if they wish."

"My!" Gerry exclaims. "That is certainly quite restrictive. Do you mean that our customers would have first claim to any data that we hold on them, and we would have to get their consent if we are to use it, even for their benefit? What if they refused and wanted their data back? Don't you think that if such rules were really necessary here that they would be in place already? If people truly cared about such data protection they would have claimed it as a right ages ago! We are not exactly shy of bringing law suits here in the USA. Lots of organisations have been using people's personal data for a whole variety of different purposes without bothering to inform them or get their consent. Society hasn't exactly fallen apart. It's accepted and typically people are not concerned about it, some may even welcome it. They don't want to be bothered by having to give consent to all and sundry when they share their personal information."

On the face of it, this might seem to be a simple discussion between two people comparing data privacy attitudes and legislation in two different continents, Europe and the USA. But we want to point to a more fundamental difference in the thinking of the two executives. We are not claiming here that one person's position is more correct than that of the other but rather we want to show you how their thinking differs.

In the first instance, Gerry reasons *inductively* by stating that since no US state specifically legislates that personal data belongs to the individuals and gives them specific rights over it, the company would not be breaking any laws by doing so. He then also reasons *deductively*. He draws the conclusion that customer data belongs to the company, because the company has both done work to accumulate it (by building and maintaining a database) and bought it at the price sought by data brokers. He appeals to a general principle that "you own what you create or what you pay for that someone else has created". Then he points out that the company's database has been created by the company and that much of the data that is in it has been paid for, either directly to data brokers or indirectly by providing customers with an efficient and economic service.

However, Jean thinks differently. She sees a bigger picture in which people have rights to know how their data is to be used. She believes that when they give personal data to a company with which they wish to do business they accept that the company has a need to know such information but only for the purposes of providing the service that they, as customers, are interested in receiving. In other words, the context in which the data is transferred to the company is important. The company should not assume that it automatically has the right to do what it likes with its customers' data. Hence, for Jean, the company must be transparent about the use to which it puts its customers' data, and customers should be able to veto such use if they don't want their data used in such a way.

In addition, Jean brings a second way of thinking to bear. She points to the fact that things are always changing. Not only have new technologies emerged that enable the collection and analysis of vast swathes of data, but also data of a personal nature has become much more revealing about the individual to which it refers. Companies are now able to make inferences about the purchasing needs and preferences of people from the data they post on social media. And predisposition to illness and disease can be predicted from DNA testing. The data that people provide for free can therefore carry considerable commercial value to organisations supplying products and services. This is something that the general public is only beginning to become aware of.

Jean then involves a third way of thinking, that of pointing to a relationship. People's rights to their data are related to their rights as human beings. She argues that the right to own one's own data is related to the right to privacy, which is a fundamental human right, and the two cannot be completely separated. So, effectively, people must own their personal data else their rights to privacy are potentially infringed. If companies are allowed to use a person's data in any way that they wish, then that person will have lost an element of privacy that is important to them.

At this point, it looks as though Gerry's position has been defeated. Whilst he has employed logical inductive principles to show that the organisation is not breaking the law, and *deductive* principles to argue that the company owns their customers' data, Jean has shown him some potential implications and has given an explanation of the thinking behind the European GDPR legislation.

She might, however, have gone one step further, which was to say how the concept of personal data has been transformed into something that can be bought and sold like a commodity. Prior to the arrival of the internet, organisations would compile mailing lists in the form of names and addresses of individuals, and sometimes these mailing lists might be sold or rented by mailing list brokers. But the individual people on those lists typically had little say over whether their details were or were not included. They had even less chance of receiving any money when their names and addresses were traded. As far as individuals were concerned, their data had no material value.

Since the internet became established, the extent of personal data has expanded far beyond a simple name and address. And so has the commercial value of such data. Not only does the availability of personal data allow companies to target their advertising very specifically at individuals who are likely to want their products and services, but it also enables them to target individuals who might be very influential in promoting those products and services in their communities. Personal data can even be used to help politicians win elections. Hence the concept of personal data has grown in importance and significance. One could say that 'personal data' has been transformed from being relatively unimportant to being of significant commercial and political value. Hence there is now a need to protect it and the people to whom it belongs against unfair exploitation and to give such people rights over how it is used, and to ascribe responsibility to organisations over how they use it. We can now see that the concept of 'personal data' has developed, changing over time, taking on new meanings in different contexts, and becoming related to such things as human rights. Such a transformation is not just at a conceptual level. The need for data privacy and control is being enshrined in new legislation and has changed the way that individuals and organisations behave. People are now in a position of being able to sell their data in the marketplace.

How might one have foretold that personal data would one day become a commodity that could be bought and sold? It is hard to see how inductive or deductive thinking would have enabled a person to come to such a realisation. There is a huge gap between the idea of mailing lists and the idea of an individual being able to sell their personal data that such logic cannot fill. What is missing is the understanding that personal data itself is changing in quantity and quality, that it has value in different contexts, and that there is a relationship between it and the concept of the human right to privacy. When these elements are included then the transformation of personal data becomes easier to see. This is not to say that logical thinking does not have its uses. It is one of the cornerstones of our understanding about the world and our ability to solve problems. Logical thinking enables a person to move sequentially in thought from a particular premise or set of premises to a necessary conclusion. But such thinking is not the only kind of that humans can use, and it has its limitations. We argue that there are advantages to being able to think more fluidly than logical reasoning allows.

Table 2.1 summarises the different forms of thinking that our two executives have used.

By contrast with Jean's thought processes, we think that Gerry's thinking is rather restrictive. He does not look beyond the current situation in terms of legal requirements, his definition of ownership and his perception that people are happy to allow organisations to use their personal data much as they have been in the past. The transformative revelation that personal data is something that individual people might see as their property, free for them to buy and sell, but not for organisations to use as they think fit, eludes him. At the time of writing, we don't know whether the USA will follow the EU in bringing in similar legislation to the GDPR, nor what other countries may decide to do. But the issue of data privacy is likely to be an important one for generations to come. Ella Road, a British playwright, describing a situation in her dystopian play "The Phlebotomist", envisages a world where people are rated genetically on a scale of 1–10.[1] Data drawn from their blood tests can make the difference for them between having a high-flying career and being unemployable due to susceptibility to a specific disease. To what extent would you want to give control over such data to a third party?

Our aim as Metathinkers is to be able to shift from one type of thinking to another in order to set our thinking free to see reality in new ways. Accordingly, we will now look in more detail at the differences between two types of thinking—logical and dialectical thinking.

[1]Road, 2018.

Table 2.1 Six types of thinking about data privacy

Gerry's thinking	Jean's thinking
Inductive There are no explicit legal requirements in any of the 50 states in the USA to prevent organisations using people's personal data, so we are not breaking any laws by doing so	*Structural* The context in which an individual gives their personal data to a third party is important. The individual proceeds on the assumption that the data will be used for a specific purpose that they are agreed with. Organisations that collect personal data should not do so for one reason and then use it for another without the individual's consent. This requires transparency
Deductive Ownership is created by an individual's own work and passes from one person to another when the buyer pays the seller the agreed price for the property Our company has either collected all customer data itself or paid for it Therefore, the data is the property of our company	*Processual* Data technology has developed rapidly in recent years and continues to evolve. One cannot predict how data might be used in the future. Current data protection laws may prove to be outdated and require reformulation in order to be fit for purpose in the future
Abductive Generally, people see the benefit of allowing companies use of their personal data. This has not led to any significant problems so far, and we don't have any complaints, therefore people don't really care and if we carry on as we are it is unlikely to lead to any significant problems in the future	*Relational* People have the right to privacy as human beings. Personal data, privacy and identity are related and mutually contribute to each other. Hence people have a right to ensure that there is "privacy by design" in the way their data is stored and used by organisations

Logical Thinking

Whilst much of our thought is automatic, as Daniel Kahneman[2] would say, a more deliberate thinking process takes place when people are faced with something that they do not understand. It may be that they have to travel somewhere that they haven't been before and do not know how to get there. Or it may be that they experience an event for the first time that does not make sense to them, for example they try to start their car and nothing happens. Everyday life is full of such problems which can be solved in different ways. People will go about finding a solution in way that applies what they already know. A car mechanic will attempt to identify which part of the car's ignition system has failed—the starter motor, the battery, the fuel pump etc. Someone who knows nothing about cars will contact someone who they think might be able to help because they have specific knowledge. In these cases, thinking involves deciding what to do next based on an explanation of what has happened or what will happen. There is an analysis of cause and effect that

[2]Kahneman, 2011.

takes the form of "if this, then that". In the former case, the thought process is one of "if the car does not start, then call the recovery service". In the latter case, the thought process is more complex. The person is able to make some distinctions about the nature of the problem. Instead of thinking simply that the car is broken, the thought process is one of "if part of the car is not working properly, then a process of elimination is required to find out which part it is. Start with checking the fuel supply etc." A little knowledge can be both an advantage and a dangerous thing. The person who thinks he knows why the car will not start may try to solve the problem but end up making things worse if his diagnosis is wrong. A person who immediately decides to call the recovery services may find he gets the problem fixed more quickly, albeit at greater expense.

It can be seen from the example above that thinking follows certain patterns and structures. "If this, then that" is a basic logical structure which assumes a connection or a chain of causality. Another basic pattern is that of making a distinction. The more knowledge one has about a subject, the more distinctions one can make. A professional sommelier or wine-taster can distinguish aromas and flavours in a wine that would not be noticed by someone who was new to the drink, and has a rich language to describe such teste and smell sensations. Our human senses enable us to distinguish all manner of physical characteristics in the environment, and language gives us the means to refer to those characteristics.

The Swiss psychologist Jean Piaget noted how children acquire patterns of thought that follow logical principles in what he termed the "*concrete operational*" stage attained at around the age of 7.[3] A typical example of such a logical principle is the conservation of quantity. When water is emptied from a short fat glass into a tall thin one, the height of the water in the glass increases. To some children, it appears as though the amount of water has also increased because they incorrectly associate a higher level with more water. However, those who have grasped the principle of the conservation of quantity understand that it is the shape of the glass that has changed, not the quantity of water. As a child's development progresses further the principle becomes established at an abstract level. This is to say that children subsequently apply the conservation principle with other entities such as number, length, mass as well as volume of liquid. Piaget labelled the stage at which children progressively apply such logic to abstract concepts, the "*formal operational*" stage. For the purpose of distinguishing the type of thinking that applies these types of specific rules, we refer to it as "logical thinking". Please bear in mind, however, that the precise set of rules that can be described as "logic" is a matter of some debate. The origin of the term "logic" is the Greek word for "reason". When we refer to logic we are referring principally to deductive and inductive reasoning, and secondarily to abductive thinking.

A classic example of deductive logical thinking is presented by Gerry, "To own something is to have bought it or created it. We have bought some data. Therefore we own that data." This form of logic knows no contradiction. Inductive logic works similarly but is not quite so certain. Here, Gerry argues on the basis of

[3]Piaget, 1968, 976–79.

probability "50 States have no specific laws against using a person's data, so the company is not breaking any laws by doing so". Here Gerry relies on his sampling of the legal requirements in the United States of America to determine what is legal, but overlooks the possibility of international laws and the laws of other countries. The third form of logic, abductive logic, follows a plausible rule but is still less definite. Gerry uses abductive logic when he asserts, "People don't seem to complain about the way their data is being used, hence generally they are unconcerned about it". His assumptions are twofold. Firstly, that the lack of visible complaining means that people are unconcerned about the way their data is being used. Secondly, that such a situation might not change substantially in the future. Whilst such assumptions seem plausible, they cannot be taken for granted, hence abductive logic is a somewhat weaker form of argument than deductive and inductive logic.

Secondary educational systems in society today are heavily geared towards developing students' abilities in Piaget's "formal operations" and teaching facts. The intended advantage of such a focus is to consolidate students' understanding of basic logical principles as well as to equip them with useful knowledge. Another benefit is that the assessment of students' progress by examination is made relatively easy when there are questions that have answers that are either right or wrong, and that require facts to be correctly regurgitated by students. The principles of deductive and inductive reasoning are reinforced by the belief that knowledge and truth are absolutes that can be established with certainty by experts, if not by oneself.

A view of the world where there are certainties and facts that can be known for sure carries with it a fair amount of reassurance. Most people gain satisfaction from thinking that they are right and that the people with whom they disagree, are wrong. And yet, as people go through life they find increasingly that there are many questions and issues where they are in disagreement with others and no clear way to establish who is right. They also encounter paradoxes and apparent contradictions that confound the basic logical principles that they were taught in school.

Consider the statement "A tadpole is not a frog". The logical rule underlying such a statement is called the law of the excluded middle. The law, which has been attributed to the Greek philosopher Aristotle, states that for any proposition either that proposition is true, or its negation is true. This makes common sense to most people. To them, an object is always what it is (law of identity), no statement can be both true and false (law of non-contradiction), and every statement is either true or false (law of the excluded middle). A tadpole and a frog appear to be two very different creatures, hence to negate the proposition by saying that a tadpole and a frog are the same thing would be a contradiction. And yet, we know that tadpoles eventually undergo metamorphosis and transform into frogs. So in the course of that transformation, the tadpole and the frog are one and the same thing. Here, then, the real world seems to defy the clear logical rules that confer clarity and certainty.

Much more recently the cognitive scientists, George Lakoff and Mark Johnson, have proposed an explanation for why such logical rules make such common sense.[4] They argue that Aristotle's rule is based on a physical metaphor. The

[4]Lakoff and Johnson, 1991, 381.

metaphor works likes this. Imagine two buckets standing side by side. Inside one is a ball. If the two buckets are separate, and the ball is in one bucket, it cannot be in the other bucket. Now think of a proposition substituting for one bucket and the negation of the proposition for the other, for example "This is a tadpole" is the first bucket, and "this is a frog" is the second bucket. And then substitute the word "true" for the ball. When a statement is true, metaphorically the ball is in the appropriate bucket. But the ball cannot be physically in both buckets when they are separate, hence if the ball is in the "This is a tadpole" bucket, that statement is true, and the other statement "this is a frog" is false. The organism cannot be both a tadpole and not a tadpole by being a frog.

Lakoff and Johnson's work shows us that the human mind naturally comes to adopt rules of logic such as the law of the excluded middle. They suggest it does so because as infants develop a sense of the physical world, they make distinctions such as "me and you", "up and down", "night and day", "subject and object", and so on. These distinctions are immensely helpful in putting structure and order on the world, but they also create categories that are understood as separate and independent. Language, by ascribing different words to different things serves to preserve and enhance these distinctions. A cat is different to a dog, cold is different to hot, and white is different to black. When something is in one category, and another thing is in a different category, the mind has few reasons to find a connection between the two. And yet, the possibility of making connections is ever present. Much of the way we describe the world is through the use of bi-polar constructs, extravert versus introvert, peace versus war, love versus hate, light versus dark, beauty versus ugliness, happiness versus sadness, young versus old, good versus evil etc. Even our political world is separated into left versus right, Republican versus Democrat.

In language and thought, we often proceed by making connections. For example, one might say "life is a journey". This statement connects two different concepts, life and journey. Clearly, in a major sense, life is not a journey. Human life has to do with conception, birth, growth, decline and eventual death. These are not features of journeys. By connecting the concept of life and journey together the thinker is employing a metaphor in an attempt to describe a particular aspect of life. In this way thought proceeds by mapping (another metaphor) one idea onto another. Dialectical thinking, which we will now describe, features strongly such connecting of ideas or concepts, even of apparent opposites, in space, time and meaning.

Dialectical Thinking

Culturally, differentiations and polarisations appear more prominent in the thought of European and American (Western) societies than Chinese (Eastern) societies.

Consider the symbol of *yin and yang in* Fig. 2.1.

Fig. 2.1 Yin-Yang symbol (© Wikipedia)

The symbol denotes a whole (the complete circle) divided into two components. Each component stands in a relationship to the other and even contains a tiny portion of the other. But neither component can exist without the other. There can be no shadow without light, no good without evil, no positive without negative. Consequently, it is the relationship between yin and yang that defines yin on the one hand, and yang on the other.

In Chinese culture, for example, the opposites of *yin* and *yang* describe contrary aspects of human experience that are also interconnected and interdependent. The interaction of *yin* and *yang* gives rise to a whole that is more than the sum of its parts and in so doing, *yin* and *yang* transform each other. Such thinking appears to be much less a part of Western society where thinking seeks to resolve and remove contradictions as opposed to accepting or even welcoming them. One can argue that both intellectual approaches have their strengths and weaknesses (another pair of opposites). The analytic tradition of Western thought separates, isolates, and reduces complex concepts to their constituent parts and gives us clarity about cause and effect, priorities, and order. The more holistic approach of Eastern thought draws attention to the importance of contexts and the idea that there is a bigger picture, and gives rise to tolerance of differences and acceptance of contradictions and paradox.

The name we give to the type of thinking that is more typical of Eastern and particularly Chinese cultures and that is characterised by tolerance of ambiguity and contradiction is that of "dialectic" which comes from the Greek, meaning "through speech". The philosophical use of the term often refers to the process of *Socratic dialogue* by which the Greek philosopher Socrates would show someone how their beliefs and ideas were contradictory. However, dialectical thinking shows up much more recently in the work of the German philosopher Georg Wilhelm Friedrich Hegel, and subsequently that of the political thinker and originator of what subsequently became Communism, Karl Marx. Aspects of dialectic also appear in ancient Hindu and Jain philosophy.

Hegel's notion of dialectic is commonly described in terms of a three-step process involving considering first a "thesis", then its opposite or contradiction, the "antithesis", and then finally the creation of a new idea or "synthesis" that encapsulates both the thesis and the antithesis. This is a good starting point for understanding dialectical thinking, however in contrast to the rules of formal logic, and almost by definition, there is no single definitive form of dialectical thinking, it stands apart. Nevertheless, in the western analytic tradition, we will define its key principles. In doing so, we will draw on the work of three people, the British philosopher, Roy Bhaskar[5]; the American psychologist and psychotherapist, Michael Basseches[6]; and the social scientist and artist, Otto Laske.[7,8] Most recently, Laske developed a framework of dialectical *forms of thought* from pioneering work by Michael Basseches, and grounded this framework in Bhaskar's philosophical formulation of dialectic, resulting in a classification of four different but related types of thought structure. It is these thought patterns that we now refer to as dialectical thinking.

As we have stated, the characteristic feature of dialectical thinking is the ability to deal with contradictions in reality and in thought. You can find such contradictions easily in everyday life:

- What is correct in a small world is wrong in a bigger world.
- What is certain today is obsolete tomorrow.
- What seems to be a simple thing actually is an element of a complex network.
- What seems to be unchangeable is creatively developed further by human actors.

Consider as an illustration the concept of "potential". We often say of some people that they have "potential". What we mean is that we anticipate that they will one day be able to do things that at present they cannot, or do not, do. The contradiction is that we are saying that they have something that currently they do not. Another way to express this is to say that they are missing something currently that they will gain in the future. There is therefore something absent that will eventually emerge.

Patterns of thought that help to overcome both contradiction and absence can be considered dialectical as opposed to logical. Such thought patterns lead to "deeper" thinking by delving under the surface of things to look at what is contradictory or absent. Using dialectical thought patterns, a thinker sheds light on different aspects of a particular concept and finds a way to overcome contradictions. We refer to these processes as "illumination" and "remediation".

Following the work of Basseches, Laske and Bhaskar we can distinguish four principles of dialectical thinking:

1. The first principle of dialectical thinking is that of *holism* by which we mean that, dialectically, nothing can be viewed in isolation. There is always a bigger whole to be considered and each thing that one looks at is just a part of that whole.

[5]Bhaskar, 1993.
[6]Basseches, 1984.
[7]Laske, 2008.
[8]Laske, 2015.

2. The second principle is one of *dynamism* or constant change. Everything that exists can be considered to be in a state of motion, never static but always, in a sense, becoming what it is not already and, at the same time, leaving some of what it is behind.
3. The third principle is that of *relationship*, or common ground, whereby each and every thing is related in some way to everything else, and it is those relationships that give the thing its essence.
4. The fourth principle is that of *transformation*. This principle is rather harder to grasp than the other three because in some ways it is a combination of them. It is the principle of significant change occurring via a movement through forms, to which all living systems are subject. Transformation is very often developmental in that there is movement towards a new form that transcends and includes the previous form, but it can also be regressive in the sense of a form breaking down, collapsing or reversing its previous growth.

A baby grows into a child, which then becomes a teenager, which then becomes an adult, which then becomes a geriatric, and which then eventually dies. These are the transformations of human life and they occur in part because individual people are always part of a bigger whole, always changing, and always in relationship to other things in their environment. When applied consciously, dialectical thinking explores and opens up reality in way in which logical thinking cannot, since logical thinking must follow precise rules, whereas dialectical thinking is constantly taking concepts and exploring what is missing or absent in terms of the context, dynamics, and relationships, and hence how that concept might be transformed.

Dialectics and Dialogue

In fact, dialectical thinking is thinking in dialogue with another person or even with yourself. One person may state a point of view, and the other will reply with a different, opposing point of view. As both parties listen to each other's thinking, a third point of view may emerge that is, in some way a combination of both the earlier points of view. Dialogue enables people to identify and reveal absences in each other's thought processes, leading to a richer and more nuanced appreciation of a topic, without which a person's thinking may remain very partial. We see dialog as a process of *opening up the mind* of another person.

The Russian psychologist Vygotsky[9] describes thinking as internalization of socially rooted and historically developed activities. Vygotsky theorized that our inner speech derives from our external speech and that, as young children, we are only really able to think out loud.

[9]Vygotskij, 1981, 52–57.

Following on from Vygotsky, researchers Per Linell,[10] Ivana Marková,[11] Hubert Hermans and Thorsten Gieser[12] have advanced the idea that thinking is predominantly dialogical. We make sense of our world by constantly talking to ourselves in our heads. But the roots of thinking are found in social interaction with other people, which provides us with a model of the dialogue we then have in our minds. We replay conversations, think of things we wish we had said (but didn't), think of what we will say and make plans as if we were talking to someone else. The writer Samuel Beckett captures such internal dialogue brilliantly in his novel "The Unnameable" where the central character speaks as if to himself; "You must go on. I can't go on. I'll go on."[13]

Since dialectics are all about discovering what is missing in thought, we have found that the most useful way to develop one's thinking dialectically and become a Metathinker is to ask certain questions. One can ask questions to oneself, or better still, engage a conversation partner in asking each other questions to open up thinking. We call this process "mind opening" after Laske[14] and it follows the classic tradition first exemplified by Socrates in advocating questions for dialogue that provoke deeper and broader thinking. At a period in time when people habitually turn to the internet to "download" standard answers to particular questions, we see the use of questions for dialogue as a vital practice to counter blind following of so called "best practice" and to encourage people to think for themselves.

Definition of Metathinking

So far, we have started to distinguish two types of thinking: logical thinking that follows specific systematic rules that determine whether a conclusion is justified given its premises and what we have termed "dialectic" thinking which seeks to explore and expand how a person sees and understands reality. It is tempting to see one or other of these two forms of thinking as superior to the other, however we prefer to see them as complementary.

This takes us to the very heart of what we mean by the term "Metathinking", since in thinking about our thinking, we are able to move to a higher level where we can choose which system of thought to apply. We can choose to apply logical or dialectical thinking, or even use a combination of both types. The kind of thinking where we are actually thinking about the different systems of thought and which to use, is "meta" because it both includes and transcends the thinking we do within a particular system of thought. Figure 2.2 separates out the two types of thinking and

[10]Linell, 2009.
[11]Marková, 2005.
[12]Hermans and Gieser, 2014.
[13]Beckett, 1997.
[14]Laske, 2008, 377.

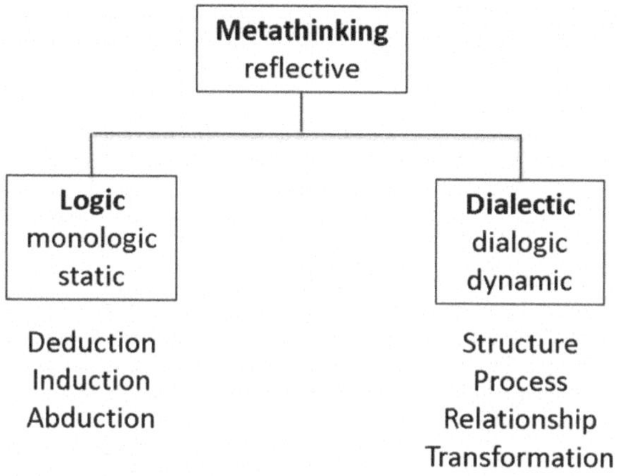

Fig. 2.2 Types of thinking (own representation based on Laske, 2008, 179)

identifies a number of components divided between logical thinking on the one hand, and dialectical thinking on the other.

In this book we distinguish four dialectical thinking modes, structural, process, relational and transformational or SPiRiT for short. For each thinking mode, we describe three thought patterns and hence arrive at a total of twelve individual "thought patterns". These thought patterns can be used as a means to open up and re-organise a person's thinking about any particular concept. In each case,

- the first thought pattern makes a distinction that serves to connect the concept that is being thought about with a particular thinking mode,
- the second thought pattern elaborates that distinction by going into more detail, and
- the third thought pattern integrates the concept with other elements to make a new more complex concept or conceptual system.

We are indebted to Iva Vurdelja for the idea that there are twelve fundamental thought patterns. Basseches and Laske identify as many as twenty-eight, and there may well be more but for the purposes of this book we prefer to focus practically on twelve. We will now describe in detail the four SPiRiT thinking modes and twelve associated thought patterns.

References

Basseches, M. (1984). *Dialectical thinking and adult development* (3rd ed.). Norwood, N.J: Ablex Publishing Corporation.

Beckett, S. (1997). *Molloy; Malone dies; The Unnamable*. New York: Knopf: Distributed by Random House.

Bhaskar, R. (1993). *Dialectic: The pulse of freedom*. London: New York: Verso.

Hermans, H. J. M., & Gieser, T. (Eds.). (2014). *Handbook of dialogical self theory*. Cambridge: Cambridge University Press.

Kahneman, D. (2011). *Thinking, fast and slow*. New York: Farrar, Straus and Giroux.
Lakoff, G., & Johnson, M. (1991). *Philosophy in the flesh: The Embodied mind and its challenge to Western thought*. New York: Basic Books.
Laske, O. E. (2008). *Measuring hidden dimensions of human systems: Foundations of requisite organization* (Vol. 2). Medford, MA: Interdevelopmental Institute Press.
Laske, O. E. (2015). *Dialectical thinking for integral leaders*. Tucson, AZ: Integral Publishers.
Linell, P. (2009). *Rethinking language, mind, and world dialogically: Interactional and contextual theories of human sense-making*. Charlotte, NC: Information Age Publishing.
Marková, I. (2005). *Dialogicality and social representations: The dynamics of mind*. (Paperback version). Cambridge: Cambridge University Press.
Piaget, J. (1968). Quantification, conservation, and nativism. *Science, 162*, 976–979.
Road, E. (2018). *Phlebotomist*. London: Oberon Books Limited.
Vygotskij, L. V. (1981). *Mind in Society: The development of higher psychological processes, Nachdr*. Cambridge, MA: Harvard University Press.

Structural Thinking

3

The first mode of dialectical thinking is called *structural thinking*. Essentially, structural thinking involves thinking about things in the world as if they had a particular physical structure and/or are part of a particular structure. But we can apply structural thinking also to elaborate and explain abstract, intangible concepts.

Illustration

Consider for a moment the beautiful structure of a snowflake. This typically has a radial symmetry with six arms. The arms themselves have smaller branches, which may themselves have smaller branches still. Hence within the structure lies a hierarchy. And a single snowflake is rarely found on its own, it will be part of a snow cloud or a bank of snow, for example, each of which has a structure of its own. So structural thinking is about looking for the structure of things and seeing things as being part of larger structures (Fig. 3.1).

Frequently structural thinking is applied to much more abstract things in a way that seeks to make them more understandable. The American writer and philosopher Ken Wilber epitomises the height of structural thinking in his "AQAL" model (his Integral theory of all quadrants, all levels) that classifies and fits together all human knowledge and experience.[1] Wilber's diagram specifies a structure of four quadrants each of which characterises a particular aspect of human beings. In the upper left quadrant, he places all the subjective aspects of consciousness or individual awareness. He calls this the "I" quadrant. In the lower left, he places all the aspects of collective human experience—the "We" or cultural quadrant. In the upper right quadrant, he puts all the

[1]Wilber, 2005.

N. Shannon and B. Frischherz, *Metathinking*, Management for Professionals,
https://doi.org/10.1007/978-3-030-41064-3_3

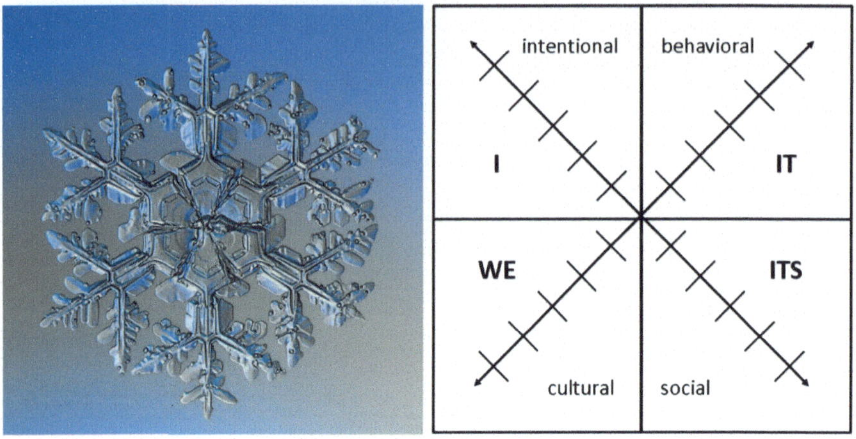

Fig. 3.1 Structural thinking images: Snowflake (© Alexey Kljatov/Wikimedia) and all quadrants, all levels (AQAL) (own representation based on Wilber, 2005, 26)

exterior correlates of human awareness—aspects that are external and objective. This is the "IT" quadrant. Finally, in the lower right quadrant, he places all the objective correlates of collective experience, the social systems and institutions that anchor subjective cultural experiences, labelled the "ITS" quadrant because of its objective, plural nature. The detail of Wilber's model is not important for our purposes at this point, but notice how the structure mirrors the image of the snowflake. Lines, levels and quadrants are placed in such way as to organise an array of different concepts, illustrating their hierarchy and relative positioning. By using structural thinking, Wilber finds a way to organise an array of different concepts into a coherent whole. Structural thinking is relatively common, indeed we are using a lot of structural thinking ourselves in organising the material in this book.

Structural Thought Patterns (S)

Table 3.1 Structural thought patterns (S)

	Structural thought patterns
S1	Differentiation of elements in a whole representing a stable entity in its own right
S2	Elaboration of elements with reference to the structure, hierarchy and functionality of the elements
S3	Integration of different elements and perspectives into a structured bigger entity as a system

Table 3.1 summarises three levels of structural thought pattern.

Let us take a closer look at examples of the three thought patterns of structural thinking.

S1 Differentiation of elements in a whole representing a stable entity in its own right

The *first structural thought pattern (S1)* is one where the thinker simply identifies that a particular element or aspect of the world is not isolated but is part of a bigger whole. This way of thinking counteracts a tendency in science to be reductionist—that is, to see and explain things in terms of only what is inside them, as opposed to what lies outside. You can, for example, think of yourself as an individual human being operating independently in the world. In contrast, the structural thought pattern S1 would, when applied, enable you to view each human, including yourself, as being fundamentally inseparable from the society or culture in which they were situated. How one behaves, therefore, is never entirely down to you, but is partly dependent on the norms of behaviour of those around you. The key to such thinking is one of expanding the boundary that you initially draw around any object in order to get a better understanding of what that object is. Hence, when you think of the snowflake that we mentioned earlier, your thought moves from considering the snowflake in isolation to considering it as part of a field or cloud of snow. Structural thought pattern S1 enables the thinker to conceptualise an object in a more meaningful way because it locates the object in a larger context or whole with which the object itself is in some way interacting.

S2 Elaboration of elements with reference to the structure, hierarchy and functionality of the elements

The *second structural thought pattern* (S2) takes the additional step of spelling out the structure of whatever is being considered as the larger whole. Here the thinker envisages the way the larger whole is organised. Such organisation could be a physical, causal or temporal structure. A prime example of this thought pattern is that of systems thinking, which seeks to map out how different parts of a system stand in relation to, and influence, each other. Very often such structures are organised hierarchically, in layers or strata. And so it is with Ken Wilber's AQAL model, which first separates the concept of "consciousness" into quadrants of interior and exterior, individual and collective, then into lines and levels of development. Structural thought pattern S2 shows how one part is related to another and the context surrounding them, and lends a certain stability to the entire structure. It is perhaps a paradox of such "holistic" thinking that the eventual boundary of the system is inevitably drawn arbitrarily by the thinker. In defining a whole system that system is immediately sealed off from the larger whole in which it is set, and to some extent a form of reductionism is ever present.

S3 Integration of different elements and perspectives into a structured bigger entity as a system

The *third structural thought pattern* (S3) develops the idea that there is always a larger whole by taking the additional step of recognising that there may be several different contexts in which one can consider the same element. A classic example of such thinking is in the book "Images of Organisation" by Gareth Morgan.[2] Morgan describes how one can view an organisation from a variety of different perspectives that reflect different fundamental images or metaphors. An organisation can be seen, for example, as a machine, an organism, a brain, a culture, a political system, a psychic prison, a system in flux and transformation, and as a domineering entity. These different perspectives constitute different organisational contexts and hence contribute to a richer understanding of the nature of an organisation. The bigger "system" that is described by structural thought pattern S3 here is not a physical system, but one of the multiple mental representations of an organisation spelling out its complexity. Morgan's model can be contrasted somewhat with Wilber's since Morgan does not impose a structure on the different perspectives in the way that Wilber does. There is, for instance, no hierarchy of perspectives in Morgan's work. They are simply laid out together. Wilber's AQAL model goes somewhat further because, in separating out levels, he specifies hierarchies where one perspective transcends and includes the others.

Mind Opening Questions

To illustrate the power of mind opening questions, we will imagine a dialogue between two people where the first has raised an issue of some significance and importance to him or her. For example, suppose a speaker has declared:

> "We are facing a crisis in our country's prisons. Prisoners have been rioting and escaping, and drug use is widespread. We are seeing an increase in violence resulting in injury and even death. Attacks on staff are up by 40%".
>
> Question 1:
>
> *"If you were to look at this problem from an even higher level, what is the bigger picture that you can describe here?"*

This question challenges the first speaker to set the problem of prison violence in a broader context. Possibilities include the context of the country's judicial system that has instituted changes in sentencing policies, resulting in over-crowding in prisons, or the context of the immigration into the country, creating a larger and more diverse population and greater social inequality.

[2]Morgan, 2006.

Question 2:

"If this problem is part of a larger system, how would you describe the structure of the whole system?"

This question encourages the first speaker to look at the problem of prison violence from a systemic point of view. For example, the issue might be seen as one due to a lack of money for prisons, where there are linkages between the country's economic performance, government revenues from taxation, investment in new prison capacity, staffing levels and training of prison warders.

Question 3:

"How does your view of this situation/event/person change if you consider it in different contexts?"

This question goes deeper still by inviting the first speaker to see the problem of prison violence arising from multiple contexts. The two previous questions yielded the contexts of the judicial system, the immigration system and the financial system. The speaker might also explore the political context, in the sense of different governments having conflicting attitudes towards criminal behaviour, or the technological context, in which new technologies (such as remote control drones) make it easier for prisoners to get access to drugs, or a social context in which crime is increasing at the same time as it becomes harder to recruit people to be prison warders.

References

Morgan, G. (2006). *Images of organization*. Thousand Oaks: Sage Publications.

Wilber, K. (2005). Introduction to integral theory and practice. IOS Basic and the AQAL Map. *Journal of Integral Theory and Practice, 1*(1), 26.

4 Process Thinking

The second mode of dialectical thinking is called *process thinking*. The essence of process thinking was captured by the Greek philosopher, Heraclitus, who is quoted as saying that one cannot step twice into the same river. Heraclitus' doctrine is one that "everything flows". Change is a central aspect of reality, and although we habitually see many things as being static, inevitably everything is in flux moving towards something different from what it is now. Process thinking encapsulates the concept of emergence and includes the classic form of the dialectical process—the flow from thesis to antithesis or opposite, and on to synthesis.

Illustration

In contrast to the static image of a snowflake that we chose to represent structural thinking, we use a weather pattern, the spiral pattern of a cyclone to illustrate what we mean by process thinking. The spiral is constantly on the move, retaining its form whilst changing its shape, becoming larger or smaller, spinning faster or slower. The cyclone seemingly emerges from nothing and eventually disappears completely (Fig. 4.1).

The developmental psychologist Robert Kegan used a spiral image to illustrate the concept of a pattern in the development of human consciousness over a lifetime. His book "The Evolving Self" (1982)[1] describes an evolving sequence of changes in the way a person relates to his or her social environment, switching between a focus on "self" (independence) and the "other" (inclusion) as life unfolds and building stage by stage a more complete and complex consciousness. Development occurs through time, with new ways of thinking, feeling and behaving emerging as

[1]Kegan, 1982.

N. Shannon and B. Frischherz, *Metathinking*, Management for Professionals,
https://doi.org/10.1007/978-3-030-41064-3_4

Fig. 4.1 Process thinking images: Cyclone Catarina (© Pixabay) and Evolving Self (own representation based on Kegan, 2001, 109)

people progress in age. Each stage transcends what went before such that, as people progress up the spiral, they become more capable of taking responsibility for their lives and able to relate to other people in more sophisticated ways. Kegan also describes human development in terms of a movement between what a person is *subject to* and what it is that they can make an *object* of. Whilst this use of the terms "subject" and "object" is philosophically abstract, it highlights the notion of the formation and then combination of pairs of opposites that is a hallmark of developmental thinking. At each progressive stage, what a person was subject to previously becomes something that they can then make object. For instance, a child who says "I love my mummy" is subject to her feelings, whilst a teenager who says "I feel loving towards my mummy" has been able to make an object of her feelings. In adult life, an important step of development will be the move from a sense of identity that is guided by what a person thinks other people think about them to one where their sense of identity is generated by themselves independently.

Process Thought Patterns (P)

Table 4.1 Process thought patterns (P)

	Process thought patterns
P1	Differentiation of a changing element, linking its current state to the past and future
P2	Elaboration of one or more elements in their developmental aspects
P3	Integration of changing and interconnected elements in an unceasing movement as a system

Table 4.1 summarises three levels of process thought patterns.

Let us take a closer look at examples of the three thought patterns of process thinking.

P1 Differentiation of a changing element, linking its current state to the past and future

The *first process thought pattern* (P1) is one where the thinker explicitly acknowledges the existence of continuous change. For example, it is prevalent currently for people to talk and write about the changing nature of work. It is claimed that a number of factors are responsible for this, technology, specialisation, globalisation, demographics and social values to name just five. Historians might also point out that work has always been changing. Going back to the pre-industrial times when agriculture was the main form of work, this emerged from hunting and gathering activities then developed in scale from small holdings in select locations to larger enterprises with the advent of irrigation systems, and subsequently changed again to a year-round activity with the advent of crop rotation. More recently it has become characterised by large scale intensive methods using fertilisers, insecticides and machinery. Hence, process thought pattern P1 takes a concept, such as work, and illustrates how that has changed from what it was in the past and how it will continue to change in future.

P2 Elaboration of one or more elements in their developmental aspects

The *second process thought pattern* (P2) goes into more detail regarding the process of change itself. When one thinks of something changing, it has the paradoxical characteristic of becoming something new and different, and at the same time retaining its identity. In going through life, a human changes from being a baby to a child and then a teenager and finally an adult, whilst remaining the same person. The mature adult is not discernible in the baby. It is as if the adult emerges almost out of nothing, but all the time there is a movement where one thing is on the way out and another thing is on the way in. Physically, the human body is continually growing new cells and old cells are breaking down. Change thus occurs out of a series of interactions between what exists and what it is about to become, and the second process thought pattern focuses on such interactions. Let us consider for a moment, a marriage between two people. In marriage, people interact and change each other, and yet they retain their individual identities. Hence, a person might say, "*when I got married, I knew that my partner would expect certain things of me, that previously I had been free from. And in a similar way, I expected things from my partner that I had not previously expected. So I changed, both because I was aware that I should behave differently from that moment on, and also because I had developed expectations of someone else that were new*". Here, the person is reflecting on a developmental sequence instigated by the interaction with another person. Similarly, one can see that personal development occurs through interactions with work. At work, people engage in tasks of problem-solving that, over time, increase their knowledge and capability. Accordingly, using process thought pattern P2, we might say that there is no such thing as bringing one's whole self to work (much as that sounds an appealing proposition) because a person's whole self is only realised when that person engages with work.

P3 Integration of changing and interconnected elements in an unceasing movement as a system

The *third process thought pattern* (P3) captures an entire developmental sequence in detail by describing a series of processes that occur over time, resulting in a number of phases, stage and levels being attained sequentially. For example, as Robert Kegan sets out, the human being develops through a number of stages each characterised by a different way of feeling and behaving in relation to the social world. One can apply the same thinking to the development of a team of people, or a whole organisation. In relation to teams, the psychologist Bruce Tuckman set out a four phase model of small group development where a team progresses from forming—characterised by relatively independent behaviour, to storming—characterised by the playing out of power struggles and dispute about goals, then norming—characterised by the establishment of working agreements, standards and cooperative behaviours, and finally performing—characterised by effective collaboration and task achievement.[2] In this model, the team is viewed as being in motion, undergoing unceasing change as it moves inexorably towards an eventual state of equilibrium where it "performs"—achieving the task set of it. It is worth noting that Tuckman later added a fifth stage "adjourning" that was characterised by team disbandment. Developmental change is not solely in one direction but inevitably results in regression. Whilst Tuckman set out a general model of team development, subsequent researchers have focused on the specifics of changes in the team as it moves from one stage to another. Process thought pattern P3 shows that there are multiple influences at work including the specific interpersonal dynamics between team members, the organisational context and the time available to complete the team's primary task.

Mind Opening Questions

How can one stimulate process thinking in oneself and others? Let us again imagine a dialogue between two people where the first speaker starts by saying:

> "There is something strange going on in the politics of the western world today. We are seeing a rise in extreme populist movements. People are shifting to support leaders who are attacking what were once respected institutions and who speak a new language that focuses on nationalism and authoritarianism. These leaders use a language that appears to have little respect for truth, tolerance, or moderation. I never expected such movements to succeed but all of a sudden they are attracting support and sweeping into power".

Question 1:

"How do you see this problem stemming from what has happened in the past?"

[2]Tuckman, 1965, 384–399.

This question challenges the first speaker to see the current political situation as an emergent phenomenon, connected with the past. On reflection, the first speaker might have commented that it was inevitable that the values of liberal democracy, present for so many years in the USA and Europe, would at some stage come under attack from their opposite or antithesis. Development occurs in a spiral, swinging from one pole to another, and hence eventually dissatisfaction or boredom with the status quo leads to a reactionary movement towards another extreme. Constant change is therefore the norm and what we took for granted yesterday, cannot be assumed to be preserved today.

Question 2:

"Is there anything that you think is missing from what you can see at present, that could be a part of, or emerge out of this?"

This question invites the speaker to look deeper into current political events and to identify patterns of interaction that are generating change. Here, the speaker might note the pervasive influence of social media as a vehicle that influences the minds of people in unpredictable ways. The speaker might also note that "Wikileaks" ability to crack open access to politicians' private emails has increased the distrust that the public has in establishment figures and institutions and is causing a populist backlash.

Question 3:

"If you think forward in time, what possible events do you see emerging?"

Here, the first speaker might take a longer-term perspective on the development of democracy, citing that democracy always exists in tension with its opposite, autocracy or dictatorship. He might also reflect that progress does not occur in a straight line and that there is an ebb and flow to social development that periodically results in a regression, such as a war or significant social upheaval.

References

Kegan, R. (1982). *The evolving self: Problem and process in human development.* Cambridge, London: Harvard University Press.

Tuckman, B. (1965). Developmental sequence in small groups. *Psychological Bulletin, 63*(6), 384–399.

5 Relational Thinking

The third mode of dialectical thinking is called *relational thinking*. Essentially, relational thinking is required because when we identify something as an entity in its own right, we separate it from other things on which, in one way or another, it depends for its character and identity. Simply put, a thing cannot be completely isolated from the totality of which it is a part. Reality is made up from an array of interconnected elements that depend on a common ground for their existence.

Illustration

Let's have a look first at a Paramecium, a very small water-borne organism which belongs to the group of unicellular ciliated protozoans. A Paramecium is a tiny creature with a differentiated internal organisation and manifold relationships to its environment to keep it alive. It propels itself by movements of its cilia. When it encounters an obstacle, the paramecium swims backward for a brief time, before resuming its forward movement. To gather food, the Paramecium uses its cilia to sweep its prey into the mouth opening. A paramecium reacts immediately on touch, temperature and light. Therefore, it is often used in classrooms as a model organism. Fresh water is the common ground of the Paramecium's world, and it will die if the water is polluted. One cannot therefore conceive of a Paramecium except in relation to its environment of water—a Paramecium outside of water is no longer a Paramecium. Relational thinking explicitly recognises this relationship with water in making the Paramecium what it is (Fig. 5.1).

On a more abstract level, another form of relational thinking occurs when we conceive of the interconnected phenomenon of dialogue. Dialogue happens between two or more people trying to establish a mutual understanding. In dialogue, two people encounter and then reconstruct what each other has in mind. They compare and integrate what each other holds to be "true" about their experience of reality. There cannot be a dialogue with only one person, that would be a

N. Shannon and B. Frischherz, *Metathinking*, Management for Professionals,
https://doi.org/10.1007/978-3-030-41064-3_5

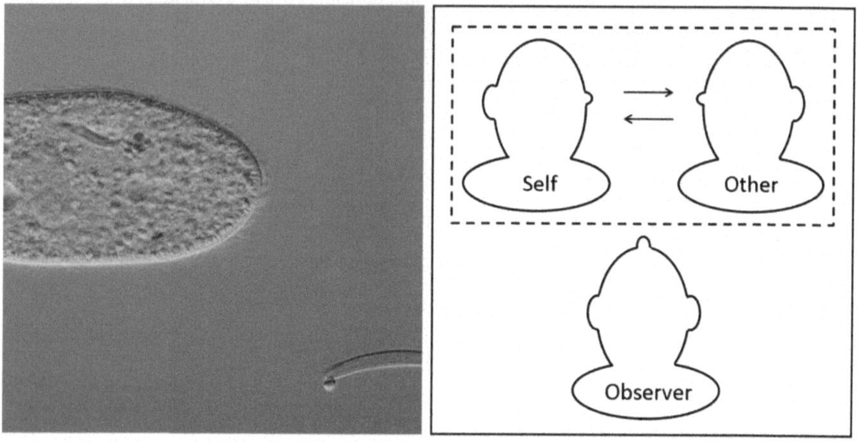

Fig. 5.1 Relational thinking images: Paramecium (© Wikimedia) and Perspectives in Dialog (own representation based on McNab, 2005, 127)

monologue. In dialogue, there is a tension between comprehension and incomprehension, and feedback mechanisms will indicate whether an interaction was successful or not. Misunderstanding, partial understanding and repairing sequences are normal phenomena of this process. If we introduce an observer into the dialogic situation, we have three perceptual positions from where the participants can perceive the dialogue: that of the self, the other and the observer.[1] In this view, a dialogue is an opportunity to provide information from three different perspectives: from the first-person perspective as the person appears in the mind of herself; from the second-person perspective as the person appears in the mind of a dialog partner and from the third-person perspective as the person appears in the observer's mind. The interrelation of these three different perspectives provides a richer picture of the social situation than a single view from only one of these positions. This insight is the basis for many coaching and group development processes. Relational thinking establishes dialogue as a shared, mutual process that establishes common ground between participants.

Relational Thought Patterns (R)

Let us take a closer look at examples of the three thought forms of relational thinking.

[1]McNab, 2005.

Table 5.1 Relational thought patterns (R)

	Relational thought patterns
R1	Differentiation of relationships between two or more separate elements
R2	Elaboration of specific relationships between interconnected elements
R3	Integration of interconnected elements and their constitutive relationships into an entity as a system

Table 5.1 summarises three levels of relational thought patterns.

R1 Differentiation of relationships between two or more separate elements

The *first relational thought pattern* (R1) highlights the idea that in the real world, things are closely linked. Often you cannot separate things without destroying them because they are tightly interconnected. If you take the Paramecium out of water or cut it off from its food, it will die and decay in a short time. In the same way, the concept of dialogue depends on the interaction of two people and if one person leaves the situation or refuses to interact, dialogue ceases to exist. The example of dialogue also illustrates that often it is valuable to bring two elements that were previously separate into a relationship. Many examples taken from everyday life, business and politics could be cited here. The prerequisites for dialogue are mutual interest and understanding. Relational thought pattern R1 indicates that dialogue needs partners with a mutual interest to communicate as a common ground.

R2 Elaboration of specific relationships between interconnected elements

The *second relational thought pattern* (R2) spells out the nature of relationships in more detail. For example, in communication, normally one person responds to the stimulus of another person and their communication is structured by taking turns to speak. One party may provide feedback to the other if he or she did not understand or accept the meaning of what the other person said. In this case, normally that person will try to repair the communication to re-establish mutual understanding and agreement. If the parties react always in similar ways to the stimulus of each other, communicative patterns and long-standing relationships will develop. The typical behaviour attached to certain roles in organisations is a good example for this routinised form of communication. On the one hand, this routinised form of communication makes reactions between a supervisor and the employees predictable and stabilises the cooperation of a group. On the other hand, routinised reactions can also lead to conflict. Imagine a supervisor and a new employee. The supervisor wishes to help the new employee to do his job and criticises him when the employee's work does not meet the organisation's standards. The new employee then becomes unsettled by the supervisor's direct critique and tries to keep out of sight in order to avoid the supervisor's control. But the supervisor decides to keep a special eye on the new employee and correct his work whenever he doesn't see the results he expects. In return, the employee then avoids direct contact with the supervisor because he is afraid of even stronger criticism. This behaviour provokes ever tighter control by the supervisor. The vicious circle leads to mutual mistrust between the supervisor and the employee. Hence, the deeper reasons for this disturbed relationship are illuminated when we apply relational thought pattern R2. The supervisor sees the employee as a problem that must be controlled, and the employee sees the supervisor as a threat that must be avoided. There often exists only one way to correct the relationship, which is for a third person to act as an observer and comment on the dynamic process between employee and supervisor. Watzlawick[2] describes such a process as a "meta-communication" with which the two conflicting parties can clarify their intentions and interpretations and establish a new relationship.

R3 Integration of interconnected elements and their constitutive relationships into an entity as a system

The *third relational thought pattern* (R3) integrates interconnected elements into a system. For example, staying with the example of the supervisor and the employee, we can see that their interaction and relationship are elements of a much bigger network of interactions in an organisation. Their interactive behaviour is shaped by the roles they play in that organisation. As private individuals, they are separate in their relationship, but in their roles as supervisor and employee they are joined together and bound to their roles in the company. Their interactions will be shaped by the standards of the hierarchical role models offered by their organisation, which itself is set in the context of a specific social culture. The supervisor and the employee may disagree in their interpretation of each other's behaviour and speech. But their interactive behaviour has a common ground, i.e. their language and their culture. Despite their disagreements and different perspectives, they use the same language and presuppose a hierarchical role model as their frame of reference for the situation in which they find themselves.

Mind Opening Questions

How can one stimulate relational thinking in oneself and others? Let us again imagine a dialogue between two people where the first speaker starts by saying:

> "Today people use smartphones almost everywhere. They talk to their gadgets in the street, in the bus, in the restaurant, at the family table and even in meetings with friends. People can't live any more without their smartphones, they depend on them completely. They don't even notice when they are using them that they are being impolite and antisocial towards people in their company."

Question 1:

"In your opinion, what aspects of good communication do people forget about when using their smartphones?"

This question prompts the respondent to explore the relationship between the concept of good communication and the behaviour of people using

[2] Watzlawick et al., 1967.

smartphones. On the one hand, the respondent may believe that face-to-face conversations with direct eye contact are much richer than speaking by mobile phone. On the other hand, he might consider that when people communicate by mobile phone in a public place, they are inadvertently also communicating with the people standing or sitting nearby in negative way, because these people are being disturbed from their peace or from having their own conversations.

Question 2:

"How do you see the relationship between mobile communication and other developments in society?"

This question invites the respondent to explore the interrelationship between social and technological developments. Technological innovations make possible new forms of communication, but they also challenge traditional forms. Mobile phones fit perfectly to the acceleration of people's working and private lives, and they create the means to satisfy people's needs for social contact everywhere at any time. The downside of their widespread adoption may be one of information overload and social disconnection with people in the immediate vicinity of users. In essence, mobile communications can connect people over long distances but at the same time separate them from their fellow human beings nearby.

Question 3:

"Under which conditions would you personally appreciate mobile communication?"

This question invites the speaker to bring together his own ideas of good communication with the use of mobile communication. The common ground of face-to-face and mobile communication is the human need for contact and exchange. Advantages and disadvantages of both forms of communication have to be evaluated. Mutual respect is necessary in any case.

References

McNab, P. (2005). *Towards an integral vision: Using NLP and Ken Wilber's AQAL model to enhance communication*. Victoria, BC: Trafford.

Watzlawick, P., Bavelas, J. B., & Jackson, D. D. (1967). *Pragmatics of human communication: A study of interactional patterns, pathologies and paradoxes*. New York: Norton.

6 Transformational Thinking

The fourth and, for our purposes, final mode of dialectical thinking is called *transformational thinking*. Schoolchildren first encounter the concept of transformation in nature classes when they learn about tadpoles becoming frogs. Transformation is also a frequent theme in mythology, fairy tales and, of course, religion. In Greek mythology humans are frequently transformed into animals and vice versa. Ovid's grand narrative poem the "Metamorphoses" carries transformation as its central theme, and writers and artists throughout the centuries have made use of the concept as a source of inspiration. Today, the concept of transformation is frequently used in connection with significant change in organisations, with leadership, with politics, and in relation to the environment. Transformational thinking includes and connects the three modes of thinking that we previously discussed. When a thinker applies transformational thinking, he or she is able to conceive how something might radically change its form. The essential meaning of the concept is that of "movement through forms", hence to think transformationally, a thinker must consider the bigger structure of which some entity is a part, the developmental changes occurring to that entity over time, and the relationship of that entity to other entities in its environment.

It can be seen that transformation occurs in the natural world both with and without human intervention, the metamorphosis of a caterpillar into a butterfly being just one instance of the latter. The concept of the Anthropocene epoch illustrates the idea that the human race is acting to transform the environment both intentionally and unintentionally with the effects of such action being seen in climate change and the reduction of bio-diversity to name but two. In engaging Metathinking, we believe that people can become more consciously aware of how they can actively and intentionally transform themselves and their environment, and be more cognisant of the consequences of so doing. We use the term "human agency" to refer to the action of humans in transforming their environment, be that the natural, social, economic or any other kind.

N. Shannon and B. Frischherz, *Metathinking*, Management for Professionals,
https://doi.org/10.1007/978-3-030-41064-3_6

Illustration

We take as our first example of transformation the natural phenomenon of a geyser. Geysers are relatively rare geological features that involve a fountain-like spray of water and steam from below ground. Geysers are caused by seepage of water from a reservoir under the ground into rocks heated by magma (which is present close to the earth's surface as a result of volcanic activity). The water is heated to boiling point and bubbles up, eventually releasing pressure and resulting in a sharp release of steam and water through a vent in the surface. Eventually the escaped water cools and seeps back into the reservoir for the process to begin again some time later. In geysers we see the transformation of heat energy into the kinetic energy of the steam and water as it rushes up into the air. We also see the transformation of water into steam and back again (Fig. 6.1).

Our second example is taken from the work of Otto Scharmer, whose U-School is a system of communities created and managed with the aim of transforming the "underlying causes of the ecological, social, and spiritual crises of our time". Scharmer's "Theory U"[1] outlines a process for bringing about transformation in "business, society and self". In a series of on-line courses, Scharmer invites participants to engage with other people in a mutual effort to uncover a deeper calling in life and from there to question the assumptions and beliefs about the world that preserve the status quo. A process of self-reflection then follows during which participants summon the courage to take action by prototyping the kind of future that they would wish for. Finally, they act to establish their prototypes and in doing so, transform themselves and their social environments. What is distinctive about

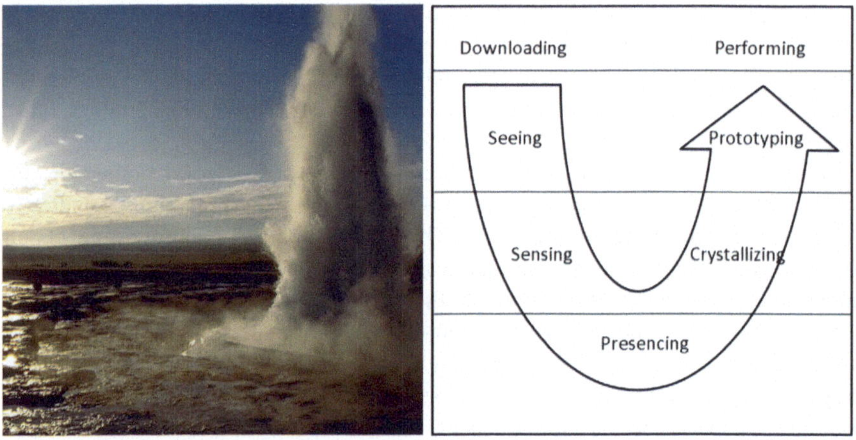

Fig. 6.1 Transformational thinking images: Geyser (© Wikipedia) and Complete U (own representation based on Scharmer, 2009, 38)

[1]Scharmer, 2009.

this process is that a person brings about transformation first by conceiving a gap between things as they are (their reality) and things as they would like them to be (their vision). Reality is seen to be missing something important (or to put it another way, something is absent from a person's conception of reality) and the person makes an intention to create a new reality that fills that absence and replaces what is missing.

Tension and conflict are intrinsic features of transformation in nature and human systems. In the example of the geyser the tension exists between the heat energy in the rocks and the water that seeps through them. In the case of transformation in human systems, the conflict exists between the way a person sees the current reality and the way that the person would like reality to be.

Transformational Thought Patterns (T)

Let us take a closer look at examples of the three thought patterns of transformational thinking.

Table 6.1 Transformational thought patterns (T)

	Transformational thought patterns
T1	Differentiation of conflicting elements leading to transformation or destruction of a system
T2	Elaboration of the conflicting interaction between two or more elements and their characteristics, potentially involving human agency
T3	Integration of conflicting elements into a new dynamic system, potentially involving human agency

Table 6.1 summarises three levels of transformational thought patterns.

T1 Differentiation of conflicting elements leading to transformation or destruction of a system

The first transformational thought pattern (T1) occurs when a thinker highlights the limits of stability within an entity where there are identifiable tensions or conflict. For example, someone might refer to the team of which he is a member by saying the following; "We have all been under a lot of pressure over the last year as the business environment became more competitive. People have dealt with that pressure in different ways, many have chosen to keep their heads down and concentrate on their immediate responsibilities. As a result we have become less co-ordinated as a group and more in danger of pulling in different directions, with the possibility that we might fall apart completely if we did not actively try to work on ourselves and unite as a team." In this statement the speaker acknowledges the bigger picture of the business environment and the shifting patterns of development in people's behaviour, and pinpoints the relationship between the two aspects. He then goes on to identify that the team could be transformed both positively or negatively as a result of this situation.

T2 Elaboration of the conflicting interaction between two or more elements and their characteristics, potentially involving human agency

The second transformational thought pattern (T2) picks up where the first one left off by elaborating in more detail about the tensions and conflicts between entities. Consider, for example, a collaborative project that involves several different parties, such as the development and launch of a new product or service. Imagine, for example, a triangle with three different parties, one at each point. At the top we have the sales and marketing team, at the bottom left corner the product developers, and at the bottom right corner we have the finance people. Conscious of the competition in the marketplace, the sales and marketing team are concerned to build a product with unique and very attractive features, and to bring it to market as quickly as possible. Meanwhile the product developers are concerned to make something that delivers what has been promised and does so reliably. Their interest is in quality and they know that this will take time to get right. Add to these two entities the finance team who want to control costs on the project and maximise revenues. They need the developers to work quickly and for the sales and marketing people to specify a product which is highly attractive to customers but that can be produced economically. The thought form identifies that the different interests of three parties interact and are potentially in conflict, hence an effort is needed to co-ordinate their work. Through dialog the parties could establish their common ground and develop a way of working together that transcends their individual interests and binds them together in a new cohesive way, transforming them as a working group.

T3 Integration of conflicting elements into a new dynamic system, potentially involving human agency

The third transformational thought pattern describes how different systems can be brought together to create a new, more effective entity. The systems under consideration can be external to a thinker, for example in the merger of the systems of two different organisations, or simply in the minds of two people searching to gain a common understanding, or a combination of internal and external, as when a person seeks to bring a personal vision to reality. The essence of the thought form is that the thinker compares two or more systems side-by side and puts forward a novel way of combining them. Social entrepreneurs are often seen as typifying this kind of thinking because they seek to instigate sustainable change that transforms society for the better. A good example of the kind of transformational thinking prevalent in government today is the concept of public-private partnerships. The traditional model of government procurement for infrastructure such as hospitals, roads, and railways is viewed as flawed because such projects typically run heavily over budget and over time for delivery, with considerable conflict between the client (government) and the supply chain (its contractors). A public-private partnership seeks to integrate the systems of asset finance, construction and maintenance, leaving these in the hands of the supply chain, in return for a commitment from the supply chain to deliver a level of service from the asset or return the asset to the government in good condition for a set sum of money at the end of an extended period of time. Essentially the concept of partnership seeks to eliminate or at least reduce the conflict between the interest of the private sector (to make a defined return on investment) and the interest of the public sector (to provide the tax payer with a high quality value for money asset). Critics of such arrangements argue that they often fail to achieve this outcome because, in the final analysis, private companies that offer the best value for money go out of business and have to be bailed out by the government.

Mind Opening Questions

We can imagine a conversation between two people where one speaker says to the other,

> "Artificial intelligence technology is now moving at such a fast rate that we can imagine new products and services, and ways of delivering them, that we thought were in the realms of science fiction just a few years ago. Organisations are now collecting data about their customers on such a scale that they can quickly establish who might buy their products and connect directly with those customers to provide them with something tailored exactly to their needs."

Question 1

"What conflict do you see emerging from the adoption of artificial intelligence and big data systems between corporations and their customers"

This question challenges the speaker to start spelling out some of the dangers of the introduction of these new technologies in the relationship between supplier and customer. At what point, for instance, does an individual's privacy become compromised by the recording of data on the way they live their lives? And to what extent is their autonomy threatened by the customers' continual exposure to products that the supplier's systems determine might be useful to them, even though the customers were not aware that they needed such products in the first place? How might those conflicts play out?

Question 2:

"What implications and consequences do you see occurring on a broader scale from these shifts in the way companies sell their products?"

This question encourages the speaker to go deeper into spelling out the nature of the potential conflicts. The speaker might explore the possibility that a supplier might use its knowledge of its customers to exploit them in some way. Customers could be led into buying products on credit that they could not afford, and therefore becoming dangerously indebted to those corporations resulting in legal disputes. Another possibility is that customers find themselves becoming dependent on the services of particular suppliers, purchasing far more of particular products than is good for them. On the other hand, customers might develop higher levels of sophistication in the way they relate to their suppliers, learning to control the data that their suppliers have about them, and judiciously switching suppliers if they felt a supplier was taking advantage. Such a trend might encourage suppliers to act in a more ethical fashion. Finally, governments may find themselves legislating to manage the relationship between suppliers and customers in a more ethical way.

Question 3:

"What new system do you think might emerge that would be able to accommodate and reconcile all sides of the conflict?"

Here the speaker must think creatively about a potential transformation in the way that people shop and have their requirements met by suppliers. Perhaps with an emphasis on sustainability, the speaker might imagine a world where the information that passes between customers and suppliers enables a beneficial match between what customers really need and can afford and what they are supplied with. In this world, suppliers would ensure that their customers were supplied with goods that were appropriate to their position in life and their income. For example, a supplier might recognise the stage at which a customer was starting a family and help that customer to budget appropriately so that he or she was provided with adequate products and services without being under pressure financially. Suppliers might become true "partners" to their individual customers, helping them through life. Such a shift might be part of an even greater social transformation towards a more sustainable world where people have increasing choice over their privacy and the way in which their personal data is used, perhaps by having the option of varying degrees of privacy and data control.

Reference

Scharmer, O. C. (2009). *Theory U: Leading from the future as it emerges*. San Francisco, Calif: Berrett-Koehler.

Setting Thinking Free

7

We began this book by discussing two different types of thinking: logical thinking and dialectical thinking. Whilst logical thinking is constrained by rules, dialectical thinking is looser, contains connections and follows certain patterns. In respect of these patterns, we maintained that dialectical thinking can be categorised into four different modes, each based on an underlying principle or belief in the shape that reality takes. In the structural mode of thinking, whatever is the subject of our thought is part of a larger structured picture or whole. In the process mode of thinking, whatever we think about is not static, but is in a state of constant change however imperceptible. In the relational mode of thinking, the subject of our thinking is always understood in relation to something else, for example 'male' is understood by reference to 'female' and vice versa. Lastly, in the transformational mode of thinking, whatever we think about is a system in transformation no matter how stable or constant it might look on the outside. In this mode, what we might see as isolated and unchanging entities are really living systems engaged in constant transformation as part of an effort to reach a new equilibrium within themselves and with their environment.

We can see that logical thinking has its own trajectory in human development. Educational systems and cultural influences apart, people typically become more fluid dialectical thinkers as they progress through life. Nevertheless many people find it hard to let go of some of the basic principles of logic set out by Aristotle so many years ago. We believe that people can make a choice regarding how they think, and we refer to this as *Metathinking*. The human mind can act on itself by noticing its thinking and consciously applying different ways to think. Such a capacity, like any other, has to be learned, and in the third part of this book we will show you how to do so.

N. Shannon and B. Frischherz, *Metathinking*, Management for Professionals,
https://doi.org/10.1007/978-3-030-41064-3_7

Constructing Worlds

When people understand that their thinking "constructs" the world as they see and understand it, they may become curious as to how their thinking operates. Once they have learned to recognise the patterns that thought can take, which can be achieved by listening to other people's thinking, they are able to start seeing how their own thinking is operating, and to engage conscious choices about how to expand their thought processes.

Take a look at Fig. 7.1. The image at the top is the famous Necker cube (first published by the Swiss Louis Necker in 1832). When people first look at the cube they see it having a single orientation (that of either the cube on the left or on the right, below). As they look longer at the cube, the orientation will shift to its opposite. For some people, the orientation may change from one to the other very rapidly, whilst for others a single orientation may remain relatively stable. Focusing on different parts of the cube may induce change or stability. The reality is that the picture is only a series of black lines on a white background, whilst the cube in whichever orientation is created in the mind of the viewer. We can say, therefore, that the cube is "constructed" in the mind of the viewer, and its orientation in one or the other position is somewhat arbitrary.

In a similar way, we argue that what matters to people as they go about their daily lives, is not purely what they "see" or more generally experience, but it is how they interpret and understand such experience in terms of what it means to them. Take for example, the word "love". Many different meanings may come to mind when one reads or hears that word. To love ice-cream is not quite the same as being

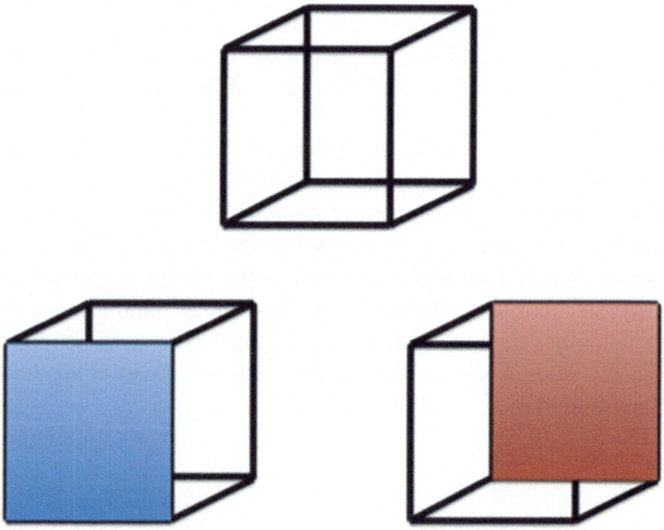

Fig. 7.1 Necker cube (own representation)

in love with someone or loving the game of football, for example. The meaning that a person attributes to the word "love" varies depending on the context in which it is presented, as well as the connotations that come to the mind of the person him or herself. Hence, despite the use of a common language in communicating ideas, people's thoughts are always unique to them in terms of the meaning they generate. For most people these meanings are generated automatically and rarely questioned.

Transforming Thoughts

We have seen how formal logical thinking follows specific rules to move from a set of premises to a conclusion. Whilst dialectical thinking does not follow rules in quite the same way as logical thinking, nor does it seek to arrive at specific conclusions, the patterns that it follows can provide a kind of framework by which thinking can organise itself and become more complete and creative.

Imagine, for a moment, that you are an astronaut looking out of your space capsule on the launch pad before being launched into space. As you look out at the Earth, you see it as largely flat. But then the rockets fire and you take off into space. You keep looking out and your perception of the Earth starts to change very fast. As you travel, you start to see the world in a different context. The Earth becomes a moving object—undergoing change. You realise you are in relationship to the Earth, the nature of which affects your perception of it. The horizon starts to appear curved as you continue on your way. Finally, you reach orbit and start to circle what you now see as a spherical globe. The Earth has been transformed in your mind.

Figure 7.2 illustrates this process figuratively. Initially, a concept is looked at two dimensionally. It has no depth. In terms of you as an astronaut, it is as if you looked out of the window and just saw a flat canvas, represented by the square. But as the rocket starts to rise, so your perception of the Earth changes into something much more three dimensional. You see things that you did not see before as you take on different perspectives (structure). You see movement in what was

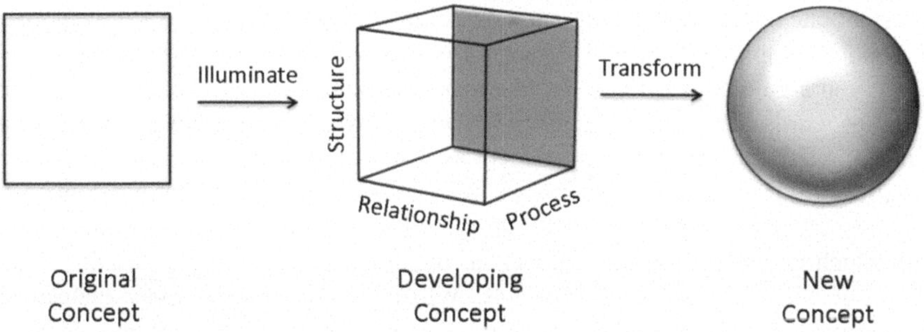

Fig. 7.2 How metathinking can transform thought (own representation)

previously a static picture (process). And you realise that your relationship with the Earth is in transition (relationship). In noticing what you couldn't see before and what was missing from your original picture, we could say that your concept of the Earth is continuously being illuminated and remediated. A more complex picture emerges as represented by the cube, and this is eventually transformed completely into a sphere where your perception of, and relationship with, the Earth is radically changed.

In the first instance Metathinking is about applying different thinking modes to a particular subject or concept in a conscious manner. Instead of seeing the Earth as a flat two dimensional object, consider seeing it as something that is part of a system and which can be viewed from different perspectives. Consider how the Earth is continually changing and evolving. Consider how you are in a relationship to the Earth, both distinct from it and yet part of it, and consider how, over time the Earth is being transformed.

However, we can go a stage further still, since Metathinking also involves transforming thought through a process of first consciously making a distinction to define a concept, then elaborating on the distinction, and finally using that distinction to integrate the concept with other concepts in a way that transforms the initial conception into a new more complex conception.

Imagine yourself again as an astronaut, this time orbiting the Earth in a spacecraft. As you look at the earth from a distance, you see that it is just one of many objects set in the dark and mysterious void that we call "Space". By seeing the Earth as set in Space you are making a distinction that connects the concept of Earth to the idea of the earth being part of a larger structure. You see the Earth as being separate from its surroundings and yet part of the bigger picture of Space. As you continue to gaze across space you notice the moon, other planets, and the sun, and you start to perceive a structure to the whole solar system. You might even try to elaborate that structure by describing the relative positions of the different planets. Then finally, after watching for some time, you start to understand that the Earth, moon, planets, and sun make up a more complex system in which the sun is at the centre and the various planets are all rotating around it.

To illustrate our point, try substituting the concept of "love" for the Earth and going through the same process. What would you say distinguishes love, how can you elaborate on that distinction, and how might you describe love as if it were part of a more complex conceptual system? Do you find this somewhat harder? Certainly, you are not alone if you do. We make the point because everyday language is full of words that stand for concepts, such as love. Once we have a word for a concept, we frequently treat that concept as if it were a physical "thing" with very specific and identifiable characteristics. We tend to assume, too, that everyone has the same understanding of the word. So, while language provides a convenient code with which to convey concepts, it also has the drawback of hiding or limiting what we mean when we use such concepts. When we consciously apply dialectical thought patterns in thinking and speaking we can *illuminate* what has been hidden, and *transform* what has been limited by our use of language to develop and then elaborate a new concept.

Table of Dialectical Thought Patterns

Table 7.1 summarises the twelve dialectical thought patterns that we have illustrated. When consciously applied, these patterns can move your thinking to a new level.

Underlying these thought patterns is the notion of living systems. When we explore everyday concepts referencing living systems, we move from talking about a concept as if it were an isolated physical "thing" to understanding it in a more dynamic sense. Take, for example, the concept of monetary inflation. One cannot see, hear, touch, smell or taste inflation. Yet we talk about controlling inflation or targeting inflation as if it had a physical presence. If we think of inflation in terms of a living system, it becomes easier to see how inflation is a component part of the bigger picture of the economy (another abstract concept); how it is not fixed but always in constant flux; how it is related to other aspects of the financial system;

Table 7.1 Table of dialectical thought patterns

	Structural Thinking
S1	Differentiation of elements in a whole representing a stable entity in its own right
S2	Elaboration of elements with reference to the structure, hierarchy and functionality of the elements
S3	Integration of different elements and perspectives into a structured bigger entity as a system
	Process Thinking
P1	Differentiation of a changing element, linking its current state to the past and future
P2	Elaboration of one or more elements in their developmental aspects
P3	Integration of changing and interconnected elements in an unceasing movement as a system
	Relational Thinking
R1	Differentiation of relationships between two or more separate elements
R2	Elaboration of specific relationships between interconnected elements
R3	Integration of interconnected elements and their constitutive relationships into an entity as a system
	Transformational Thinking
T1	Differentiation of conflicting elements leading to transformation or destruction of a system
T2	Elaboration of the conflicting interaction between two or more elements and their characteristics, potentially involving human agency
T3	Integration of conflicting elements into a new dynamic system, potentially involving human agency

and how it might be transformed and be transforming. Our Metathinking choice lies in how we think about inflation; whether we allow ourselves to go beyond a bald intuitive declaration such as "inflation is a bad thing" to a logical explanation "inflation is caused by an excessive money supply", or to a dialectical elaboration "inflation emerges due to the interaction of many factors, the availability of credit, expectations of purchasers, supply of goods and services, as well as government policies in relation to interest rates, borrowing, public sector budgets and taxation". We believe that a conscious Metathinking choice to employ the four modes of dialectical thinking and the 12 dialectical thought patterns leads both to a more critical and a more creative depiction of what is going on in the real world.

The Dialectical Thinking Cycle

Metathinking is a dynamic iterative process by which the thinker takes a concept and develops it by applying the dialectical thought patterns. We recommend that you develop your Metathinking through a practice of cycling through the four modes of dialectical thought applying thought patterns from each one to a specific concept sequentially, starting with structure and ending with transformation. We use the template (Fig. 7.3) as a guide.

One can also use this cycle when in conversation with other people to expand the thinking about a particular topic and to find ways to achieve a synthesis between different points of view. When used in dialogue between two or more people, Metathinking opens up contradictions and absences (things that are missing from one or other person's description of what they are thinking and speaking). Metathinking in this sense is a method for acquiring, broadening, refining, and assessing knowledge of reality. The opposing views of two different parties in a discussion stand as a thesis and an antithesis, with the possibility of the discussion leading to a synthesis—a new perspective that combines both of their views and on which they can both agree. The discussion starts with open questions and answers. Different aspects of a particular point of view are illuminated as the pros and cons of the argument are explored. The absences in the parties' thinking are gradually revealed as one person explores the thinking of the other. If all proceeds well, the participants may find a conjoint solution that integrates their previously separated views. This integration of opposites represents a transformation of their original thinking, such transformations being the goal of dialogic discourse. A dialogue between people of initially opposing views that is focused on listening and communicating what is missing from either side's perspective assures a broader view of situations and leads to practical solutions. Whereas monologic views of the world remain fragmentary and partisan, the use of dialectic in dialogue helps to establish a more complete understanding of reality by encompassing different perspectives.

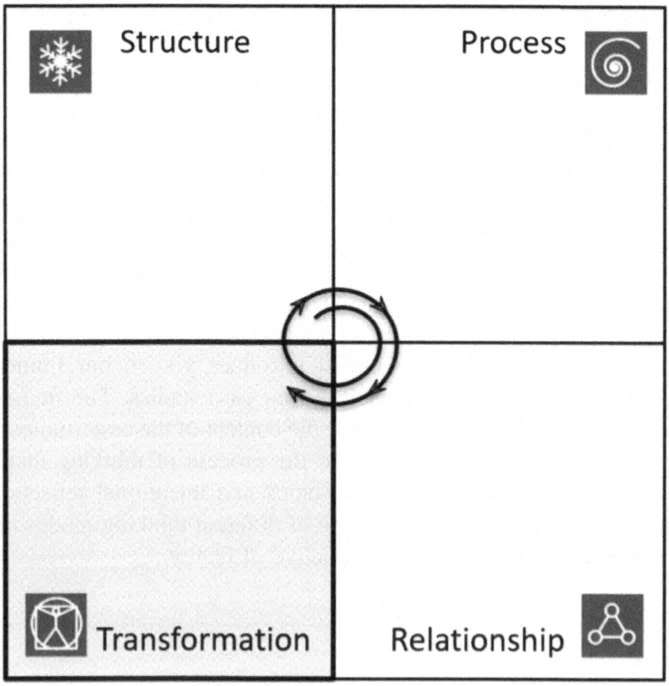

Fig. 7.3 Dialectical thinking cycle (own representation)

The Importance of Metathinking

It often said that we create our own reality. At the same time there is the saying, attributed to Alfred Korzybski, that the "map is not the territory".[1] We think that Korzybski meant that what we hold in thought and convey in language or graphics is just a representation of how we see the world or how we would like it to be, not the way the world is. And yet, humans take action in the world and are effective in changing their environment. Hence, thought is both part of reality and instrumental in transforming reality. We may only be able to make a crude representation of reality in our minds but that does not stop us being able to change our world. As people's awareness of their social, political, economic and ecological environments has grown, so people have come to see the enormity of the challenges that face humanity. We need to bring all of our thinking processes to bear if we are to create a better, more sustainable environment and make a good life possible for all people,

[1]Korzybski, 2005.

i.e. a life in which people can pursue their own interests and meet their needs compatible with the needs of all other people.

The philosopher Roy Bhaskar titled his book "Dialectic: The Pulse of Freedom".[2] to highlight his claim that dialectical thought enables humans to rid themselves of the limitations on their existence. In sharing this view, we do not hold any kind of political agenda. Our position is that Metathinking enables conscious choice about how we represent the world in our minds and, in particular, that dialectical thinking points the way to seeing what is not there, and yet could be there, in way that logical thinking does not. In other words, dialectical thought focuses us on removing what constrains and limits us, and Metathinking gives us the power to become more diverse in the way we think.

In the next part of this book, we will introduce you to our framework for Metathinking which we will use to analyse four case studies. The framework applies Wilber's integral quadrants to analyse the content of the case studies, and then uses dialectical thinking modes to analyse the process of thinking that the case studies describe. Metathinking is the conscious and intentional reflection on the form that thinking takes and the application of different thinking modes in order to develop a richer and more complex perspective of reality.

References

Bhaskar, R. (1993). *Dialectic: The Pulse of Freedom*. London and New York: Verso.

Korzybski, A. (2005). *Science and sanity: An introduction to non-Aristotelian systems and general semantics* (5th ed.). Brooklyn, NY: Institute of General Semantics.

[2]Bhaskar, 1993.

Part II
How to Apply Metathinking

The Metathinking Framework

8

In this section, we present four case studies in order to illustrate the development of thinking in action. Using structural thinking to define our choice of topics, each case study focuses on one of four units of analysis: individual, team, organisation and society. In each case study, we present an analysis based on the thinking modes and thought patterns.

Integral Quadrants

We will start by outlining the framework and methodology for our analysis which borrows from the structural model "AQAL" (all quadrants, all lines) proposed by the philosopher Ken Wilber that we referenced in Part I. According to Wilber, everything can be viewed from four different perspectives[1,2]:

- That of individual personal experience (individual interior or upper left UL). He describes this quadrant as "intentional" because it deals with what the individual thinks, feels and has in mind to do.
- That of collective personal experience (collective interior or lower left LL). He describes this quadrant as "cultural" because it reflects what a group of people do together.
- That of the objective reality of individual entities (individual exterior or upper right UR). He describes this quadrant as "behavioural" because it has to do with one is observable in terms of how a person or object behaves.

[1]Wilber, 2005.
[2]Wilber, 2007.

N. Shannon and B. Frischherz, *Metathinking*, Management for Professionals,
https://doi.org/10.1007/978-3-030-41064-3_8

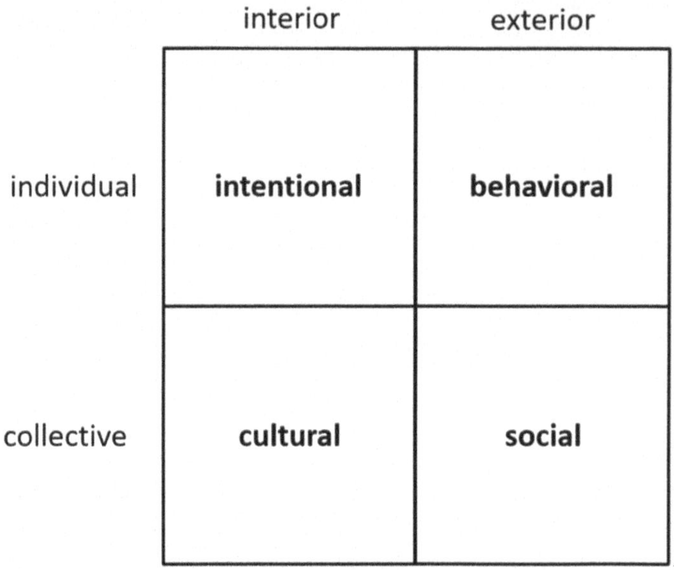

Fig. 8.1 Integral quadrants (own representation based on Wilber, 2005, 26)

- That of the objective reality of collective entities (collective exterior or lower right LR). He describes this quadrant as "social" because it has to do with observable structures in our social world.

Wilber proposes (in what is a classic example of structural thinking) that one can think more holistically by taking into account all four perspectives, and hence, he calls this an "Integral" model. The model of the four perspectives is set out in Fig. 8.1.

Quadrants Combined with Thinking Modes

Wilber's model illustrates the different ways in which we construct our knowledge of the world. We can consider objects in the world as either parts or wholes and view them from an internal (or subjective) or external (or objective) perspective. As *Metathinkers*, we are interested not just in the four perspectives themselves, but in the structure of each perspective, the movement inside each perspective, the relationships within each perspective and the potential for developmental transformation in each perspective. But not only that, we can also consider the structure of the whole four perspectives, the movement from one perspective to another, the relationships between the perspectives and the potential for developmental

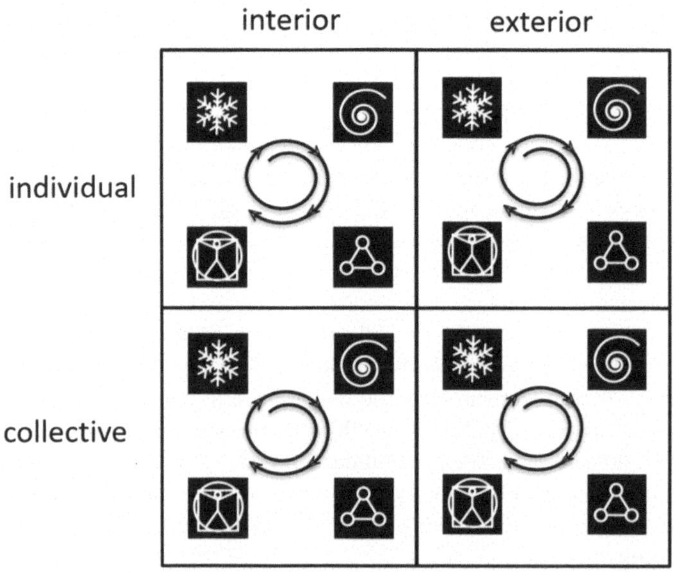

Fig. 8.2 Integral quadrants and thinking modes combined (own representation)

transformation of the entire four perspectives as a whole. In other words, we can combine Wilber's integral categories with our thinking modes by applying the thinking modes to the content within each quadrant as well as to the whole four quadrants. Essentially, we see the thinking modes being applied *fractally* to a whole and the part within a whole (Fig. 8.2).

In this book, we refer to the "Metathinking Framework" as the combination of Wilber's integral quadrants for the structure of content and the four dialectical thinking modes (SPiRiT) for the thinking process.

By way of example, let us imagine an engineer with an unusual illness. He has a vision that perhaps one day such an illness could be managed, rather similar to diabetes, providing a way could be found to test blood for the presence of a particular substance that would signal whether someone with the illness should take a particular medication or not. Currently, no such device exists that would do the job in the same way that someone with diabetes can use a glucometer to test blood sugar. His vision, an individual interior (upper left) perspective, is of such a device. How might he proceed? As a first step, he might investigate the available forms of blood testing technologies (exterior individual—upper right quadrant). He would look at the different kinds of technologies (structural thinking), how the technologies are developing and what is missing from them (process thinking), how those technologies are related to other technologies (relational thinking) and how they might be transformed with new developments (transformational thinking). With good fortune, he might identify that an emerging combination of technologies could make the device viable.

His next task would be to align a team of people to his vision. Here, he starts to connect with the interior collective lower left quadrant. The challenge he faces would be to establish a team with the right people and mix of skills (structural thinking), to develop them into an effective unit (process thinking), to motivate them by connecting their aspirations to the achievement of his vision (relational thinking) and to transform their potential by providing developmental support (transformational thinking).

Finally, moving into the exterior collective lower right quadrant, he would need to go out into the world to market the product and change the way people with this illness manage their treatment. Here, he would have to consider industry structures and the characteristics of different health systems (structural thinking), emerging trends in healthcare and social attitudes (process thinking), the relationships between things like people's ability and willingness to purchase the product and their desire to improve their well-being (relational thinking) and whether people will transform to making greater efforts to manage their health (transformational thinking).

Holons—The Units of Analysis

Wilber uses the concept of a "holon" to describe the general properties of a unit of analysis.[3] Holons are both units on their own and simultaneously part of a bigger whole (as one would be given to think using structural thinking) and nested in "holarchies". Hence, individual, team, organisation and society are holons within a holarchy. Figure 8.3 graphically represents the four layers of the holarchy, each layer divided into four perspectives.

In the following chapters, we will present a case study at each level of the holarchy, individual—team—organisation—society, to show the application of the Metathinking Framework. In each case, we will investigate the extent to which the subjects of our study, the people engaged in specific discourses, make use of the four perspectives and the four thinking modes. Our position is that, when a perspective or thinking mode is absent, such absence represents a potential source of error and a potential opportunity for those individuals to get a better grasp on reality and find a better solution to the problem facing them. Such analysis is both critical in the sense of exploring the deficits in thinking and creative in the sense of pointing to how thinking could become more complete.

[3]Wilber, 2007, 34.

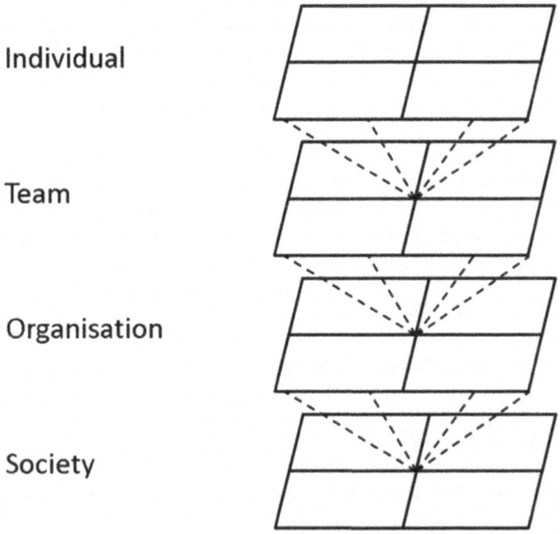

Fig. 8.3 Holarchy: individual—team—organisation—society (own representation)

Introduction to the Case Studies

The goal of the case studies in the following four chapters is

- first, to demonstrate the methodical application of the Metathinking Framework to different holons such as individual, team, organisation and society;
- second, to analyse existing and missing contents and thought structures in the discourse of an issue pertaining to a particular holon;
- third, to show possible transformations of the holon by relating different perspectives to each other.

Wilber's AQAL scheme (all quadrants, all levels) can ideally be complemented by a scheme of all thematic quadrants and all thinking modes or AQAT for short.

The combined models of the integral quadrants and the dialectical thinking modes now provide the Metathinking Framework for the presentation and discussion of our four case studies. Our first case study addresses how an individual's thinking transforms as she progresses in her career to a managerial position. We track the changes in the person's thinking over a period of four years. Readers who are themselves taking on managerial duties may find that the case study helps them locate gaps in their thinking and how they might overcome them. Our second case study focuses on how a management team think about developing their collective resilience. We describe the process of an offsite team workshop where the managers explore what resilience means from their personal perspectives, that of their team as a whole and that of their organisation. Thirdly, we look at the topic of "digital transformation". Here, we draw on a variety of sources that describe how to, and how not to, conduct the digital transformation of an organisation. We draw variously on business school articles, a paper produced for the European Commission called the "Onlife Manifesto", a discussion by five CEOs at the Davos Economic Forum in 2016, and an interview with a consultant previously engaged to run a major digital transformation project for a client. By comparing and contrasting the thinking behind this rich variety of sources, we show how a structured Metathinking approach can help to avoid some of the failures that occur when organisations attempt their own digital transformation. Finally, we take a Metathinking approach to analyse the discourse surrounding three different national health systems. The systems in Switzerland, the UK and the USA are all under pressure and facing transformational change. Yet, it seems that satisfactory solutions to the rising cost of health care are proving elusive. We look at what might be missing from the thinking about such transformations and suggest that the current debate misses important perspectives on individual attitudes and responsibility towards personal health care. Transformation is being considered in public discourse in terms of the provision of health care and its cost, but not in terms of individual attitudes and action.

References

Wilber, K. (2005). Introduction to integral theory and practice. IOS Basic and the AQAL Map. *Journal of Integral Theory and Practice, 1*(1), 26.

Wilber, K. (2007). *Integral spirituality: A startling new role for religion in the modern and postmodern world.* Boston, MA: Integral Books.

Personal Transformation—Becoming a Manager

9

Cognitive Interviewing

In this case study, we focus on the upper left quadrant—that of the individual herself. To do so, we make use of a technique to assess a person's level of cognitive development developed by Otto Laske.[1] The cognitive assessment is made through a semi-structured interview where an interviewee is guided by an interviewer to describe his or her world of work. The resultant conversation has the characteristics of a "Socratic" dialogue in the sense that the interviewer tries to understand the sense or meaning that the interviewee makes of certain work-related concepts. The interview proceeds by inviting the interviewee to talk about three separate but related categories of their working life, referred to, respectively, as the "Task House", the "Organisational House", and the "Self House". Structurally speaking, these three categories can be mapped to Wilber's four integral quadrants. The upper left quadrant maps onto the "Self House", i.e., the inner life of the individual. The upper right quadrant maps onto the "Task House", i.e., the individual's roles at work. The lower left and right quadrants map onto the "Organisational House", i.e., the organisation in which the individual works (Fig. 9.1).

The process of such an interview is simple in that the interviewer asks the interviewee to say something about various details of each "house" in turn. For example, when focusing on the "Task House" the individual is asked to describe her job in detail, focusing in particular on her role in making decisions, interacting with other people, and managing information. When focusing on the "Organisational House", the individual is asked to describe the bigger picture of her job, for example, the organisation's culture, or the political and social dimensions of her

[1]Laske, 2008.

N. Shannon and B. Frischherz, *Metathinking*, Management for Professionals,
https://doi.org/10.1007/978-3-030-41064-3_9

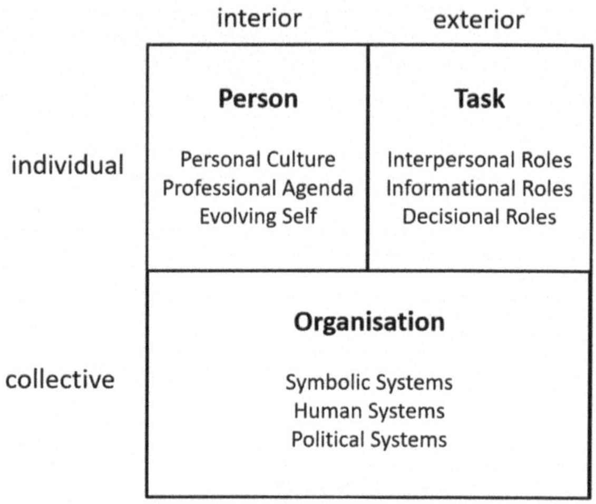

Fig. 9.1 Topics of the cognitive interview (own representation based on Laske, 2008, 277)

community. Finally, in relation to the "Self House" the focus turns to the individual herself, for example, her own development, values and goals in life.

In order to conduct the assessment, the interview is recorded, transcribed and then analysed to identify thought patterns used by the interviewee. We score the interview by noting the number and type of thought forms present in the thinking of the interviewee as she talks about each of the different houses. We have found that, typically, people have a distinctive footprint in terms of their use of thought patterns. They will use the thought patterns from one thinking mode when they describe one aspect of their life but not for others. This absence of thinking modes in specific areas can relate to imbalances in their life. For example, they may find themselves moving ahead very successfully at work which they can describe with a broad variety of thought forms, but being unsuccessful in their personal relationships which they appear to think about with a much more limited set of thought forms. This allows us to make some observations and give people feedback on their use of the thinking modes and thought patterns, which appears to have a developmental impact on them. In becoming aware of their selective use of thought forms to think about different parts of their lives, they may become able to reframe and rethink aspects of their lives which are causing them difficulty or where they find themselves stuck.

Now, we will introduce you to Sonja, whose cognitive development we assessed using this methodology in two interviews, performed with an intervening period of four years.

Sonja's Cognitive Footprint

When we first met Sonja, she was working as a product development engineer for an international pharmaceutical firm, where her responsibilities were mainly technical in nature. She had the help of an assistant but did not see herself as being that

Table 9.1 Sonja's cognitive footprint I

Quadrant	Structure	Process	Relation	Transformation	Total
Person	1	0	0	3	4
Task	2	1	2	1	6
Organisation	3	3	1	0	7
Total	**6**	**4**	**3**	**4**	**17**
%	**35%**	**24%**	**17%**	**24%**	**100%**

person's manager. Aged 29, like many people of that age she enjoyed her work and the learning she gained from it but was not particularly career minded, neither was she particularly optimistic about her prospects for advancement. Outside of work, she had sporting and cultural hobbies that were also important to her and she wished she had more time to pursue those interests.

What was distinctive about Sonja's thinking at the time was that her use of transformational thought patterns was reserved principally for her descriptions of herself. She described her job mostly in terms of structural and relational thought patterns and her environment in terms of structural and process thought patterns. In other words, for Sonja the most significant transformations in her life were the ones to do with herself and her own development. She described herself as "constantly evolving" and "always learning" both at work and in her private life. Her intentions at work were to gain more knowledge of the medical field and to become a specialist in the management of development projects but she had little interest in becoming a business manager or working in marketing. At the same time, she was aware of the tension between the demands of her employers and her desire for more time to pursue outside interests. She seemed to see her workplace as rather static and the environment outside of work as more fluid and therefore perhaps of more interest to her. Table 9.1 shows what we call Sonja's "cognitive footprint". It counts the number of thought patterns she used distributed between the three different "houses" and allocates them to the relevant thinking mode. In a one hour interview of this type, a sophisticated thinker might demonstrate thirty or more instances of thought patterns. As we can see, Sonja used thought patterns from each of the thinking modes, but the distribution varied according to the subject on which she was focused.

Sonja's Cognitive Development

We wondered whether Sonja's footprint of thought patterns would change at all as she made the transition from her twenties into her thirties, and we were lucky enough to be able to interview her a second time, some four years later. By then, she was aged 33 and things had changed for her at work. In the intervening period, she had become a team leader and her role encompassed the organisational aspects of production as well as the technical ones. Managing people is significantly more complex than managing technical issues. The latter most frequently can be managed following a strict protocol and rule set, and therefore there is often a clear right and a wrong way to act. But humans are much less predictable and variable than machines. Very often, they do not wish to be managed by someone else. So we were intrigued to know if Sonja was thinking about her work in a different way, and whether she was being successful or not.

Let us listen a little as Sonja explains her roles at work. She said, "I am in charge of the whole planning of the process and the scheduling of the personnel. I have managerial responsibility for these people. I am responsible for ensuring that everything is running smoothly so that we produce the right quantity in the right time. Often, I have to decide whether a process has failed. Then I have to fill out a report indicating the anomaly in our production process. I have to judge whether we still comply with our defined processes or not. Then whether to make a change or not. These are decisions I have to take every day. In addition, I now have to take decisions relating to people. For example, I had to decide who had to leave the company when the project volumes decreased. These are difficult decisions concerning people".

As the team's leader, Sonja's responsibilities had significantly increased. In being responsible for the overall performance of her unit, Sonja now had to make choices about which people to have in her team and then to ensure that those selected worked effectively and productively. The way Sonja had started to think about such issues showed up when we asked her to describe the relationships she had to manage in her work. For example, she frequently had to take action to resolve tensions between team members. She talked about it as follows:

> "Two employees told me, independently of each other, that the other was not talking to them anymore, and that they were unhappy with the situation. They were not unpleasant towards each other, but both had a feeling that something was wrong with their relationship. My feeling was that they should resolve the problem themselves so I encouraged them to talk to each about the problem without telling either one that I had also spoken to the other. So they did speak to each other and, afterwards, both were very much relieved. Such situations are very common. I encourage the people to solve problems themselves. If they can't solve a problem themselves or if the problem escalates, then they come to me and we talk together. But first, I always try to stimulate conversations between the people themselves".

Sonja's new-found responsibilities have caused her to turn her attention towards managing conflicts in the workplace. Previously, her transformational thinking was very much focused on herself, but at the time of the second interview she was applying such thinking towards other people and the relationships between them. Her intervention was subtle but apparently effective. She gave another example where a member of her team was unsettling others by becoming overly emotionally reactive. Normally, Sonja's organisation would have applied a formal process of instituting a performance improvement plan which, if unsuccessful, would have led to the employee's dismissal. However, after Sonja had spent some time discussing the matter with the person he resigned and the situation was resolved without further problem.

Table 9.2 Sonja's cognitive footprint II

Quadrant	Structure	Process	Relation	Transformation	Total
Person	0	3	2	1	6
Task	3	0	3	4	10
Organsiation	2	0	4	0	6
Total	**5**	**3**	**9**	**5**	**22**
%	**22%**	**14%**	**41%**	**23%**	**100%**

In this second interview, we found a total of four instances of Sonja's transformational thinking in relation to her work role, by contrast with our earlier interview when there was only one. She spoke excitedly about her role as a problem solver and resource for knowledge, whilst at the same time being aware that if she was able to pass on everything that she knew to people in her team she might eventually become superfluous. Her work seemed to have grown in importance and significance to her. She talked enthusiastically about her appetite for roles where she had an impact and was able to move things along and add value. "I would not do a job where I could not make a positive difference", she said. She was also anticipating a promotion to a role with increased responsibilities with the authority to initiate projects and where she had control of budgets. Her vision for that role was a transformational one in the sense that she saw herself resolving a chaotic situation by creating a structure and systems and processes that would facilitate work for all concerned. Table 9.2 shows Sonja's second cognitive footprint, taken four years later.

The qualitative shift in Sonja's thinking over the four-year period is summarised in Fig. 9.2, showing the number of thought patterns used throughout the interview.

The overall number of thought patterns increased from 17 to 22, and the number of relational thought patterns grew from 3 to 9 showing how Sonja's relational thinking became dominant in the second interview. The complexity of her thinking

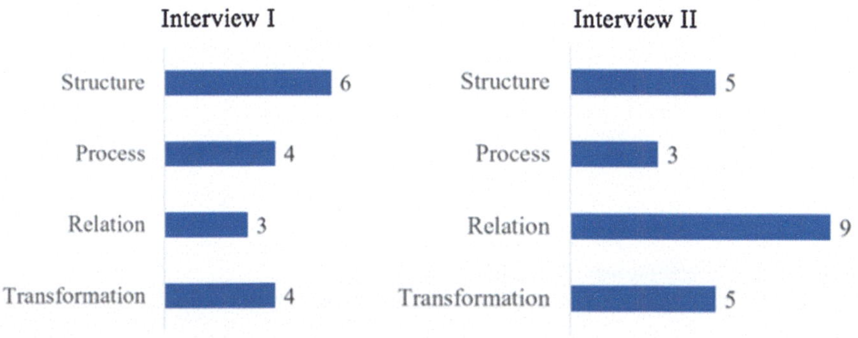

Fig. 9.2 Sonja's cognitive footprints I and II (own representation)

and her ability to see connections between different aspects of her work and life had grown substantially. Moreover, her focus had shifted from the changes she saw in herself towards the changes she could make in her job and her work with other people. Hence, her sense of herself as an agent of transformation acting on the world around her had increased.

Cognitive Behaviour Table

We can go into further detail about Sonja's thinking processes by mapping her use of thinking modes against the topic on which she was focused during the interview in a table. We call this a "cognitive behaviour table". Table 9.3 lists bits of her

Table 9.3 Sonja's cognitive behaviour Table II

	Structure	Process	Relationship	Transformation
Task				
#01	S1			
#02	S2			
#03	S2			
#04			R2	
#05			R2	
#06				T2
#07				T2
#08			R1	
#09				T2
#10				T2
Organisation				
#11			R1	
#12			R2	
#13	S1			
#14			R2	
#15			R1	
#16	S1			
Self				
#21		P2		
#22				T2
#23		P2		
#24		P2		
#25			R2	
#26			R3	
Total	**5**	**3**	**9**	**5**
%	**22%**	**14%**	**41%**	**23%**

thinking from the interview with their corresponding thinking mode to make visible the flow of her thoughts; what she talked about and how.

In the interview, Sonja uses all four thinking modes, with the relational thinking patterns being far the most frequent, making 41% of the total. Relational thought patterns describe the internal and external relationships of a system and their common basis. What is striking about the table is that various thinking modes are distributed unevenly across the three houses. In the Task House, relational and transformational thinking dominate which suggests that Sonja consciously and purposefully influences what happens in the workplace. Sonja's use of the process thinking mode only occurs in the Self House. Process thought patterns describe how things arise and disappear without human intervention. Our analysis shows that Sonja uses the transformational thinking mode specifically when referring to topics in the Task House which relate to her role at work, whilst her thinking about herself (in the Self House) is much less complex and involved relatively small changes. This was a surprising insight also for Sonja herself.

Cognitive Coaching and Personal Transformation

Working with clients, we have found that the analysis of a person's dialectical thought patterns is a very useful tool to get a feel for their level of cognitive development and to provide the basis for professional coaching in more sophisticated thinking. Firstly, it provides the means by which a coach can construct an integrated model of a client complete with the developmental challenges that the client faces. Secondly, such work is an act of "process consultation" in the sense used by Edgar Schein by which a client may come to understand better the assumptions, values, attitudes and behaviours that are helping or hindering their success.[2] Thirdly, using this method a coach can provide a client with the means to examine their own thinking and to see what might be missing in terms of thinking modes and thought patterns, thereby enabling the client to explore and expand further their conceptual landscape of a problem. A cognitive coach provides feedback, educates and directs the attention of clients towards their own thinking processes, thereby providing a "royal road" to what had previously been unconscious. By using sets of questions that are based on the four thinking modes, the coach opens the client's mind to a more nuanced and complex notion of the reality of their world. We present below some examples of the "mind opening" questions that we might use in coaching conversations with clients to stimulate their thinking.

[2] Schein, 1998.

Mind Opening Questions

We invite you to imagine that you are a coach working with employees within an organisation. Consider the following mind opening questions as a means to stimulate and develop your client's thinking (Table 9.4).

Table 9.4 Mind opening questions: personal transformation

UL	**Intentional**
S	What different parts of yourself do you find that you bring to your work?
P	When you look back over recent times, in what ways have you found yourself changing the way you work?
R	Are there any ways in which you can relate the way you are at work to the way you are in other areas of your life?
T	What struggle do you anticipate between your ambitions on the one hand, and your desire for work/life balance on the other, and how do you see that being resolved?
UR	**Behavioral**
S	What different parts of your role can you describe?
P	In what ways would you say that your role is evolving?
R	Can you connect what you do in your role to the broader vision for your team/department or organisation?
T	What different activities might you also engage in that would lead to a transformation of your role?
LL	**Cultural**
S	Can you describe how the different parts of your work team fit together?
P	Is there something that is currently excluded from the team, that would be useful to include?
R	When you think of the other teams with which your team interacts with, how do they influence each other?
T	What would you say are the limits to the stability of your team?
LR	**Social**
S	What elements of the environment must you take into account as far as your organisation is concerned?
P	What longer-term changes do you anticipate for your organisation?
R	How would you see what your organisation is doing relating to the needs of its clients?
T	How would your organisation be strengthened or weakened if it was to merge with another?

References

Laske, O. E. (2008). *Measuring hidden dimensions of human systems: Foundations of requisite organization* (Vol. 2). Medford, MA: Interdevelopmental Institute Press.

Schein, E. H. (1998). *Process consultation. Vol. 1: Its role in organization development* (2nd ed.). Reading, Mass.: Addison-Wesley.

Team Transformation—Building Resilience 10

Workshop for Team Development

In this case study, we explore a senior executive team development exercise that we undertook for a division of large private sector organisation with several thousand employees. The team, comprised of seven people led by its chief executive, was a mix of people from different backgrounds, some of which were long-term employees of the organisation and others that were relatively new. They worked in an industry sector known for its volatile fortunes caused by exposure to the economic cycle, high levels of competition, slim margins and relatively high risks. They had a mandate to grow profitability cautiously with a focus on operational improvement. In practice that meant being selective about the work that they took on, managing risk very tightly (requiring a high degree of professionalism), meeting or exceeding their clients' expectations, and getting the best from their workforce. The chief executive was positive about the team and the prospects for the business but concerned about the level of pressure on the team and the degree of commitment required from its members. In his mind, the tough times that they had faced over the previous two years were likely to continue for a while longer and the team needed to be highly resilient. As a result, he wanted to invite the team to an offsite workshop when they could take a breather for a couple of days, strengthen their relationships, reflect a little on how they might support each other and take some time to consider how they could increase their chances of success going forward. At the same time, he was keen that they should not spend the time getting into "business as usual" discussions. He wanted to keep away from the kind of focused conversation that they had when they met as a board and conducted business reviews.

The quadrant in focus here is that of the lower left "Team" quadrant. In this quadrant, we investigate themes such as interpersonal relationships, shared worldviews and belief systems, and team climate and culture. Yet, from a Metathinking perspective, the "Team" quadrant is also intrinsically linked to the other three quadrants and cannot be fully separated from them without error. Hence, an

N. Shannon and B. Frischherz, *Metathinking*, Management for Professionals,
https://doi.org/10.1007/978-3-030-41064-3_10

initiative to develop a senior executive team, such as, in this case, a workshop, is inevitably going to impact the whole organisation (upper and lower right quadrants), as well as the mindsets of the executives themselves (upper left quadrant). Often, the composition and dynamics of the executive team sets the tone for the rest of the organisation. The team are responsible for setting the culture and climate of the whole organisation, and their own team culture and climate is often a miniature replica of what exists outside of them. If the team itself cannot change, then the likelihood is that efforts to change the rest of organisation will not yield the desired results. In theory therefore, if the executives in the senior team are able to recognise how their own behaviour affects the whole organisation, there is a prospect that they will devise interventions not just to strengthen themselves as a team, but which develop the rest of the organisation in a way that strengthens teams throughout and which is mutually reinforcing.

Team and Themes Analysis

A consultant undertaking an assignment of this nature often has to walk a fine line between simply following the brief and expectations handed down by his client and delivering a workshop that enables the team to come up with actions that will address more than just the symptoms on the surface. In the first instance, it is important to build trust and to ensure the client has confidence that nothing untoward will happen. This involves producing a draft programme for the event and talking it through with the event sponsors, who in this case were the HR director and the CEO. As a facilitator, the consultant must also try to establish some kind of rapport with the other members of the team so that his or her credibility is not in doubt when introducing and leading exercises on the event itself. A standard process that we use for doing this is to conduct a form of team analysis by interviewing members of the team individually and asking a standard set of questions to surface how they view the functioning of the team and, to an extent, the organisation as a whole. In these interviews, we get a sense of the members of the team and their way of thinking, in particular as to whether they already have some of the tools for dialectical thinking at their disposal. We also get a feel for the ability of the team to work together to solve broader organisational issues, for example, culture change. We also use the interviews to tell the participants a bit about ourselves and establish some common ground. All participants are asked the same questions (e.g. —how do you feel about the quality of senior team meetings), and the answers are collated in a report where people's responses are presented anonymously and organised into certain themes based on keywords or terms that cropped up regularly in our conversations. This feedback report is presented and given to participants to read, usually the evening before the workshop. Then at the workshop, the team are asked to address three questions:

1. What are the important findings in the report?
2. What are the implications for the team and leadership?
3. What action should they take?

However, as sometimes happens, our client was not in favour of this type of approach thinking that it would take the workshop in the direction of focusing more on the overall business and less on the individuals themselves. With retrospect, we can conclude that the CEO was sensitive to the reality that most conversations within the team were focused on the lower right quadrant, that of the organisational systems, processes and metrics of performance, and that he wanted to redress the balance by situating the event firmly in the "we space" of the lower left quadrant. In responding to this sensitivity, we put forward a second proposal on the lines that we conduct a peer feedback exercise by telephone before the event and share the results of this at the workshop itself. For this exercise, we proposed that we would ask each member of the team to give their views on three or four of their colleagues, using a standard set of questions. The questions included items such as:

- What do you value most about x in the work that s/he does?
- How much of a team player would you consider x to be both with his/her own team and across the broader business?
- How well do you think x is succeeding in creating the environment for high performance and getting the best from people?

The idea was to give each member of the team a sense of how they were being viewed by their colleagues and to leverage these insights to strengthen mutual understanding and relationships between the team as a whole. Structurally thinking, this exercise was therefore situated firmly in the left-hand quadrants, responding to the CEO's concerns.

Our client accepted the proposal for the feedback exercise and we then went on to design the whole event. Our intention was to spend the first day on interpersonal and team issues and then to see if the team were ready to move onto more organisational issues on the second day. A criticism that we frequently hear levelled at such executive team offsite events is that, although participants generally enjoy the workshops and feel they spend the time well, little changes after the event. We chose to try to evade this criticism by giving a large part of the second day over to "action planning" concluding with allocation of responsibilities for particular tasks to specific members of the team. Our hope was that, if the team navigated their interpersonal issues and relationships successfully on the first day, then they would be ready to address some of the wider organisational issues on the second day. We decided that we would add in two extra questions when we conducted the peer feedback exercise prior to the event:

1. What's your view on the functioning of the senior team? What, if anything, would you like to see improved?

2. What would your hopes be for the workshop itself? What would you consider to be a successful result of the workshop, given that you will be giving up two days of your valuable time? Is there anything that you would not like?

The first question was intended to give us a sense of how positive or negative people felt about the team itself, and therefore how much time would likely be taken up dealing with team issues. The second question would test people's perceptions of the purpose of the event and make us aware of any taboo or "no go" areas. Depending on the quality of the replies, we would then have a sense of whether our design for the workshop would be appropriate.

In the event, the peer feedback telephone interviews went well. People were well disposed towards each other and positive about the team. In each case, we were at pains to emphasise that the idea was not to report back who said what verbatim, but to collect the themes that people thought were important and to prepare a report for each member of the team that captured these themes and presented them anonymously together with some actionable recommendations. Hence, a measure of confidentiality would be preserved. But, in any case, we ensured that the feedback always included some positive strengths as well as some perceived areas for improvement. The responses to the two extra questions showed that people in the team were positive about the team as a whole and had few requirements for the offsite meeting itself. Most felt it would be time well spent almost irrespective of the output, whilst one or two indicated that they would like to generate some actions that could be implemented going forward.

Reflecting All Quadrants

We knew then that our plans for the workshop content would most likely be well received. We planned to start the first day by getting people to "check in" by saying how they were feeling and how they would like to be feeling at the end of the two days. This would then enable us to introduce the idea of resilience being a positive response to emotional states elicited by negative events. In other words, whilst people can always be expected to experience some negative emotion, such feelings need not necessarily result in behaviour that takes them away from what is important to them and their goals. In order to encourage people to notice the level of congruence between what they were thinking and feeling internally and what they were saying and doing in the company of others, we introduced them to an exercise called the "Left-hand column" exercise. The exercise, originated by Chris Argyris and Donald Schön, is described by Rick Ross in the book "The Fifth Discipline Fieldbook".[1] The idea is to encourage people to write down the thoughts and feelings that they experience but do not actually express in their interactions with others. By keeping a record of such internal dialogue in the left-hand column of

[1]Senge (ed.), 2007.

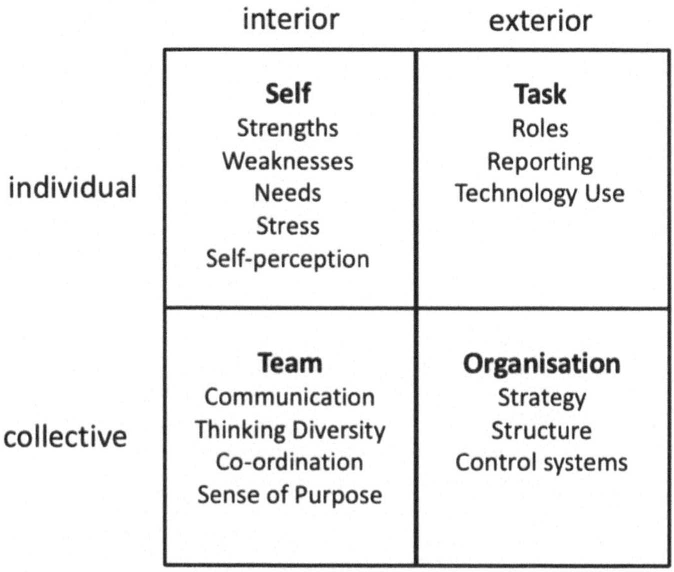

Fig. 10.1 Teambuilding topics mapped against quadrants (own representation)

their notebooks, people can become more willing to communicate those thoughts openly with their colleagues and to do so in a manner that alerts others to the possibility that the speaker is wishing to say something that is both important but also uncomfortable for them. In introducing people to this exercise early in the workshop, we hoped to create an atmosphere that was "psychologically safe" for people to speak openly and say what was on their minds.

In the rest of the workshop, we would conduct a number of exercises focused on the left quadrants—the individual and the team. Our plan was to lead participants steadily through to the point where they would consider action planning for the entire organisation and hence link their own developmental actions with changes that they might initiate in the right side quadrants, people's roles, the business processes and systems and the organisational strategy and structure. Figure 10.1 shows the four quadrants.

Team Development Activities

Table 10.1 summarises briefly all the activities that we planned. These were interspersed with some material presented by the facilitator giving examples of resilient people and emotional intelligence techniques for building greater resilience.

Table 10.1 Team development activities

Activity	Purpose	Process
Common ground	To establish what participants value in common with each other	Participants discuss in pairs what is most important to each other. Pairs then share what they discovered that they have in common and what separates them, with the whole group
Feed forward	To get ideas on what team members could improve	Participants review their individual peer feedback reports, decide on what they would like to improve and solicit suggestions from other members of the team
Team challenge	To experience a short team task	Participants are divided into two teams to see who can build the highest tower out of kit supplied, inside 20 min
Team reflection	To analyse their strengths and limitations as a team	Participants rate their team on four dimensions Communication Diversity of thinking Coordination Strength of mutual purpose
Poster presentation	To summarise current self-perceptions and get additional colleague feedback	Participants prepare and present a poster describing how they see the purpose of their role, how they think they are doing, how they think they are viewed, and how they would like to be viewed
Difficult conversation case study	To get advice on how to deal with a stressful conversation	Participants prepare and present a short description of conversation with a third party that they found or would find stressful and get advice from colleagues

Action Planning

The final activity for the workshop was an action planning exercise designed to get the team to establish a specific set of tasks that individual members would take responsibility for delivering. The activity had four parts:

(a) An initial "visioning" exercise where the participants were invited to consider a point in future two to three years hence, when their organisation might be considered the most resilient of its kind in the industry and therefore a leader;
(b) A "reverse planning" exercise when they plotted how the organisation would have arrived at the state they envisaged in (a) applying four "mindsets" or thinking modes;
(c) Creation of a list of activities that they thought feasible and desirable to undertake;

(d) Evaluation of those activities in terms of impact (the extent to which they believed the activity would help them reach their vision) and their ease of implementation, in order to prioritise and allocate responsibility.

In order to get the participants to understand and use the thinking modes, we prepared a short presentation with a summary and examples of ideas relevant to each thinking mode as follows:

Action Planning: Four Mindsets to Drive Future Planning and Action

Table 10.2 sets out the four thinking modes explained below.

1. **Structural Thinking Mindset: Four Perspectives on Resilience**

Following the model in Fig. 10.1, you can think about resilience from four different perspectives. Firstly, that of your self, which includes things like your physical health, sleep patterns, diet and mental attitudes. Secondly, you can think of resilience from the perspective of your team, involving the extent to which people in the team are supportive of each other, can communicate openly and are bound by a common sense of purpose. Thirdly, you can think of resilience in terms of the demands the organisation makes on people in terms of the tasks, processes, and tools available to help their work. Finally, you can think about resilience in terms of larger themes to do with the way the organisation as whole works.

2. **Process Thinking Mindset: Emergent Themes**

You can focus on what is currently changing in your environment, and how those changes bear on you and your resilience. Examples of relevant trends emerging in your industry are being indicated by:

- Reports by official bodies such as the Health and Safety Executive "Managing Construction Health Risks—Wellbeing", and NBS (National Building Specification): "Mental Health matters in the Construction Industry";
- Attitudes of the Millennial Generation: Emphasis on value of "Wellness";
- New technologies: bringing new tools and new demands.

Table 10.2 Four mindsets to action planning

	Structural thinking: everything is part of larger structure/multiple perspectives. Focus on the bigger picture
	Process thinking: everything is constantly on the move. Focus on what is emerging
	Relational thinking: everything is connected and influences everything else. Focus on common ground and connections
	Transformational thinking: everything can be transformed. Focus on radical change

3. **Relational Thinking Mindset: Connection and Common Ground**

You can now start to make connections between the different elements that you have identified and consider how they influence each other. For example, consider the connections that exist between:

- Mind and body;
- Individual/team/task/organisation;
- Resilience and productivity;
- Resilience and efficiency;
- Resilience and learning;
- Resilience and competition;
- Resilience and development.

What would you say are the implications of these connections where action to improve resilience is concerned?

4. **Transformational Thinking Mindset: Intentionally Creating a New Future**

Finally, you can think about how you might transform your future by developing a vision and identifying how it might come about. Consider the following questions:

- Vision—Where do you want to be? When?
- Imagine if you are there, what steps would have taken place for the vision to have been realised?
- What would have to have been TRUE for this to come about?
  - What structures?
  - What processes?
  - What relationships?
- What action will you take?

In addition, the team were given a set of mind opening questions to stimulate their use of the thinking modes.

In order to consider these questions efficiently, the team was split into three groups. The first group addressed upper left quadrant issues around individual resilience, the second group addressed bottom left quadrant issues around team resilience and the third group addressed upper and lower right quadrant issues around organisational resilience.

Results

It is always difficult immediately after an intervention such as a team development workshop to know whether the team has really benefitted. Typically, people appear to enjoy the workshop, say that they got new insights and that they decided on some

Table 10.3 Activities to develop organisational resilience

Aim/aspiration	Action	Impact	Ease
A culture where psychological safety is the norm	Resilience training for employees	High	Med
	"Permafrost" education	High	Low
Reduction of waste	Communications etiquette	High	High
A productive, healthy, "smart" working week for all	Understand the fifty-hour week	High	High
	Retake control over diaries	Med	High
Reduction of waste	Reports: purge of what's not needed	Med	Low
Focus on well-being	Identify and promote "Be Well" champions	Med	High
Better work-life balance	Revise policies on, and improve implementation of, holidays, lunches and breaks	Med	High
Clarity of roles	Weekly call for senior team	Med	High
	Appoint moderator	Low	High

actions, and indicate that it was worth spending the time. But it is hard to know whether real change and transformation has occurred or will occur. A lot depends on the willingness of the team to follow up by meeting again to discuss progress and on their resolve to continue taking action. As soon as people leave the workshop external events come into play that may increase or decrease the chances of developmental movement. In addition, people may leave the team and new people may join. Hence, there are many dynamics that come into play.

This particular team came up with the actions to take and aims on which they were based, shown in Table 10.3 categorised by estimated impact and ease of implementation. At the time of writing, the team had already met some four weeks after the event to revisit the individual feedback and follow up on progress, so there were indications that they had moved forward.

In Table 10.3, the activities have been categorised according to the anticipated impact and ease of implementation, as agreed by the team at the offsite. In the first instance, the team recognised that addressing the organisational culture to bring about a climate of greater openness was essential. They wanted "psychological safety" to become the norm and they saw the route to achieving this being some form of "resilience training". However, they also saw that a significant constraint on the effectiveness of such training was what they termed the "permafrost layer". This term referred to a cadre of generally well-established middle managers who the team considered to be very resistant to any sort of change. Effectively, they were both dependent on this group of managers to run operations, and yet critical of them because they appeared to be resistant to new ideas and ways of working. In the eyes of the team, tackling this group and "re-educating them" was both important and yet too difficult to take on. They decided to "park" such action until a more appropriate time. In our experience, it is not unusual for members of a senior leadership team to see a tier of their managers in such a way that is "beyond help". Typically, the senior team do not recognise their own role in contributing to the stance of such resistance to change in their managers and instead see it as a characteristic limitation of such people. As facilitators in such a situation, we face a dilemma between drawing the attention of workshop participants to a potential blind spot in their thinking with the risk of the group getting sidetracked into an unproductive debate about the limitations of their mid-level managers, or accepting the situation pragmatically and pressing on with developing an action plan that the team feel comfortable with. In this instance, we decided not to dwell on the issue and pressed on.

A second theme that the team identified as creating unnecessary pressure was the way that new communications technologies were being used. Here, they were aware of a relationship between people's use of "always on" email and internet and their (and that of others) sense of overwhelming workloads. In this instance, they felt the problem could be addressed by setting out a protocol for the use of email, addressing issues such as the need to send copies to a wide variety of people. It is interesting to note that this upper left quadrant solution was not connected to any upper right quadrant actions, such as people learning how to handle email in more effective ways.

Thirdly, the team felt that people were accustomed to working an overly long working week, in the region of five ten-hour days. Whilst there was a belief that there must be a better, more productive way for people to work, it was acknowledged that the problem was not well understood. Initially, the team felt that one of them should research the problem themselves, but after some discussion, it was decided to use a cohort of managers to look into the problem as part of a leadership development exercise. The need for members of the team to examine the extent of their ability and willingness to delegate and therefore, reduce their own workload, was not raised as an issue, however the team did agree that they needed to "retake control" over their diaries. This followed the observation that, by allowing their assistants to run their diaries, they often found themselves with suboptimal appointments including a lot of travel.

Another source of time wastage that the team felt pervaded their work and that of their employees was that of management reporting. This was described as a major source of stress both for the team and for those people reporting to them. Over time, an ever-increasing number of reports had been created, with the effect that more reports were being produced than were ever read or digested. They agreed that by rationalising the reporting, time could be saved in compiling and sifting through them and that a thorough purge of what was redundant should be undertaken.

Finally, the team identified that they could build on an existing organisational initiative that had created a cohort of "Be Well" champions to encourage more healthy living and working styles throughout the organisation. Thus, they established a useful first quadrant relationship between healthy lifestyle and resilience and they determined to raise the profile of the "Be Well" champions by more active involvement and promotion.

Mind Opening Questions

We invite you now to imagine that you are part of a management team thinking about how to develop greater resilience for yourself and other people in your organisation. Consider the following mind opening questions as a means to explore the issues you might have to explore as you set about establishing a plan of action (Table 10.4).

Table 10.4 Mind opening questions: team transformation

UL	**Intentional**
S	In what contexts do you feel more stressed and when are you more resilient?
P	What events and occurrences are emerging that might affect your resilience?
R	How is your resilience related to other aspects of your work?
T	Where are your personal limits and what action might you take to raise them to a complete new level?
UR	**Behavioural**
S	In what ways have the tools you use to do your work added to the organisation's stress? For example, your email system?
P	For your team to be more resilient, in what new ways do you have to behave, and how would these emerge from the old ways?
P	What new interactions between you and different parts of the organisation need to occur?
R	What new relationships between you and different parts of the system need to be forged?
T	What conflicts might arise and how you might resolve them?
T	What personal development would you have to undergo?
LL	**Cultural**
S	What attitudes to the way work should or should not be conducted threaten people's resilience and how might you change them?
S	What are the different perspectives within the team on its resilience?
P	What are the historical events and influences that have caused the current culture to emerge and how is the culture developing currently?
R	How is the way you make changes in your organisation related to the stress people experience?
T	How can you take a whole systems approach to transform your resilience?
LR	**Social**
S	How does the way your team is structured affect its resilience?
S	How could the systems within your organisation, e.g. for remuneration, recruitment, performance management be improved to support greater resilience?
P	What new processes would have to occur within your organisation?
P	What strategies are missing in your current organisation that need to be established?
R	What common ground can be found between the goals of different parts of your organisation?
T	What different systems within your organisation could be better coordinated or integrated?
T	How could your organisation become, at the same time, more inclusive, integrated and differentiated?

Reference

Senge, P. M. (ed.). (2007). *The fifth discipline fieldbook: Strategies and tools for building a learning organization*. London: Brealey.

Organisational Transformation—Going Digital

11

Metathinking Text Analysis

In this case study, we review several sources of information about the practice of "digital transformation" and practice "Metathinking" by analysing the thinking implicit in their content, with reference to Ken Wilber's four-quadrant "integral" model and the four SPiRiT thinking modes. We use Wilber's model to categorise the content of a person's thinking, and the four thinking modes to categorise the way they think about their subject. Together, the two forms of analysis give us the "what" and the "how" of someone's thinking. We begin by drawing on a selection of published articles by experts on the subject, primarily addressing what the experts consider as "best practice". We then examine a panel discussion at the World Economic Forum in Davos (2016) involving five CEOs of large multi-national companies. In this discussion, each of the five CEOs relates how they and their organisations are bringing about digital transformation. We finish with excerpts from an interview that we conducted with a consultant actively engaged in helping clients digitally transform their organisations. In this interview, the consultant describes a digital transformation that failed and explores the reasons why.

The standard unit of this Metathinking analysis is a paragraph of text or a passage in a spoken conversation. In each case, we have identified the underlying thinking mode in use and the integral quadrant being referenced by the author or speaker section by section and counted these instances to give totals for the number of occurences in each of the texts and conversations. Where a paragraph or spoken passage contained more than one thought pattern or a combination of thought patterns, we assigned a count of 0.5 to both of the concerned thought patterns. In the same way, we counted up the integral quadrants used in each section of text. There are obvious limitations in this kind of quantitative analysis since different paragraphs and passages may be of different levels of importance and sophistication, and therefore qualitatively different. Nevertheless it gives the reader a feel for where the focus of an article or speech lies in terms of thinking modes and

N. Shannon and B. Frischherz, *Metathinking*, Management for Professionals,
https://doi.org/10.1007/978-3-030-41064-3_11

quadrants, and therefore points to what might be missing in terms of thought and understanding.

This kind of text analysis is a relatively new field of application of Metathinking. In applying such analysis, we can extend the process of Metathinking beyond excerpts from interview dialogue to any written text. By means of text analysis, the thinking modes and thought patterns used in a text can be counted and categorised, and different texts can be compared with each other in terms of the depth of the thought process that they express. This analysis shows the strengths and weaknesses of texts from a Metathinking point of view, for example, the extent and range of thought patterns can be contrasted with any thematic absences and one-sidedness. However, there are limitations in that one cannot probe the author of the text to elaborate on what a certain passage means in the same way as one might in interview.

Visuals on Digital Transformation

By way of introduction, we show below a series of diagrams and infographics that are typically used as visual examples of thinking about digital transformation. Even these diagrams and infographics can be categorised according to thinking modes. As an example, we ran a search on Creative Commons Search images with the keywords "digital transformation".[1] Among the first hits were the following graphics, which can easily be assigned to a certain thinking mode.

The first diagram "The Three Elements of Digital Transformation" shows a number of entities grouped under three categories and organised spatially. It spells out a "big picture" of digital transformation and is thus an example of structural thinking (Fig. 11.1).

The second diagram is organised as an input–process–output model. Although it has structural elements, we see it best as an example of the process thinking mode because it points to change occurring over time (Fig. 11.2).

The third diagram spells out the relationships between different elements of digital transformation showing how they are connected. It is therefore an example of the relational thinking mode (Fig. 11.3).

For our fourth diagram, we have a more abstract image—that of a man diving into a "digital sea". The representation is therefore one of transformation (Fig. 11.4).

[1]Creative Commons, 2018.

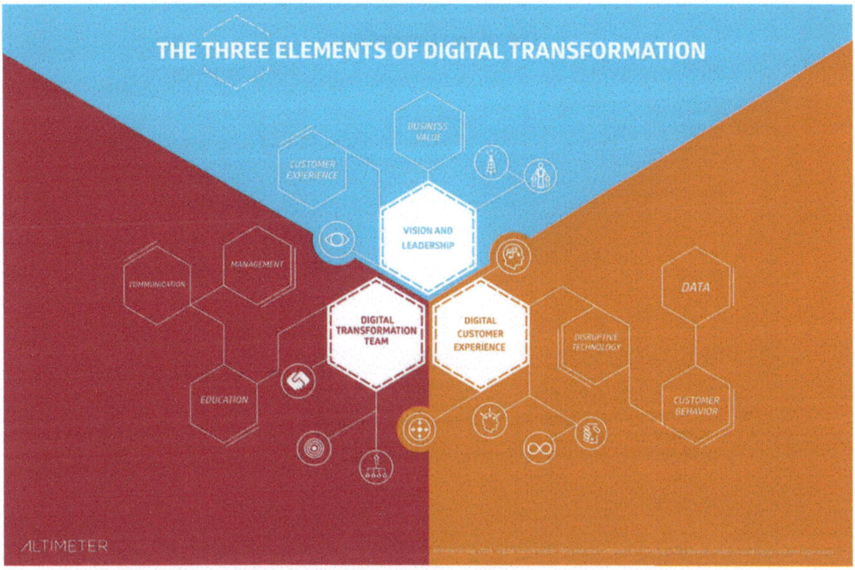

Fig. 11.1 Digital transformation: Structure (© Altimeter)

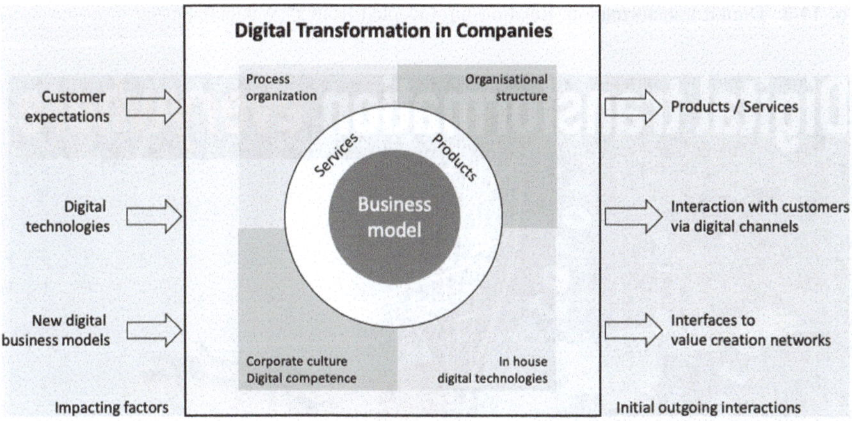

Fig. 11.2 Digital transformation: Process (adapted from © Wikipedia)

The examples show that there are prototypical visual forms of representation for the thinking modes that we can understand intuitively. But the visual forms emphasise different aspects of a topic and hide others. They are used specifically to illuminate different aspects of how their author conceptualises the issue they wish to describe.

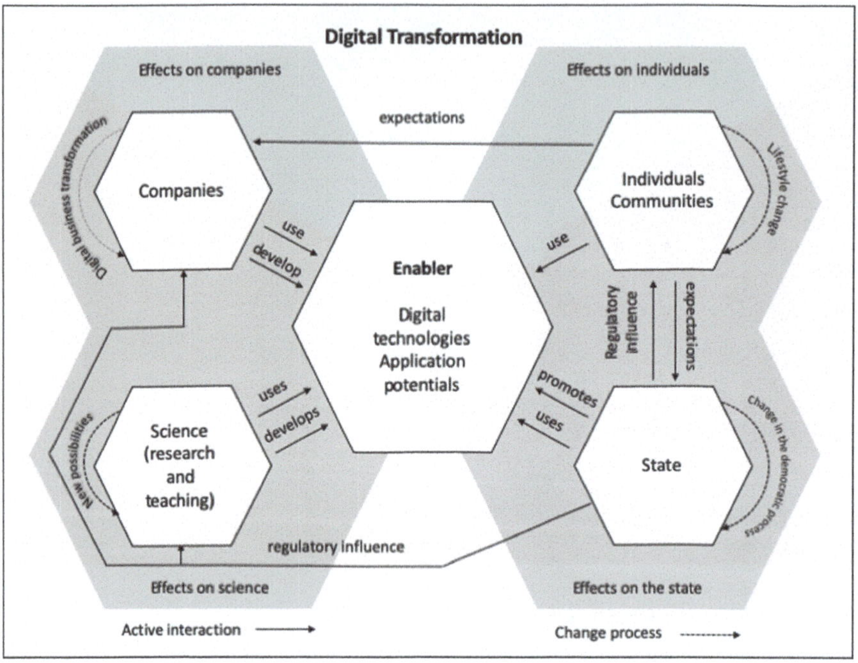

Fig. 11.3 Digital transformation: Relationship (adapted from © Wikipedia)

Fig. 11.4 Digital transformation: Transformation (© Gerd Leonhard)

As the visuals show, thinking modes pervade writing and discussion about digital transformation. We present this analysis, not with a view to identifying good or poor practice in carrying out an organisational digital transformation, but as a means to show how thinking about digital transformation, as reflected in the discussion and written comment is selectively focused in specific ways. The benefit of such analysis is that it enables us to see what might be missing from the current discourse and to suggest ways in which a broader and more inclusive understanding of digital transformation might be achieved.

"Best Practice" Papers on Digital Transformation

At the time of writing, digital transformation is a prominent and widely reported topic. There are many experts in the field writing about good and bad practices of digital transformation. We have chosen two authoritative papers to show how Metathinking text analysis helps to illuminate the strengths and weaknesses of thinking about this topic:

- Westerman, Bonnet and McAfee (2014). The Nine Elements of Digital Transformation (MIT Sloan Management Review).[2]
- Davenport and Westerman (2018). Why So Many High-Profile Digital Transformations Fail (HBR March 2018).[3]

The authors of the first paper "The Nine Elements of Digital Transformation" set out the areas in which they think organisations can find opportunities for digital transformation based on research interviews with executives in large companies. They identify something they call "Digital Maturity"—a quality of organisations involving a combination of digital activity and leadership that creates business transformation. In their view, such digital maturity enables better performance and entails leaders having a vision for which digital activities represent good opportunities for their companies. They then analyse the opportunities under three areas, with three opportunities in each area. Essentially, this is a piece of structural thinking where a bigger picture of all the opportunities facing such companies is presented. We also notice that the authors link successful digital transformation with their concept of digital maturity involving the knowledge and skills of company executives. This is a piece of relational thinking.

In the first area identified by the authors, labelled "Transforming Customer Experience" the authors note that companies are using digital means to identify and analyse the needs and preferences of different customer segments and to market to these segments more selectively. For example, a company may dynamically alter its pricing in relation to the specific characteristics of a local market, which might

[2]Westerman, Bonnet and McAfee, 2014.
[3]Davenport and Westerman, 2018.

include variations in customer demand due to factors such as the time of day and the weather. This analysis shows elements of structural and process thinking modes. The authors also note changes in the enhancement of the sales process largely through the use of new digital technology. They cite the use of digital technology by salespeople, in stores and on e-commerce sites to encourage customer interest and purchases. Here again, the authors apply structural and process thinking in relation to the different emerging trends in different marketplaces. Finally, the authors describe how companies are changing the process by which customers conduct their shopping, offering combinations of online home and in-store shopping, some even coupled with opportunities for other leisure activities. Here, the thinking emphasis is very much on the transformational mode, integrating different systems to provide a very different experience for the customer.

The authors conduct a similar description of two other areas for transformation, operations and business models. In each area, they point to a multitude of emerging changes in working practices and the products and services offered by businesses. Their preoccupation is principally with the process and structural thinking modes, and they have less to say about how different areas relate to each other (relational thinking mode) or how the complete transformation occurs. They do, however, conclude with a statement about the requirement for strong leadership and vision. Here, they hint at, but do not elaborate on, the inner changes that might need to occur within corporate executive teams and the way individual executives think about their businesses.

In summary, the Metathinking text analysis is revealed in Fig. 11.5.

When we look at the summary statistics on the thinking modes in use and the quadrants in focus in the paper, we can see that structural and process thinking modes dominate and that the focus is almost entirely on the lower right quadrant—that of the objective aspects of the external environment in which companies operate. In the first instance, what is missing from the authors' focus is an analysis on the upper left quadrant—the subjective perceptions and thinking of executives in an organisation. Similarly, there is no analysis on the lower left quadrant—the internal dynamics and values of executive teams in the companies. These omissions are ironic because the authors highlighted at the start of their article the concept of "Digital Maturity" and this clearly has something to do with how executives think

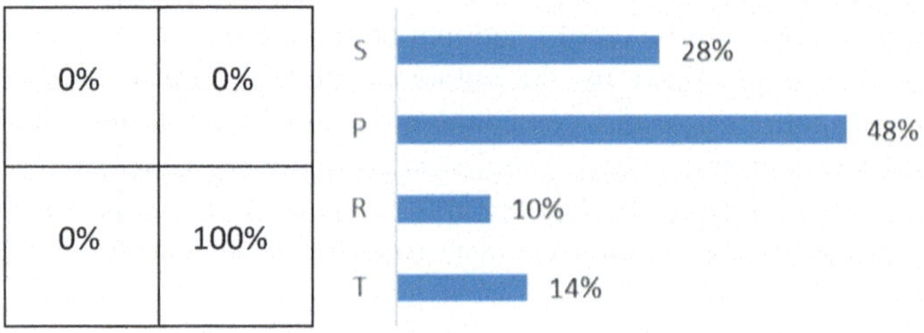

Fig. 11.5 Thinking profile: The nine elements of digital transformation (own representation)

and approach the work of digital transformation. In our view, the selective focus on the external quadrants is reflected in little use of the relational and transformational thinking modes. For example, where the authors talk about transforming the customer experience, they might have related this concept to the attitudes and values that executives in the company have towards customers. Do they, for instance, think of customers as being rationally or emotionally influenced? We suggest here that if the customer experience is to be truly transformed, then the way that executives think about their company's customers and the values that they apply must also be transformed.

In the second paper, which was written some four years later, Davenport and Westerman argue that there have been repeated patterns of failure when organisations have attempted digital transformations. They offer a variety of reasons for this, pointing out firstly that there are always many factors affecting an organisation's success and hence an expectation that digital transformation is necessarily going to lead to better performance is misguided. Secondly, they indicate that digital transformation involves changing the way an organisation does business, and hence requires investment in many different areas such as skills training for people and new business processes, as well as new digital technology and infrastructure. Thirdly, they point to a need to coordinate investment in digital transformation with what is happening in the organisation's external environment—its markets, customers and competitors. Here, they suggest that organisations frequently forget to ensure that their digital initiatives fit with their chosen strategies. Finally, they say that executives make less rational decisions about investments in digital transformation because of uncertainty about how a particular technology might be taken up within a market. Digital technologies change rapidly and are frequently superseded with something better, and hence, executives may make poor choices because of uncertainty about what is the best technology to follow.

We believe that the thrust of the Davenport and Westerman paper is aimed at changing the behaviour of CEOs and executive teams such that when they make investments in digital transformations, they do so in a better informed and more sophisticated way. Although they do not go so far as to make it explicit, the authors are suggesting that decision-makers should transform their own thinking in order to be more successful at digital transformation. One might expect therefore that the authors would focus on the upper and lower left quadrants in terms of the psychology of executives and cultures of their teams. Our analysis shows rather more focus on the right side quadrants. This is to say that their main preoccupation is with the objective elements such as behaviours, technologies, business processes and aspects of the external environment. They do have a little to say in upper left quadrant terms in relation to the individual psychology of executives making investment decisions about digital technology. For example, they comment about how such executives lose their rational thinking processes and are influenced by the hype promoted by vendors, consultants and high-profile cases in the media. But they say nothing about the (lower left quadrant) aspects of culture in an organisation attempting a digital transformation or the impact on people and teams (Fig. 11.6).

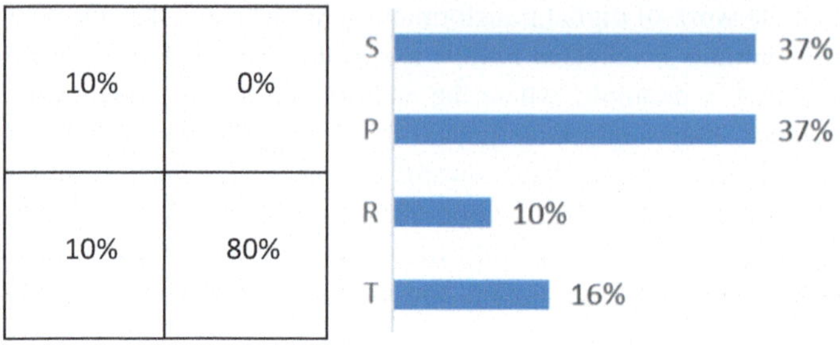

Fig. 11.6 Thinking profile: Why so many high-profile digital transformations fail (own representation)

In terms of the thinking modes, the authors' first point is a structural one. They identify that digital transformations must be considered within the context of the "bigger picture" within which the organisation is operating. This bigger picture includes the overall economy, the specific industry and the actions of competitors. Next, Davenport and Westerman note that digital transformations involve more than technology investment, they change the way business is done and hence involve changes in many other activities of the organisation, such as staff skills, business processes and machinery. Here, the authors hint at the need to coordinate change in different systems across the whole organisation—very much a transformational thinking mode. The authors also note the relationship of digital transformation to business strategy, and the link between the latter and the market in which the organisation is operating—clear evidence of the relational thinking mode. Lastly, they highlight the emergent nature of digital technologies and, in particular, the sheer uncertainty surrounding which form of digital technology will win out in the end.

Comparing and contrasting the two papers, we can see that the latter paper on the failure of digital transformations represents an improvement in terms of the balance of thinking modes and structural quadrants. The earlier paper, listing elements of digital transformation, appears entirely to miss an examination of the internal aspects of executives and their teams. In it, much is said about changes in the external environment, but nothing is expressed about changes in the way that organisations think about the process of digital transformation. Right side quadrants and structural and process thinking modes prevail, at the expense of noticing the relationship between transforming the way a business works with the attitudes, values and mindsets of its management team. Instead, the concept of "digital maturity" is invoked but left without detail explanation or exploration.

Perhaps, therefore, it comes as no surprise that, some four years later, researchers are exploring the reasons for the failure of multiple digital transformations. Even in this case, the paper we have chosen falls short of an in-depth exploration of the parallel process of transformation that might need to occur in the thinking and decision-making of executives and their teams. There is evidence of greater emphasis on the left side quadrants, but right side "external" elements still predominate.

By way of contrast and for a broader, more strategic, perspective we chose a third paper written by an expert group:

- The Onlife Manifesto: Part 1, The Onlife Initiative.[4]

This publication emerged as part of the output of a research project organised by the European Commission to explore the impact of information and communication technologies (ICTs) on the human condition. The perspective taken by the authors of this paper is that ICTs are more than tools (for example, to aid and accelerate communication or reduce the cost of business transactions) and are elements of an environment that the human race has created which increasingly affect our sense of ourselves as human beings and how we operate in the world. In this perspective, one cannot isolate the physical aspect of digital transformations from their effect on people and their lives. There are therefore social, ethical, legal and political implications of some significance that, typically, are not recognised let alone articulated. A simple illustration of this point that may help is as follows: many of us are now avid users of various forms of social media. We post our views and respond to the postings of others, often with "likes" or "retweets", exposing our thinking to a potentially vast audience. Hence, we influence and are influenced on a much wider scale than ever before. Our online presence creates a "cyber-personality" that may be somewhat different from our actual sense of who we are, and yet which may also represent a target that can be persuaded to behave in certain ways. We are seeing such potential for manipulation not just in online advertising for products that, otherwise, we might never have contemplated, but also in the political arena and electoral voting intentions.

In the first section of this paper, the authors argue that the thinking that defines what they refer to as "modernity"—perhaps simply defined as the set of assumptions underpinning modern social organisation—is itself becoming increasingly challenged. They suggest three ways in which this is occurring. Firstly, the traditional distinction between what is nature and what is human artefact is no longer valid. Secondly, the idea that humans are rational actors, and therefore ethically accountable, has given way to the idea that ethics are better understood as socially determined. And thirdly, the mechanical and hierarchical models on which much of social and political structures are based are giving way (to more organic metaphors) under the influence of ICTs. There is plenty of structural and process thinking in this section. Existing structures are seen as breaking down and new ones emerging. There are also elements of relationship and transformational thinking. The development of ICTs is linked to the creation of new and very different social and political structures. All four quadrants are under consideration here—upper left in terms of mental models and assumptions; lower left in terms of cultural attitudes

[4]Floridi (ed.), 2015.

and perspectives; upper right in terms of artefacts and nature; and lower right in respect of societies and nation states.

In the second (brief) section on fears and risks in a hyperconnected era, the authors comment on the social impact of online systems and the behaviours of those entities that control, manage and use them. They point to a general blurring of who has control over what, and a lack of clarity in responsibility and accountability. They also suggest that concepts such as personal freedom and equality become undermined in an online world where selective use of data is made to profile, target and selectively group individuals. Here, they apply structural, process and relational thinking and link all four integral quadrants in proposing that emerging technologies impact on social systems, culture and individual experience.

The third section of the manifesto deals with "Dualities", a more philosophical notion, that of the distinction made between pairs of objects which appear to be in opposition, i.e. the posing of a dichotomy and the benefit of "re-integrating" the opposites, so that they become in a sense "overlapping" or, to apply a metaphor, two sides of the same coin. The authors point to several distinctions, for example, that between humans and their artefacts, and between public and private. They argue that artefacts have come to take on a life of their own, and hence biological and evolutionary metaphors apply to them as well. The authors call for a rethink of the concepts of responsibility, duty, control and freedom in such a new world. In itself, such a rethink is transformational. The assumption that humans are free, autonomous agents must be revisited. We consider that, in terms of integral quadrants, the emphasis on public and private is an attempt to link right and left quadrants, to show how they are interrelated. Hence, this section is also particularly strong in terms of relational thinking. It defines the common ground between public and private life by stating that people's privacy needs both exposure to and shelter from the public gaze.

The final section covers a number of the themes under the heading "Proposals to better serve policies". The authors point to the paradox of human freedom—the idea that we are both free and yet not free because human action cannot be completely separated from the social and physical contexts in which it arises. This again links left and right quadrants in relationship to each other. They also propose that information and communication technologies influence and shape us as humans, much as we as humans shape such technologies. Here, they link upper and lower left quadrants in relationship. Finally, they consider the impact of the digital economy on human attention, something they claim that is now treated as a commodity. This links the upper left quadrant of "attention" with the lower right quadrant of "technologies", and hints at connections to the lower left quadrant in terms of the cultural processes by which people apply and regulate the use of technology.

In summary, our Metathinking analysis of the "Onlife Manifesto" is shown in Fig. 11.7.

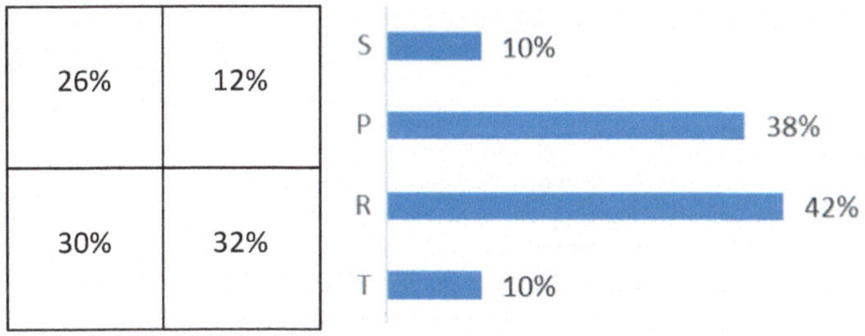

Fig. 11.7 Thinking profile: The onlife manifesto (own representation)

In respect of the integral quadrants, all four perspectives of the topic have been touched. As one might expect of a political document, the emphasis is very much on the lower collective quadrants, culture and social systems, and on the upper left quadrant—the internal processes of individuals. There has been less emphasis on the upper right quadrant—the physical aspects of the systems themselves.

Interestingly, relationship and process thought patterns dominate clearly over structural thought and transformational patterns. The authors are focused very much on the relationship between shifts in technology and how these might change the nature of what it is to be human. Their implication is that such changes should result in a transformation of politics and social policies, but they have less to say about the exact nature of those transformations.

For illustration, Table 11.1 shows how we applied the coding on some paragraphs. All texts are taken from the manifesto.[5]

[5]Floridi (ed.), 2015.

Table 11.1 Metathinking coding of paragraphs

Bit	Text	Thinking mode	Thematic quadrant
0.3	The world is grasped by human minds through concepts: perception is necessarily mediated by concepts, as if they were the interfaces through which reality is experienced and interpreted. Concepts provide an understanding of surrounding realities and a means by which to apprehend them. However, the current conceptual toolbox is not fitted to address new ICT-related challenges and leads to negative projections about the future: we fear and reject what we fail to make sense of and give meaning to	P/R	UL
1.1	Philosophy and literature have long challenged and revised some foundational assumptions of modernity. However, the political, social, legal, scientific and economic concepts and the related narratives underlying policy-making are still deeply anchored in questionable assumptions of modernity. Modernity has indeed—for some or many—been an enjoyable journey, and it has borne multiple and great fruits in all walks of life. It has also had its downsides. Independently of these debates, it is our view that the constraints and affordances of the computational era profoundly challenge some of modernity's assumptions	T	LL/LR
2.1	It is noteworthy that Cartesian doubts, and related suspicions about what is perceived through human senses, have led to an ever-increasing reliance on control in all its forms. In modernity, knowledge and power are deeply linked to establishing and maintaining control. Control is both sought and resented. Fears and risks can also be perceived in terms of control: too much of it—at the expense of freedom—or lack of it—at the expense of security and sustainability. Paradoxically, in these times of economic, financial, political and environmental crisis, it is hard to identify who has control of what, when and within which scope. Responsibilities and liabilities are hard to allocate clearly and endorse unambiguously. Distributed and entangled responsibilities may wrongly be understood as a licence to act irresponsibly; these conditions may further tempt business and governmental leaders to postpone difficult decisions and thereby lead to loss of trust	R	UR/LR
2.3	The abundance of information may also result in cognitive overload, distraction and amnesia (the forgetful present). New forms of systemic vulnerabilities arise from the increasing reliance on informational infrastructures. Power games in online spheres can lead to undesirable consequences, including disempowering people, through data manipulation. The repartition of power and responsibility among public authorities, corporate agents and citizens should be balanced more fairly	P	UR/LL

(continued)

Table 11.1 (continued)

Bit	Text	Thinking mode	Thematic quadrant
3.7	Nevertheless, we consider this distinction between private and public to be more relevant than ever. Today, the private is associated with intimacy, autonomy and shelter from the public gaze, whilst the public is seen as the realm of exposure, transparency and accountability. This may suggest that duty and control are on the side of the public, and freedom is on the side of the private. This view blinds us to the shortcomings of the private and to the affordances of the public, where the latter are also constituents of a good life	S	UL/LR
4.6	We believe that societies must protect, cherish and nurture humans' attentional capabilities. This does not mean giving up searching for improvements: that shall always be useful. Rather, we assert that attentional capabilities are a finite, precious and rare asset. In the digital economy, attention is approached as a commodity to be exchanged on the market place, or to be channelled in work processes. But this instrumental approach to attention neglects the social and political dimensions of it, i.e., the fact that the ability and the right to focus our own attention is a critical and necessary condition for autonomy, responsibility, reflexivity, plurality, engaged presence and a sense of meaning. To the same extent that organs should not be exchanged on the market place, our attentional capabilities deserve protective treatment. Respect for attention should be linked to fundamental rights such as privacy and bodily integrity, as attentional capability is an inherent element of the relational self for the role it plays in the development of language, empathy and collaboration. We believe that, in addition to offering informed choices, the default settings and other designed aspects of our technologies should respect and protect attentional capabilities	R	LL

Discussion on Digital Transformation

Metathinking text analysis is not limited to written text. It can be applied to spoken texts in the form of interviews and conversations. To show how the analysis of a conversation works, we have chosen a panel discussion at the World Economic Forum 2016 in Davos on digital transformation which is publicly available as a video and in the form of a transcription on the internet.[6]

The panel was convened by Rich Lesser, the CEO of the international firm, the Boston Consulting Group, and involved a conversation with five CEOs drawn from a broad selection of prominent multi-national businesses. Lesser's intention was to

[6]World Economic Forum, 2016.

get the CEOs to talk about how digital transformation was important to their businesses, what they were doing about it, and particularly the organisational enablers they were applying to make it happen. We have analysed the entire transcription of the conversation to see what thinking modes the CEOs were applying and where their focus, in terms of integral quadrants, lay. As it turns out there are interesting differences between the speakers. Whilst a panel of such a nature does not necessarily allow all the panellists to speak equally, nor can they be expected to reveal all of their thinking, it is interesting to speculate that their views are reflected in the strategies that their organisations are applying to bring about digital transformation.

The panel began with some comments from Klaus Kleinfeld, CEO of the metals company Alcoa. He spoke principally about "right quadrant" elements, namely the impact of changes in technology such as the advent new materials as well as the reduced cost of diagnostic sensors. Together these accelerate the manufacturing development process for new products, benefitting customers but also having some implications for workers in terms of their thought processes (lower left quadrant).

Next came Jean Pascale Tricoire of Schneider Electric, an energy management firm. For him, the changes appeared to have been even more dramatic. Whereas Kleinfeld had talked about an acceleration in processes and a reduction in time-scales, Tricoire spoke about new products and services emerging out of a need for energy management, new relationships with customers and partners, and a transformed R&D function. Many aspects of his business appeared to have required rethinking resulting in transformation at many levels. Although a lot of these changes were external "right quadrant" changes, there were also links to the left quadrant in terms of how people in his organisation had adapted to the change.

The third panellist, Bernard Tyson, revealed how the customer experience was being transformed in the healthcare industry by virtue of new digital technologies. Whereas, in the past, clients had gone to their healthcare provider and had to comply with the way of working that suited the provider, Kaiser Permanente, was taking health care to their clients by consulting over the telephone and internet. Whilst technological transformation had been the driver for such changes, Tyson had also become aware of the need to make it clear to his people how their roles would be transformed. He was therefore considering more actively the lower left quadrant.

By contrast, Meg Whitman, CEO of Hewlett Packard Enterprises, was very focused on the external (right quadrant) aspects of transformation. She talked about the need to accelerate change in systems and processes through IT in order to become more automated and orchestrated. However, she also noted as an after-thought that organisational culture was important, and she admitted that when changes had not been successful, or as successful as hoped, it was often because the changes for people had not been attended to as well as had the changes in technology.

Finally Marc Benioff, the CEO of Salesforce, a company that offers cloud computing products to businesses, commented on the need for a new kind of relationship between customer and supplier—one where the customer trusts the

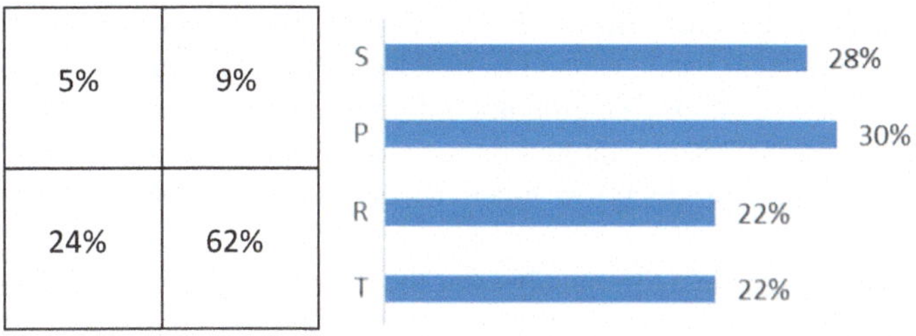

Fig. 11.8 Davos panel discussion 2016: Thinking profile (own representation)

supplier with access to their data. This, he claimed, was a transformation of trust since suppliers are getting more information than ever, of a more intimate nature, about their customers. For him, this represented a shift in values from the third to the fourth industrial revolution.

Analysing the discussion across all participants (Fig. 11.8), we can see that in terms of content, although all four quadrants have been discussed, the main focus was on the lower right quadrant, that of changes in the external environment—principally its social systems and technologies. We notice throughout a real absence of emphasis on the development of individuals, their emotions and values, their beliefs and the way they attach meaning to the transformations that they find themselves involved in. These aspects belong to the upper left quadrant—interior and singular. It is noteworthy that none of these very successful CEOs commented that they had to change themselves or to transform their own thinking in order to successfully transform their organisations. We can see a greater interest in the lower left quadrant relating to the interior collective. This is typically expressed in the discussion in terms of the importance of team, departmental and organisational culture—aspects of a group of people that they have in common in terms of shared beliefs, feelings and values. The upper right quadrant, which would reference the external qualities of a single entity, for example, a specific technology or piece of equipment, is rarely mentioned in preference to the lower right quadrant.

In general, a good cross section of thinking modes can be found in the discussion. The participants spoke about the bigger picture of digital transformation and the changes in technologies, evidence of their use of structural and process thinking modes. The use of relational thinking modes was less common but still in evidence, particularly from Marc Benioff who discussed how a business model and customers attitudes regarding trust in their suppliers are related, how common cultures between acquired organisations are important and how technology is related to the speed of strategy execution. Similarly, Jean Pascale Tricoire displayed the strongest transformational thinking modes when he spoke about several themes. Firstly he described connecting up energy supply and utilisation systems through the Internet to create an adaptive system that created energy efficiencies. Secondly, he spoke about a transformation in the relationship that Schneider has with its customers. There, the company has moved from being "on call" to correct problems or execute projects for customers to being connected to customers' energy infrastructure on a permanent basis, which has enabled it to provide a lot of new services. And thirdly, he spoke about changing not only what the company does, but the way that it does it, and that theme applied particularly to the R&D function which was now able to develop products on much faster timescales and in a much more flexible manner.

Finally, we have made a brief analysis of the differences between the thinking of the different speakers (Fig. 11.9). We have simplified the analysis by combining our count of upper and lower quadrants content to give a single figure for whether the speaker was focusing on the internal or external aspects of their organisation. We can see immediately, that the CEOs of the two major industrial firms (Alcoa and Schneider Electric) were highly focused on the "right side" engineering and manufacturing external features of their businesses. So too, was Meg Whitman, the CEO of computing and computer manufacturing giant Hewlett Packard. Only Bernard Tyson, the CEO of the healthcare company Kaiser Permanente privileged the internal personal and cultural aspects of the digital transformation, whilst Mark Benioff of Salesforce—the IT business services company spoke—relatively little about either side. What is the significance of such differences? We can only speculate because we do not know the extent to which the CEOs revealed the full extent of their thinking. However, the differences point to a surprising lack of emphasis on the implications for employees and employee culture during digital transformation in certain organisations. Only in health care, it seems, is the need to transform people as well as things really understood.

Turning to the analysis of the thinking modes, each speaker (with the exception of Tyson) appears to have a preference for a particular thinking mode over the others. Benioff stressed the relational thinking mode by pointing to the supplier–customer relationship and the need for a new level of trust. Kleinfeld spoke most about technological changes and their impact—a process thinking mode. Of all the CEOs, Tricoire was most preoccupied with the transformational aspects created for his company, Schneider Electric. He spoke of a transformation in the business model from products to services, a transformation in the relationship with customers and a transformation in the way that the R&D function operated. Meg Whitman from Hewlett focused on the structural thinking mode. For her, the important aspects were in new systems and processes, new plans and new strategies. Of all the CEOs, Tyson's thinking profile appears the most balanced. Perhaps it may be that the nature of the healthcare industry is one where the impact of digital technologies on people, the way they think and the way they behave, necessarily comes to the fore because of the personal nature of the service offered.

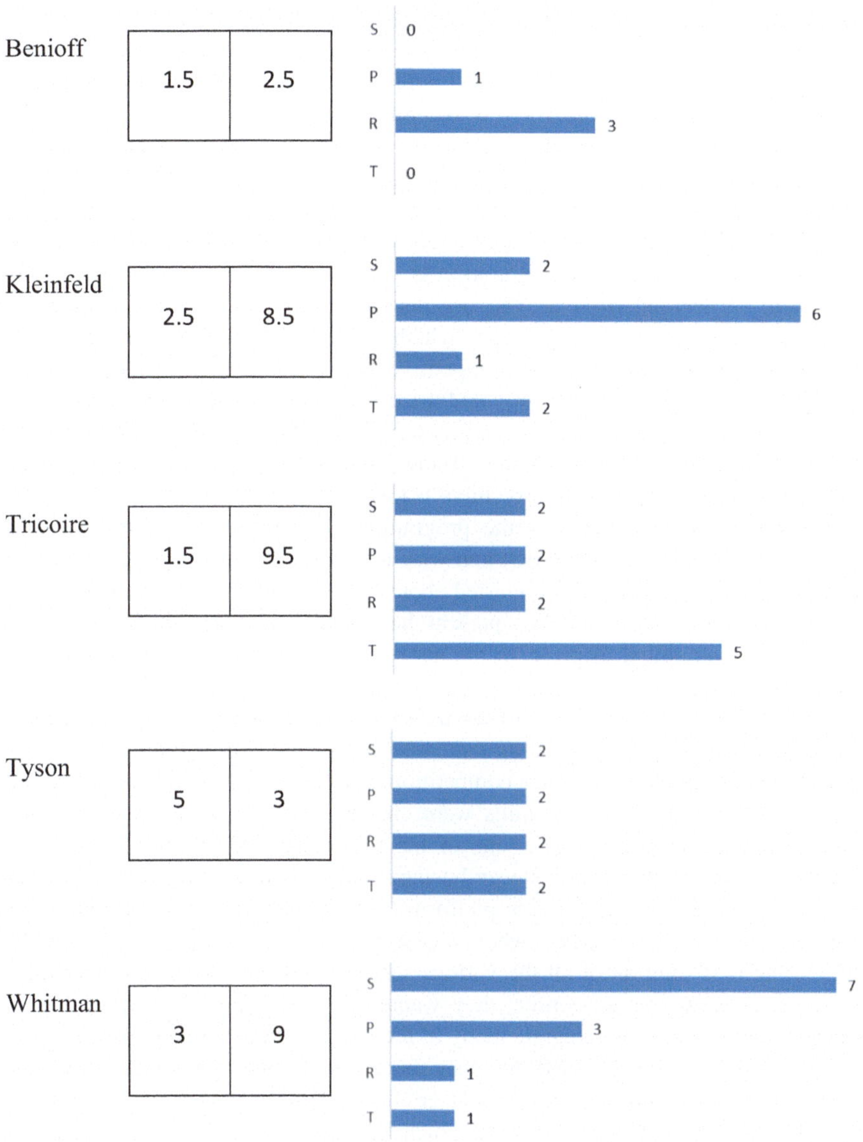

Fig. 11.9 Thinking profile of each participant of the panel discussion (own representation)

Interview with a Specialist in Digital Transformation

So far, we have presented and analysed published articles and a public discussion about digital transformation. By way of contrast, we finish this case study with commentary on an interview that we carried out with a consultant who specialises in digital transformation projects. We wanted to find out specifically how the consultant thought about digital transformation and how that compared to the thinking of his clients as he went through a project with them. In this case, the project he told us about was not a success, and hence there are some interesting lessons to be learned from it. The organisation itself was a large international business-to-business service provider which had grown swiftly in recent years through acquisition. Part of a very competitive industry, it acted as a vital link in the supply chain for its clients and provided them with a variety of related services. At the time of taking the decision to commence the digital transformation project, it had over 30 different business units, grouped into four divisions under divisional directors who were part of the executive team.

The consultant had acted as the programme director for the transformation, reporting to the CIO and the CEO, and was, therefore, one of the principle people involved. Our interview with him lasted about one hour, after which we transcribed and analysed the interview. We present here some excerpts which have been paraphrased and edited to preserve the anonymity of the client organisation concerned and its people.

We asked the consultant first to tell us a little about the reasons for the project itself. He described an organisation that was both facing stiff external competition and also suffering from internal competition. As the organisation had grown, it began to appear that different units were chasing after the same customers and offering similar services. Hence, one of the things that the executive wanted to achieve was more alignment between business units, such that they would provide more of a single face and a single platform to their customers. For example, they wanted a single online presence where a customer could go to their website and be offered the best solution of all the various services that the various business units could provide. At the same time, they wanted to reduce overall costs and were looking to outsource and integrate many of their IT functions. So, there appeared to be a rational dual objective and the business case presented by the CIO convinced the CEO and his team that they should go ahead. However, our consultant noted from the start that there was a problem which he described as follows: "… there was a lack of detail in terms of what the proposed transformation program actually meant and what changes it would drive, apart from a reduction in the headcount of 500 people through contracting with an outsourced provider. The divisional directors were not well aware of what the program would do, how it would impact their organisation and the services to their customers, or how it would impact their people. So immediately when we started to prepare some of those changes, we got a lot of push back and active and passive resistance. People did not have the feeling that they had been involved in the decision making or the development and the details of the business case".

On the face of it, this looked like a classic failure to consult with and get key stakeholders on side. And yet, when we asked the consultant if the CIO had factored in the possibility of such resistance his response was as follows "Yes, he did consider that and built that in, but I think his way of thinking around this what that, well, if he pushed on and signed the contract for the outsourcing and pushed that through then the business units would have no choice, almost, but to come on-board". We might now ask about the company's executive team: "What they thinking?" The logic for the digital transformation seemed clear, it was to create efficiencies, reduce costs and provide a better service to customers. But, on the other hand, it seems as though none of the team had really taken the time to work through the implications for themselves and for their employees. In effect, they were focusing on the right side quadrants and not on the left side. They forgot to ask themselves "what might this mean for me and my team of people?"

There were further problems to come as well. The CIO had engaged various partners on long-term contracts to outsource various components of the organisation's IT infrastructure with the idea that, in so doing, IT and communications systems would be united across the divisions on a common platform. Due to the large number of recent acquisitions the company had about fifteen different customer relationship management systems in use. Whilst it was clear to people at all levels of the organisation that there was a need to rationalise and integrate all of these different systems, the choice of supplier and the nature of the contract with the supplier was left to the CIO. When it turned out that the CIO had made relatively poor choices and signed contracts that were not particularly advantageous, it became a matter of concern that some of the financial objectives of the programme would not be achieved.

We asked the consultant why the CEO and his team had not placed a stronger governance process on the management of the transformation programme and, in particular, the choice of supplier and supplier contracts. His answer was that there were two major factors. Firstly, the technical nature of digital information technology is such that many executives do not feel confident making decisions and hence they rely on the expertise of specialists, such as the CIO and his team. Secondly, during the period of the programme, the CEO became preoccupied with the possibility of the business being acquired by a much larger foreign company. This deal, which was kept highly confidential, meant that the digital transformation programme was not seen as the most important thing on his, and his team's agendas. Here's what the consultant had to say about the implications: "… transformations (like this) take years rather than months, and the ability of an organisation and its leadership to stay focused for such a long time on the execution of a transformation is hard. There are always other business priorities, always other targets that you need to achieve that may have a shorter-term priority. If you have your transformation program to the side, there is always a risk that it gets de-prioritised and therefore you never end it. And so in my view you shouldn't actually talk about separate transformation. The organisation transforms as a whole, and it's not so much a project anymore, it's more sort of working towards a new way of operating. So, it becomes almost central to what you do in your executive team. Everything that you do in your executive team, all those other initiatives that you would undertake, all those pressures that you have around bottom-line and cost reduction and whatever, should be tied into that transformation". Here, our consultant appears to call for a much more integrated process when embarking on a digital transformation, the project of embracing new digital technologies must somehow be coordinated with the ongoing business. It is not something that can be carried out separately.

How should the digital transformation then have been carried out? Our consultant's view was as follows: "The point is that transformation is done through the leadership of the organisation, and the leadership itself should go through a transformation as well, and then drive forward from there". In this case, the leadership appeared to have seen the digital transformation as a separate project that could happen almost without their direct involvement. The consultant continued "The key aspect of this is that it would have been better to take a more integrated approach to the design of the business model, operating model, and the business architecture, including things like processes and data systems, etc. Do more of that ground work first, do more design, starting with the customer in mind, by asking what services does the organisation offer and what does it want to offer to the customer as an aligned group that offers different services. And then build on that by asking how do we want to shape the organisation from an operating model perspective? And then see how technology can be used to support that aim. The most important thing is that the executive support needs to be strong and broad and across the board. The executive team needs to understand what their role is in the transformation itself and how as a leadership team they need to transform themselves in the way they think and act".

From a Metathinking perspective, it appears that our consultant was advocating for a link between left quadrant and right quadrant actions. The "right side" quadrant IT programme needed to be coordinated, not only with other business processes but with an entire mindshift and cultural transformation on the part of the executives themselves. The mistake, such as it was, was for the executive to treat the transformation programme as something external to themselves, taking place without a corresponding change in the way they thought about their business and their behaviours. In this case, the consultant's story about his client ended badly. As it became clear that the programme was not going to be successful, he left the programme after seven months, the CIO was moved on, and a year later, the firm was acquired and is now managed by entirely different executive team. Much money was wasted on outsourced services and the contract with one of their key IT and communications suppliers was terminated.

Perhaps a disaster of this nature could have been avoided had the executive team taken a look at their thinking, noticed that their perspective was very narrow and learned to think in a more integrated and transformational manner. By failing to link the external changes to interior changes in terms of their own development and their behaviours and culture as a management team, they expected organisational transformation to happen without seeing that, as they were part of the organisation, they would need to transform themselves.

Mind Opening Questions
We invite you now to imagine that you are a CIO about to embark on a programme of digital transformation for an organisation and to consider the following mind opening questions as a means to explore the issues you might have to tackle as the programme unfolds (Table 11.2).

Table 11.2 Mind opening questions: organisational transformation

UL	Intentional
S	To what extent are your values and aspirations aligned with those of your colleagues on the executive team?
S	How appropriate is the knowledge and experience you have gathered in your career to the role that you now need to play?
P	What new skills and abilities might you have to develop as you lead this programme?
P	How is your current thinking a product of what you experienced in the past and how might you need to develop new ways to think?
R	What is the relationship between your sense of yourself as a competent executive and the kind of knowledge you might need to acquire to adapt yourself to the digital transformation?
R	How are your present attitudes related to the likely success or failure of the transformation project?

(continued)

T	What conflicts do you face within yourself about the changes you need to make to succeed in the new future?
T	What aspects of yourself might you have to transcend in order to deliver this project successfully?
UR	**Behavioural**
S	What objective measures can you take in relation to the organisation's readiness for such a programme?
S	What aspect of the competitive environment might enable or impede the programme?
P	How is the behaviour of your customer changing?
P	What business trends are emerging that need to be taken into account?
R	What is the relationship between the engagement and motivation of people at work and the kind of technologies that you are planning to use?
R	To what extent are you shaping your role in this project, and to what extent might the role shape you?
T	What new systems can be integrated to move the organisation to a higher level of development?
T	What conflicts might emerge and need to be overcome as systems and processes that were once separate are merged?
LL	**Cultural**
S	What skills, abilities and values are shared within the executive team?
S	To what extent is the executive team motivated to make this project a success?
P	What additional knowledge and skills might the executive team need to acquire?
P	How might the relationships between people in the executive team need to evolve?
R	What is the relationship between power to influence the programme and responsibility for the success of the programme within the team?
R	How might the relationship between the executive team and the rest of the organisation be affected by the programme?
T	How would conflicts within the executive team be resolved?
T	In what ways would the executive team as a whole need to develop to a higher level of functioning?
LR	**Social**
S	What aspects of the external environment might affect the way people in your organisation respond to the internal changes you bring about?
S	What accounts for the success or failure of digital transformations in other organisations?
P	How are your organisation's customers and their needs changing?
P	What technological developments are likely to occur as the programme unfolds and what impact might these have?
R	What common ground is there between current systems and processes in the organisation and the new systems and processes that the digital transformation will involve?
R	How might organisational performance relate to factors in the external environment whilst the programme is being carried out?
T	What conflicts might arise between the pursuit of the goals of the digital transformation programme and people's expectations for their work and sense of purpose
T	How might the whole organisation need to be elevated to work at a higher level of development?

References

Creative Commons. *Search*. Accessed 23 November 2018, https://search.creativecommons.org/.

Davenport, T. H., & Westerman, G. (2018). Why so many high-profile digital transformations fail. *Harvard Business Review*. Retrieved March 9, 2018, from https://hbr.org/2018/03/why-so-many-high-profile-digital-transformations-fail.

Floridi, L. (ed.) (2015). *The onlife manifesto—being human in a hyperconnected era*. Retrieved November 23, 2018, from http://www.academia.edu/9742506/The_Onlife_Manifesto_-_Being_Human_in_a_Hyperconnected_Era.

Westerman, G., Bonnet, D., & McAfee, A. (2014). The nine elements of digital transformation. *MIT Sloan Management Review* (blog), Retrieved November 23, 2018, from https://sloanreview.mit.edu/article/the-nine-elements-of-digital-transformation/.

World Economic Forum (2016). *Davos 2016—The digital transformation of industries*. Retrieved November 23, 2018, from https://www.youtube.com/watch?v=qav1y7G15JQ.

Social Transformation—Rethinking Health Care

12

In our final case study we move to the level of national infrastructure and compare and contrast the healthcare systems of three different countries: Switzerland, the United Kingdom and the United States of America.

We have chosen to analyse healthcare systems because they are much in the public eye with a vigorous debate in national and international press about their viability and sustainability. The cost of health care appears to be rising disproportionately to other living costs, putting pressure on the extent to which it is affordable by both government and private individuals alike. However, our aim is not to make a scientific study of different healthcare systems. Our objective is to show you by example how you might use the Metathinking Framework of integral quadrants and dialectical thinking modes to systematically expand and illuminate your understanding of a complex topic.

A Methodology for Data and Discourse Analysis

No debate about the need to transform healthcare provision should be undertaken in isolation to an estimation of the impact that different systems may have on public health. It is interesting therefore to compare data on public health between different countries to see how this relates to the different healthcare systems that they use. For our analysis of different national healthcare systems and the discourse about them, we use a mixed methodology. First, we will present quantitative data on the health of people in their respective countries. Then, we will present our analysis of the discourse about the healthcare systems themselves. The discourse analysis shows us how people are presently constructing their knowledge of the healthcare systems and raises questions about the influence that institutional and social contexts have on such knowledge.

N. Shannon and B. Frischherz, *Metathinking*, Management for Professionals,
https://doi.org/10.1007/978-3-030-41064-3_12

In Metathinking, data charts and diagrams can act as examples of the structural, process and relational thinking modes. In this case study, we will use line graphs and vertical bar charts to track changes over periods of time—the process thinking mode. We will also use horizontal bar charts to display graphically the structure of the thinking modes used in the discourse and their relationship to each other. The Metathinking Framework provides a good basis for systematically correlating and integrating the results of these two analyses resulting in a richer picture of the topic.

Quantitative Data

For our discussion of the three health systems, we will take a look at the health of the citizens in the three countries using data from OECD official statistics on health and healthcare systems.[1] The OECD provides rich data on various aspects of the health of citizens in different countries. We have selected data for Switzerland, the United Kingdom and the USA and present this in diagrams.

Qualitative Data

As our source for the qualitative data, we used a body of titles and lead texts from newspaper articles in the Swiss newspaper Neue Zürcher Zeitung (NZZ) in the year 2017. The NZZ is a high-quality paper with a reputation for objectivity and depth of coverage in international affairs. In order to identify relevant articles, we ran a search in the NZZ archive with the keyword "Gesundheitssystem" (healthcare system) combined with the names of the three countries CH, UK and US as additional keywords. We filtered out irrelevant articles and got as a result a corpus of about 100 articles. Then, we translated the lead texts with Google Translation into English and performed a content analysis, coding the text excerpts independently by country, focusing on particular integral quadrants and the principle dialectical thinking mode underlying the content of the articles.

For example, consider the following article summary.

"US spending on medicines spikes. The healthcare system is caught in a dilemma between affordability and promotion of innovations. No country spends as much on medicines per capita as the US. The lamentation about the high prices is widespread. There is a way to curb prices without stifling innovation, but it is controversial".

Here, the author notes a tension between price control to ensure medicine is affordable, on the one hand, and free market pricing to help drug manufacturers fund innovation, on the other. We consider that the thinking mode is transformational, since it identifies the elements of the system that could lead to a substantial change in the system itself and highlights the opposition of those elements to each other and the possibility of conflict (controversy) in their integration.

[1]OECD, 2018.

Identifying the thinking modes is not always a precise science as it depends to a certain extent on how one interprets the meaning of the texts and the author's intentions. In order to check the reliability of our judgements, we rated the articles independently and, where we had differences, we went back to the original articles in German, debated the text and decided on the correct coding.

In a second step, we have examined the values being expressed in the public discourse on health care because they are the basis for conflicting opinions between people about what needs to change and the motor for potential transformations. In order to identify articles that contained a strong emphasis on values, we performed a text analysis of the entire article using a data mining tool. We identified and selected all the articles that had higher than ten occurrences of a noun expressing an abstract value. This analysis is a simple quantitative text analysis. The new methods of mining and machine learning will offer completely new approaches for discourse analysis with reference to the Metathinking Framework.

The Three Healthcare Systems in Comparison

First, by way of background, we will briefly describe how the healthcare systems are structured in each country using information from Wikipedia articles.

Switzerland: Public and Private Health Care with Compulsory Private Health Insurance

The Swiss healthcare system is financed through a combination of public, subsidised and private elements. Health insurance is compulsory for all people resident in Switzerland. Health insurance covers the costs of basic medical care for the insured person and their stay in hospital. However, complementary medicine and dental treatment are not covered by compulsory insurance. Compulsory insurance can be supplemented by private insurance, which makes it possible to improve additional treatment or the standard of the room and service in the hospital. The insured person must cover part of the cost of treatment themselves. Insurance premiums vary between different health insurance funds and different regions. There is no free state health service. For people with low incomes, however, the state pays subsidies towards the insurance premiums.[2]

United Kingdom: Publicly Funded Healthcare System

The National Health Service (NHS) was founded in 1948 as one of the most important social reforms after the Second World War. The basic principles were

[2]Wikipedia (a), 2019.

that the services should be comprehensive, universal and free. England, Northern Ireland, Scotland and Wales, each have their own publicly funded healthcare systems. The schemes are 98.8% funded from general tax and social security contributions and by small sums from patient fees for some services. The NHS uses doctors called General Practitioners (GPs) to provide local primary care and to refer patients to other specialist services as needed. Regional hospitals then provide the more specialised services, including care for patients with psychiatric disorders and direct access to accident and emergency units (A&E). Private healthcare, where patients or their insurers pay for treatment, is also available for those people who can afford a premium service.[3,4]

United States: Health Care as a Private Sector Business

Health care in the United States is largely provided by private companies and organisations. 58% of US hospitals are non-profit, 21% are government-owned and 21% are for-profit. Although the United States is one of the world's leading economic powers, it is the only industrial nation in the world without universal health care. The Patient Protection and Affordable Care Act, often called "Obamacare", was brought into law by President Barack Obama in 2010. The aim of the law was to improve access to health care by making health insurance mandatory. By 2016, the uninsured portion of the population had roughly halved, with an estimated 20–24 million additional people insured. Insurers are obliged to accept all applicants and charge the same rates. In addition, all insurers must cover a list of essential health services. Since the new presidency under Donald Trump, Obamacare has been under great political pressure.[5,6]

We can see from the above that health care provision differs between the three countries in the extent to which it is funded and regulated by the government. In the UK, the focus is on providing free health care to all citizens, and private services are available for those who wish to pay for premium treatment. In Switzerland, health care is paid for by mandatory insurance for all residents, with subsidies by the state being made available to ensure insurance premiums are affordable for those on lower incomes. In the USA, health care is paid for by medical insurance or privately, but there is no universal coverage despite the Obamacare legislation to make insurance mandatory. Additionally, there are some government subsidies paid to insurance companies in order to make premiums more affordable, which the current administration is keen to cease, and tax credits paid to insured citizens. The net effect is to make the costs of health insurance premiums more volatile and uncertain than in Switzerland.

[3]Wikipedia (b), 2019.
[4]Wikipedia (c), 2019.
[5]Wikipedia (d), 2019.
[6]Wikipedia (e), 2019.

Statistics and Diagrams on National Health and Health Care

In this analysis, first, we present quantitative data on health and health care from an exterior, objective (right quadrant) perspective in terms of measures of national health and the cost of health care. Secondly, we look at a subjective (left quadrant) perspective on health, presenting data on how people perceive the status of their health in the different countries.

Right Quadrants: Life Expectancy, Infant Mortality, Absence from Work and the Cost of Health Care

We look here at life expectancies taken at six different points in time every decade since 1960. A life expectancy is the average length of time that the population is expected to live. Immediately, we can see that life expectancy has been changing, and getting longer, for all countries during this period. It is also noticeable that Switzerland has the longest life expectancy, and that its life expectancy has advanced the furthest in the last 50 years, from 74 to just over 84 years. The USA, by contrast, now has the lowest life expectancy having been surpassed by the UK, although in 1980 and 1990 it was ahead of the UK (Fig. 12.1).

When we look at another measure, that of infant mortality, again we see major changes over time with infant mortality rates dropping from a rate of twenty per thousand to around five or less over 50 years. Here, the USA also lags the other countries, with Switzerland and the UK having identical rates of 3.9 in 2014, whilst the USA's rate is 5.8 (Fig. 12.2).

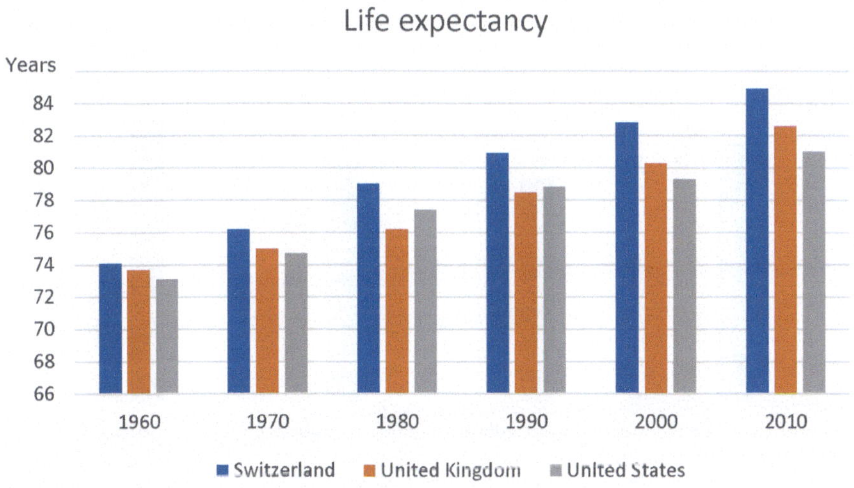

Fig. 12.1 Life expectancy (own representation based on OECD 2018)

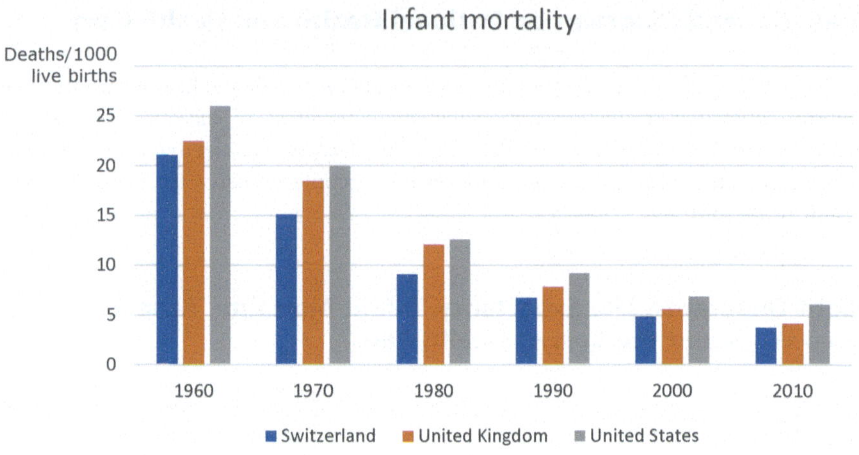

Fig. 12.2 Infant mortality (own representation based on OECD 2018)

Another interesting statistic is that of days lost at work due to absence through illness. One might expect that the healthiest population would see the least days lost at work due to sickness. But here, it turns out that Switzerland, which has the longest life expectancy, also has the highest number of days off sick, and by quite a margin, whereas the USA has the lowest. The 2010/2012 data shows the Swiss having an average of 8.8 days off per year, the UK 6.5 and the USA 3.7 (Fig. 12.3).

But how much is each country spending on its health care? Here, there are also changes. Spending, as measured in terms of the share of gross domestic product (GDP), has increased over the years. In these terms (and in absolute terms—

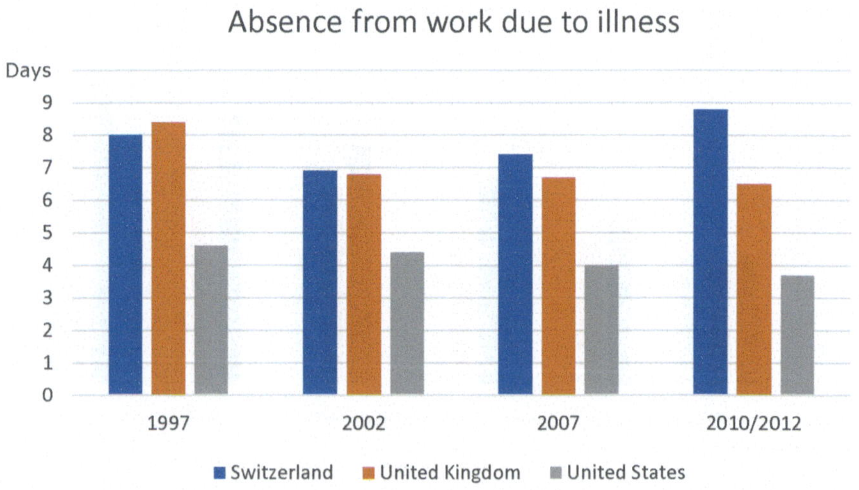

Fig. 12.3 Absence from work due to illness (days) (own representation based on OECD 2018)

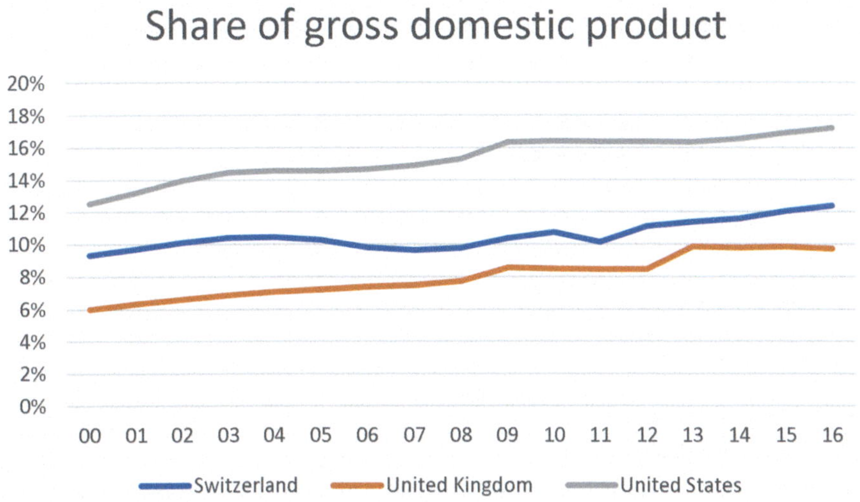

Fig. 12.4 Share of gross domestic product (own representation based on OECD 2018)

because it has the largest GDP), the USA spends far more on health care than either Switzerland or the UK. Figure 12.4 shows the development of health care costs as a share of gross domestic product between 2000 and 2016.

In conclusion, we can see substantial changes over time and significant differences between the three countries. Overall health and longevity seem to be improving whilst costs are increasing. In the USA, the costs are highest, but life expectancy is the lowest, and people seem to take the least time off work. One might ask on the basis of this data, why don't people in the USA live longer, given the extra amount that they spend on health and the fact that they take so little time off work due to sickness? Let's look at some data from the left quadrant to see if that sheds any light on such a question.

Left Quadrants: Perceived Health Status

Here, we take a measure of perceived health status for which we have data for just one year—2014. The data tells us what percentage of the population consider themselves in good or very good health, in fair health (not good or bad), or in bad and very bad health. This is a subjective measure showing how people report themselves as feeling. It is worth noting that there are some differences in methodology here in collecting such data, as well as the possibility that people's report of their health status is very variable from day to day and in different contexts (Figs. 12.5 and 12.6).

Overall, it can be seen that people in the USA report themselves in better health than those in Switzerland and the UK, and that people in the UK report themselves least well, which is ironic given that their health system is the only one that is free at the point of delivery to the user. The relations between people's experience of their

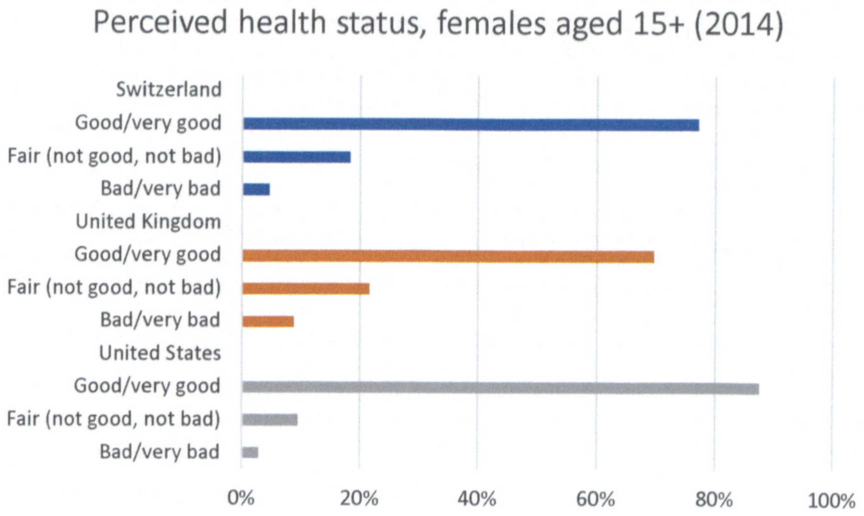

Fig. 12.5 Perceived health status, females aged 15 + (own representation based on OECD 2018)

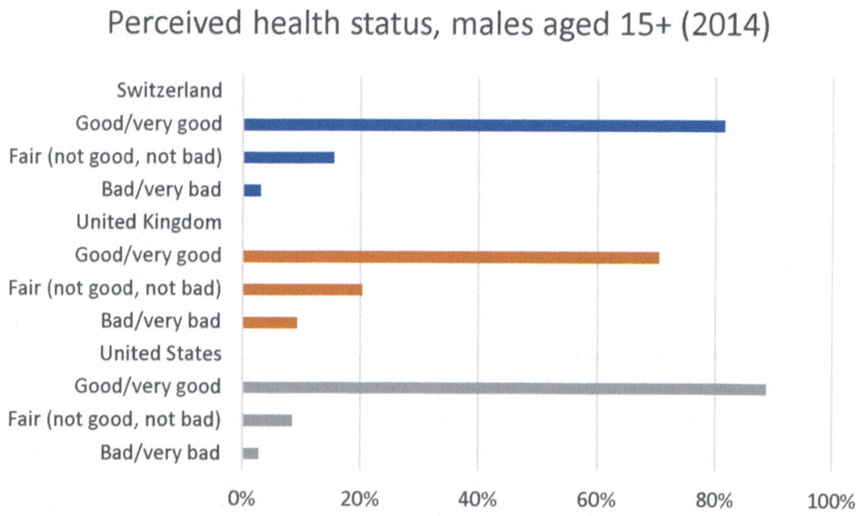

Fig. 12.6 Perceived health status, males aged 15+ (own representation based on OECD 2018)

state of health, their life expectancy and typical length of time off work through sickness during the year appear complex. The one factor that is clearly common to all health systems is the rising cost, which threatens the sustainability of the systems themselves. As we shall see in the next section, the rising cost problem is a major factor in the calls for transformation within each system. We believe that it is inevitable that, when they occur, such transformations will prove controversial and involve a degree of conflict, creating winners and losers. But, what is the quality of thinking in the public domain about such transformation?

Public Discourse on Health Care

Turning now to the qualitative data, we identified a total of 104 NZZ articles on the subject of healthcare system. The majority (77) referred to the system in Switzerland; there were 6 articles on the UK system and 21 on the system in the USA. The disparity is not a surprise because NZZ is a Swiss newspaper but, with the US presidency of Donald Trump, the discussion of Obamacare and its potential repeal and replacement received a lot of interest in Swiss newspapers.

Thinking Modes

For the following analysis of quadrants and thinking modes, we used only the lead texts of the articles. In terms of the thematic quadrants, the large majority of the lead texts (98) referred to "right quadrant" external objective characteristics of the systems. Only a few lead texts (6) discussed the more subjective elements (left quadrant) about how people felt about their health and health systems. We found it surprising that there were no articles referring to the subjective upper left quadrant which suggested to us that individual personal perspectives on health and healthcare systems were not being taken properly into account.

Let's have a look at the dialectical thinking modes now. Most of the lead texts expressed structural thought patterns (44) and process thought patterns (36). Together, structural and process thought patterns made up 75% of the lead texts. There were a smaller number transformational thought patterns (16) and only a few relational thought patterns (8). Figure 12.7 shows the relative proportions of the thinking modes.

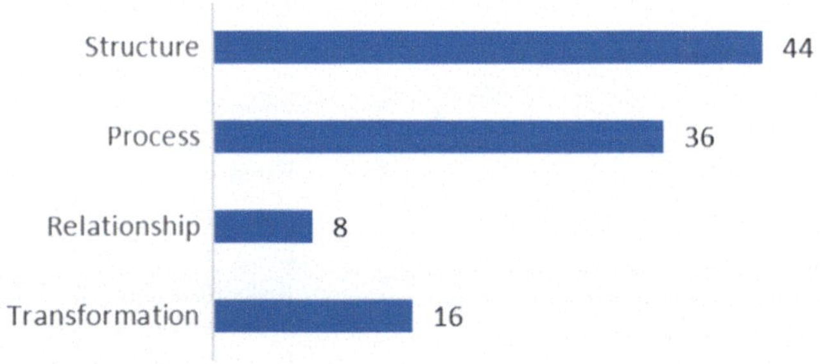

Fig. 12.7 Thinking modes in lead texts on health care (NZZ 2017, n = 104) (own representation)

Opportunities and Threats

For the following analysis, we used all the 104 articles in the corpus. Tables 12.1 and 12.2 respectively show the positive and negative values described in the discourse on health systems of our body of articles, categorised according to thematic quadrants. We can say that a positive value is an opportunity because people are likely to move towards taking advantage of it, whilst a negative value is a threat that people will seek to move away from and avoid because of the damage and loss of value that it would cause. This analysis was based on the entire content of the newspaper articles, not just on the lead texts.

Interpretation

Firstly, both the results of the lead text analysis and the analysis of opportunities and threats show that the newspaper articles represent the health care concept in a rather one-sided way. Using the integral quadrant model, one can see that there is a much stronger focus on the exterior objective characteristics of the systems than the

Table 12.1 Opportunities in the discourse on health systems

	Interior	Exterior
Individual	Liberty (Freiheit, 27) Responsibility (Verantwortung, 21)	Health (Gesundheit, 546) Life (Leben, 88) Care (Pflege, 82) Provision (Versorgung, 74) Age (Alter, 19) Assistance (Betreuung, 13)
Collective	Right (Recht, 165) Quality (Qualität, 98) Security (Sicherheit, 36) Justice (Gerechtigkeit, 15)	Performance (Leistung, 249) Development (Entwicklung, 64) Progress (Fortschritt, 31) Saving (Einsparung, 25) Access (Zugang, 24) Efficiency (Effizienz, 15)

Table 12.2 Threats in the discourse on health systems

	Interior	Exterior
Individual	Anxiety (Angst, 10)	Illness (Krankheit, 47)
Collective	–	Costs (Kosten, 461) Risks (Risiken, 39) Pressure (Druck, 31) Rationing (Rationierung, 26) Waste (Verschwendung, 16)

subjective "internal" aspects such as how people feel about their health and their health care. The public discussion focuses principally on performance and costs. Although the concept of "affordability" is often mentioned, the subjective part of this notion in respect to what individuals feel and think they can afford is not explored. In general, aspects such as attitudes, values, lifestyle and group culture were seldom addressed in the newspaper articles, and whilst there were themes about collective rights, there was much less written about individual responsibility.

Secondly, the results show that the thinking employed about healthcare systems is biased heavily towards themes around the structure of the healthcare systems themselves coupled with descriptions of trends and emerging changes. There is far less written about potential transformation within the systems themselves and very little written about the relationships between aspects of the healthcare systems and other entities such as people's attitudes, habits and lifestyles, or things such as their employment contracts, diet and exposure to things that might damage their health, such as pollutants.

Our brief analysis throws up what is missing in the discourse about the transformation of healthcare systems in terms of illuminating questions about the relationships between the external characteristics of the systems themselves and the internal thoughts, feelings and attitudes of people towards their own health care. If healthcare systems are to be truly transformed to create better quality of life for individuals and the public in general, broader and deeper questions need to be asked. We present some of these below in the section on mind opening questions.

These questions may have the potential for transformation in health care in the direction of individual and collective quality of life.

This case study was written in a Metathinking way, i.e., we deliberately used integral quadrants and thinking modes to illuminate different aspects of a topic and to develop the text. We started with structural aspects, extended the analysis by relational aspects and finally integrated process and transformational aspects of the topic.

We advocate the use of Metathinking to identify and include missing integral quadrants and thought patterns when exploring the kind of complex problems often referred to as "wicked". Such problems are typically controversial and polarising, arousing strong feelings among people but defying resolution. Many examples exist; climate change, multi-racial integration, cyber-crime, control of personal data, energy management and terrorism to name just few. Transformation in thought leads to transformation in reality when humans take action.

Hence, Metathinking is an effective thinking tool for think tanks in business and politics.

Mind Opening Questions

We invite you now to do some thinking of your own about how you might like to see health care transformed in your country by considering the following mind opening questions. These fall into two types, those relating to a single integral quadrant, and more complex questions which relate one quadrant to another (see Table 12.3).

Table 12.3 Mind opening questions: social transformation

UL	Intentional
S	In what ways and in what contexts do you imagine you could live a healthier life?
S	What is your conception of having perfect health?
P	How has your sense of yourself as being well or unwell changed in recent times?
P	How might your future state of health by governed by the states of health you have enjoyed in the past?
R	How do you connect your healthy self with your unhealthy self?
R	What, for you, is the relationship between you being able to care for yourself, and you needing to be cared for a health system?
T	What behaviours would you say that you have that are healthy on one hand, and unhealthy on the other?
T	How might you integrate a healthier way of living into the aspects of your life that are unhealthy?
UR	**Behavioural**
S	What objective measures are being used to monitor people's states of health?
S	What aspects the environment are identified as having a bearing on people's health?
P	What trends do you observe when you consider the various physical indicators of people's state of health?
P	How is technology changing the way people can manage their health?
R	How do people connect the amount they have by way of disposable income with what they are willing to spend on their health?
R	What common ground is there between the various organisations that promote health and those that deal with sickness?
T	How are new technologies making people both well and unwell?
T	What tensions exist between the medical profession and the pharmaceutical industry?
LL	**Cultural**
S	What habits, customs and pastimes do you and people in your society engage in that impact on their health?
S	What accounts for the improvements or deterioration in the health of people in your community?
P	How have people's expectations in relation to their health changed in your community?
P	What behaviours and practices in the way people live their life are emerging that impact on their health?

(continued)

Table 12.3 (continued)

LL	Cultural
R	What is the relationship between people's state of health and the level of healthcare provision in their community?
R	How is people's sense of their wellbeing connected to the availability. Quality and affordability of healthcare provision where you live?
T	What groups in your local community acting to improve health and what groups are acting to damage or limit it?
T	How might different groups in the community be coordinated better to improve healthcare?
LR	**Social**
S	What factors account for different countries approach to, and organisation of their healthcare systems?
S	What enables a country to maintain its healthcare system at the level it is now?
P	What would you say are the major trends globally in healthcare provision?
P	What new developments and factors seem to be emerging worldwide that will impact on healthcare?
R	How do the political systems of countries relate to the form their healthcare takes?
R	How are changes in demographics, lifestyles, economies, and cultures impacting healthcare provision?
T	Which are the major groups in conflict about the healthcare systems?
T	How can the different entities of the pharmaceutical industry, private and public medical organisations, regulatory bodies, insurance industry, and government be better integrated?
LL LR	**Cultural and Social**
P	How do people assess what they think is affordable and how do they weigh the personal burden of taxation against the benefit of free or subsidised healthcare?
P	How do people's notions about the effectiveness of government regulation influence their preference for different government policies, and how do these show up when they come to vote?
P	How do people see the trade-off between a highly profitable and innovative health industry and affordable or free healthcare?
P	To what extent do people feel that governments should regulate in order to lessen environmental hazards to healthy living? For example, should cigarettes be banned completely?
R	How are the different structures of the three health care systems related to people's perceptions of health care itself? For example, does having free or subsidised healthcare make people more or less responsible for their own health?
R	How are personal attitudes towards work and lifestyle (liberty, responsibility, anxiety etc.) related to collective aspects such as the cultural aspects of health (rights, security, justice etc.)?
R	How are the same personal attitudes towards work and lifestyle related to objective characteristics of health systems such as performance, quality, efficiency, costs, risks etc)?

References

OECD. OECD data. Retrieved November 23, 2018, from http://data.oecd.org.

Wikipedia (a). Healthcare in Switzerland. In: *Wikipedia*. Retrieved January 6, 2019, from https://en.wikipedia.org/w/index.php?title=Healthcare_in_Switzerland&oldid=876018779 .

Wikipedia (b). Health care in the United Kingdom. In: *Wikipedia*. Retrieved January 2, 2019, from https://en.wikipedia.org/w/index.php?title=Health_care_in_the_United_Kingdom&oldid=876437755 .

Wikipedia (c). National health service. In: *Wikipedia*. Retrieved January 6, 2019, from https://de.wikipedia.org/w/index.php?title=National_Health_Service&oldid=182994437 .

Wikipedia (d). Health care in the United States. In: *Wikipedia*. Retrieved January 3, 2019, from https://en.wikipedia.org/w/index.php?title=Health_care_in_the_United_States&oldid=876685114 .

Wikipedia (e). Patient protection and affordable care act. In: *Wikipedia*. Retrieved January 6, 2019, from https://en.wikipedia.org/w/index.php?title=Patient_Protection_and_Affordable_Care_Act&oldid=877144314 .

Deeper and More Integrated Thinking 13

We have now explored four very different case studies, each with a different point of focus. We started with the analysis of the thinking of a single person taken from interviews at two points in time and drew lessons about how the Metathinking concept could be used to get a feel for a person's level of cognitive development and help them improve their thinking. We then looked at a typical team development workshop to see how a management team could be helped to think more holistically about themselves and their organisation. We moved on to consider the very topical issue of "digital transformation"—how organisations are attempting to transform themselves in response to the advances in digital technologies. Here, we drew on the literature on the subject written over a span of 4 years, a CEO panel discussion from 2016, and an interview with a specialist consultant in transforming organisations. Finally, we examined the health services in three different countries, Switzerland, the UK and the USA, in order to explore the thinking around the problem of national health care. Here, we drew on published statistics and analysis of newspaper articles to see what was most in people's minds when they wrote about the topic. In each case, we have applied a similar methodology to show how thinking might be extended using the Metathinking Framework to develop a deeper and more nuanced understanding of the reality of the situation.

Benefits of Metathinking

What are the key insights and lessons we can take from such case studies? Firstly, the Metathinking method enables one to see what is missing from someone's or some people's thinking. In doing so, the method provides a route to develop a more complete understanding of the reality of a situation. In our first case study, we saw how Sonja moved from thinking mostly about herself and developed the capacity to think about how to support and enable people in her team to be more effective in

N. Shannon and B. Frischherz, *Metathinking*, Management for Professionals,
https://doi.org/10.1007/978-3-030-41064-3_13

their work. In the second case study, we explored how a team could move from narrow thinking about how they handled the stresses and pressure of their own working patterns towards an understanding of how they might change the way of working for the whole organisation to make it more resilient. In the third case study, we looked at how different researchers and practitioners viewed the subject of digital transformation from their own particular perspective and how they focussed on particular aspects at the expense of others, creating risks that digital transformation programmes might not succeed. And in our study on national healthcare systems, we saw how the individual perspective on people's experience of their health had largely been left out of the debate about how to fund the spiralling costs of national health care.

Secondly, our Metathinking method promotes productive dialogue between people. Whether it is between two individuals in a coaching relationship, or between members of a team, or different commentators on business, or even discourse in the public press, applying Metathinking enables people to have both a deeper and broader discussion. By identifying the quadrant in which a person is focusing, and the thinking mode that they are applying, differences in perspectives can be explored. A more complete understanding of the reality that people experience emerges as people consciously examine the what and the how of each other's thinking. People can come to appreciate that there is always something missing from their thinking and by combining their thinking with that of someone else in dialogue they can both benefit. A synthesis between opposite sides of a debate becomes possible as people move away from a position where either one person's or the other person's view is correct to one of "both my view and your view are valid and look at the same thing but from different perspectives".

Thirdly, Metathinking enables us, as humans, to see how to transform our environment. How does this occur? When we apply Metathinking, we develop a better, more complete conception of the reality in which we are immersed. We become aware of a bigger picture and how we are located within it. We notice how things are always changing and evolving. And we become aware of how everything is related to everything else in one way or another. Our awareness leads us to envisage a new reality in our minds because we can see that our reality is lacking something that we desire. In essence, we transform the world in our mind by imagining a different reality to the one which we perceive. What is then required is action on our part to realign our environment with our vision.

A Process for "Deeper", More Integrated Thinking

Let us review a variant of the diagram we showed you at the start of this section. Figure 13.1 suggests two ways in which one can proceed:

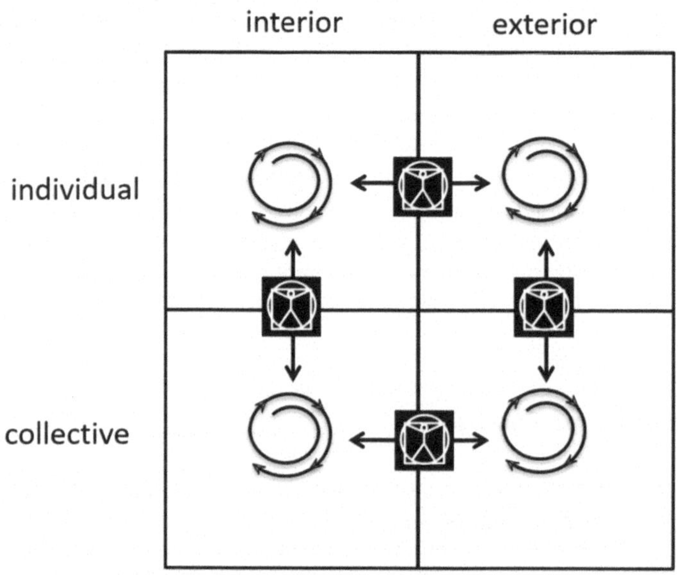

Fig. 13.1 Metathinking: all quadrants, all thinking modes (AQAT) (own representation)

(a) one can systematically rethink a problem quadrant by quadrant, applying the thinking modes to transform one's conception and understanding of each quadrant on its own, and
(b) one can rethink the relationships between the quadrants themselves and re-align them, thereby transforming one's conception of the whole.

For example, in our team case study, the executive team could rethink what "resilience" for their organisation would mean quadrant by quadrant. Starting with their own personal resilience, they could explore how they could transform themselves mentally and physically (upper left and right quadrant). They could then examine how they could develop their culture and way of working to become more resilient as a team (lower left quadrant). Then, they could look at particular roles, tasks and tools within the organisation that could be transformed to support greater resilience (upper right quadrant). Finally, they could look at the whole organisation in its broader environment to see whether the organisation was pursuing an appropriately resilient strategy (lower right quadrant).

Alternatively, taking the example of our digital transformation case study, the executives could start by considering the relationship between their new business strategy (lower right quadrant) and the culture of the organisation and how they operate as a team (lower left quadrant), in order to rethink the kind of behavioural shift required to enact the new strategy successfully. They could then proceed to think about their own individual personal development (upper left quadrant) in relation to the cultural shift they hoped to achieve. And finally, they could examine the relationship between their personal mindsets and ways of working with the new roles, tasks and tools that the digital transformation would bring.

In summary, we can say that deeper, more integrated thinking involves consciously and systematically considering "all thematic quadrants, all thinking modes" (AQAT). One starts by focusing on a specific quadrant and illuminating the contents of that quadrant by applying the three thinking modes, structure, process and relationship. One then moves to another quadrant to repeat the process. Next, one considers the relationships between different quadrants and how the concepts in each might be integrated. Such thinking is the basis of a transformative practice.

The Evolution of Thought

In the course of researching our case studies, we came to appreciate how thinking itself is continually evolving. At the individual level, we saw how Sonja's thinking developed over the course of four years, becoming stronger at noticing the links between different aspects of her life and work, and turning her ability to think of herself as an entity in transformation to thinking more of the transformational potential of her role and organisation. Even more emphatically, we saw at the organisational level in the case study on organisational transformation how the thinking about the process of going digital had evolved over a number of years. George Westerman, a senior lecturer at MIT Sloan school of management, who has been researching how large companies in traditional industries use digital technologies to transform with the aim of gaining strategic advantage for many years, coauthored two of the papers that we analysed set four years apart. It would have been interesting for us to interview George Westerman in the same manner that we interviewed Sonja to see how his thinking had evolved, but instead we can observe how the concept of best practice in digital transformation has evolved. Back in 2014, Westerman was setting out a structural template with which to analyse the emerging changes that an organisation should consider in determining its transformation strategy. Four years later, Westerman was writing about the ways in which organisations fail in their attempts to transform. Our interview with a specialist in digital transformation highlighted the mistakes that organisations make, reinforcing Westerman's thesis. We might question whether anything has been learned over the years. Our sense is, however, that current thinking on digital transformation has evolved, and that contemporary commentary is both broader and deeper and shows more evidence of the dialectical thinking modes that we have outlined.

Sometimes it seems as though it is the bitter experience of the past failures that bring people to the realisation that things are more complex than they first thought. Or perhaps people start from the position of being optimistic that they can achieve what they need by keeping things simple. We will mention one more example to illustrate this point, drawing again from the literature on digital transformation. But, we believe that there are many parallels in other fields, for example medical treatment, marketing and advertising, consumer behaviour and environmental management (particularly at a time when there is such an emphasis on the concept of sustainability). The growing application of complexity science (or complex systems thinking) to social systems is an indicator that confidence in linear and reductionist logical models have insufficient explanatory power to help solve problems.

Jeffrey Immelt, the ex-CEO of the US global corporation GE, wrote in a Spring 2019 special edition of the MIT Sloan management review that "executing a digital transformation is not only the most complex but also the most critical challenge that any manufacturer faces today".[1]

Immelt, who committed some $4 billion into GE's digital transformation, writing with Vijay Govindarajan describes three barriers to success; incumbency—the desire to stick with existing business models, systems and processes that have successfully brought the organisation revenue in the past; talent—the availability of the appropriate knowledge skills and abilities; and culture—which in manufacturing companies often reflects the long planning, investment and product development cycles as opposed to the agility, responsiveness and speed of digital technology companies. According to Govindarajan and Immelt, this leaves such companies with several dilemmas that they are inclined to resolve the wrong way and hence, in the process, talk themselves out of transformation.

Firstly, companies question whether it would be quicker and cheaper to outsource the digital capability that they require or to enter into partnerships, rather than develop it internally. This is a classic "buy ready-made or grow from seed" dilemma. From an external right quadrant perspective, there is a good case for minimising the investment by using external support. However, the authors argue that this impairs the opportunity to develop the internal left quadrants' assets of capabilities and culture. Irrespective of the risks of choosing the wrong partner (as also described by the specialist consultant in our case study), using external support leaves the organisation static in terms of the development of its own core competencies. A division is created between the outsourced suppliers making the change and those being changed—the organisation's employees. This leaves the organisation dependent on its external partners and denies it the opportunity to learn how to make best use of digital technology internally.

Secondly, the organisation may be conflicted over whether to hand the job of managing the digital initiatives over to its existing IT function or hiring outsiders and placing the initiative under a newly appointed chief digital officer. Here, Govindarajan and Immelt argue in favour of buying external talent. Internal IT staff are unlikely to have the required expertise and experience in sufficient amounts. In addition, existing IT staff will already be part of the organisation's culture and authority structure. They may be reluctant to strain existing relationships by introducing radical change. Using relational thinking, the authors connect digital transformation initiatives with processes for talent development on the one hand,

[1]Govindarajan and Immelt, 2019.

and organisational politics on the other. Seeing these relationships gives them insight into some of the problems that might emerge if the wrong choice is made.

Thirdly, the organisation has to decide whether to centralise the new digital transformation function or divide it between its various operating units. There is clear evidence of structural thinking here as the authors recognise the argument for matching the digital initiatives to the different customer groups that are served by different business units rather than having a 'one size fits all' approach. However, they argue against a distributed digital function on the basis that the function must have sufficient size and power to enact disruptive change, and that can only come by being linked closely to the centre. We are again reminded that developmental transformation seldom occurs without conflict.

Looking at the literature on digital transformation over the last few years, we detect a change in complexity and sophistication reflecting the evolution of thought and development of a body knowledge about the processes involved. We don't pretend that it is easy to answers the questions addressed by Govindarajan and Immelt, and it may be that it takes a CEO of Immelt's experience to know what is best for a specific organisational transformation, albeit Immelt left GE after 16 years at the helm with a stock price that had halved during his tenure. However, we do think that it helps to know what questions to ask at the start and to test one's thinking for what might be missing. We like to think that our case studies and the Metathinking Framework direct attention in a systematic manner to the areas that do need to be thought about if we are to transform some part of our reality successfully.

Reference

Govindarajan, V., Immelt, J. R. (2019). Leading digital change. *MITSloan Management Review. Special Report*. Accessed May 23, 2019. https://s3.amazonaws.com/marketing.mitsmr.com/offers/DeloitteCollection0319/MITSMR-Leading-Digital-Change.pdf.

Part III
How to Become a Metathinker

Learning Metathinking

14

Why go to the effort of learning dialectical thinking? Here is a short case example for you to consider:

Learning Process

Janet is having a big argument with her business partner, John, over how best to provide service to a particular client. Janet argues that the relationship with the client is all important and that even though it might cost the firm extra in time and money, they should do the best possible job in terms of quality. John, on the other hand, argues that the client will be perfectly satisfied with work of an average standard and that there is no need to go to any extra time and trouble. In fact, he argues, doing so will undermine their profit margin whilst raising the client's expectations about the quality they can expect at lower price levels.

The row is threatening to result in their partnership breaking up. Janet, to support her case, has downloaded an article from a prominent business school website that highlights the importance of customer relationships and the "customer experience" in providing quality service. Meanwhile, John has a report from a leading firm of accountants that presents evidence on the need to manage margins carefully in order to be as efficient as possible and avoid insolvency. Neither Janet nor John appears willing to back down. Janet concludes that if one of them is right, the other is wrong. Either way, the argument has shown up that they have fundamental differences regarding the way to do business. She reasons that they should never have got together in the first place because they clearly have different mindsets and different values. Clearly, their partnership is doomed and unless they split the business their firm will have no future.

However, John notices that whilst he and Janet have different instincts about the way the business should be run and can support those instincts with different logical arguments taken from the views of business experts, there could be other ways to

N. Shannon and B. Frischherz, *Metathinking*, Management for Professionals,
https://doi.org/10.1007/978-3-030-41064-3_14

think about the problem. He decides to try out some different modes of thinking. Firstly, he asks himself, "Supposing I was to zoom out and try to see the bigger picture, what insights might I gain?" He notes that the firm's clients are set in the context of a market, which itself contains many different clients with differing needs. He also notes that the firm exists within the context of a number of suppliers which constitute its competitors. Looking at that picture, he can see that it is important for his firm to position itself in way for its services to be attractive to customers and where there is a minimum of competitors offering similar services. Secondly, he thinks about how the situation might change over time. He says to himself, "what works for us today, might well be different to what worked last year, and will most likely be different to what works best for us next year". He concludes that the firm should try to be agile and evolve its offering to clients as the future unfolds. Then, he asks himself how the two themes of quality and efficiency might be related. He decides that they are unified by the common ground of improving value. Quality focuses on improving the value that a customer receives from a service, whilst efficiency focuses on reducing the cost to the firm of providing client services, so that it gets better value from its employees and suppliers. Lastly, he considers the potential for transforming the firm by working simultaneously to identify what its different clients value most in terms of cost or quality, where these needs are not being met very well by competitors, and putting in place improvement plans to increase efficiency and quality. He decides to engage with Janet again and to talk to her about how the company could organise itself in such a way as to keep developing the quality of its service whilst reducing its cost, and at the same time, targeting customers selectively with high quality or low-cost options, particularly in areas where there is the least competition.

In this example, John has "Metathought" a way to rethink what seemed like an intractable difference between Janet and him over their firm's strategy. His proposal is transformative in that it envisages a way of working for the firm that is both more differentiated and more integrated. If John can get Janet to see the same picture as he envisages, their conflict will be resolved. However, he will need first to convince Janet that it is not simply a question of one of them being right and the other wrong, since that would be to take a logical "either/or" binary perspective that reduces a complex problem to a simple one. He might argue "if the problem is that simple, how is it that we cannot look up the answer in some encyclopaedia of business?" By invoking Metathinking, and specifically by applying different thought patterns, John has found a way to reconcile the conflict between him and Janet and to create a new vision for their business. Essentially, Metathinking allows you to reorganise your thoughts at a new level as a means to avoid the limitations of intuitive and logical thinking.

Didactics of Metathinking

One of the interesting aspects of Metathinking is that it is like having a conversation with oneself. It is reflective thinking. When you are practised as a dialectical thinker this will come very naturally to you. You will be able to analyse your own thinking reflectively and use different thought patterns. However, in the early stages of learning dialectical thinking, it is easier to practise with someone else who can be a dialogue partner for you. As you listen carefully to how your dialogue partner is thinking, you will notice not only what thought patterns they are using, but also what patterns they are not using, and when you do so, you will be able to literally "open their minds" by inviting them to apply other structures. Hence, whilst some of these exercises are designed for you to do on your own, for many you will need a partner and for some others, you will find it helpful to have a third person to act as an observer.

The following three chapters list a series of exercises grouped according to three types of activity—Identify, Use and Reflect. For each exercise, we detail the task in terms of steps and provide materials. The first set of exercises "Identify" requires you to see if you can identify the modes of thinking and thought patterns presented in the form of texts, interviews, speeches and pictures. These exercises will help you familiarise yourself with the thought patterns themselves. The second set of exercises "Use" is designed to get you to try using the thought patterns in your own thinking. The final set of exercises "Reflect" gets you to reflect on your own thinking with the aim of testing and expanding it by using the thought patterns. Whilst all but one of the "Identify" exercises can be done on your own, you will need a dialogue partner for most of the "Use" exercises. The "Reflect" set of exercises are generally exercises that you can do on your own but also some that you might find useful to do with a partner (Table 14.1).

We have also graded the exercises in terms of three levels of difficulty; easy, medium and difficult.

Table 14.1 Progression in dialectical thinking

Progression features	Identify	Use	Reflect
Thought patterns	Other people's thought patterns	Others' and own thought patterns	Own thought patterns
Application	Receptive, interpretive	Public, productive	Private, reflective

Overview on the Exercises

Table 14.2 shows an overview of all exercises. We have classified the individual exercises according to characteristics:

- Social Form: individual (I)—partner (P)—group (G);
- Level of difficulty: easy (*)—medium (**)—difficult (***).

Table 14.2 Overview on the exercises

Chapter 15. *Identifying dialectical thought patterns*		
Reading		
• Exercise 15.1a: Comparing three managers	I, P	*
• Exercise 15.1b: Comparing three mothers	I, P	*
• Exercise 15.1c: Comparing three students	I, P	*
• Exercise 15.2: Analysing interview excerpts	I, P	**
• Exercise 15.3: Analysing excerpts from strategy paper	I, P	***
Listening		
• Exercise 15.4: Analysing political speeches	I, P	**
• Exercise 15.5: Dialectical listening	G	**
Interpreting images		
• Exercise 15.6: Classifying logos and symbols	I, P	*
• Exercise 15.7: Illuminating unusual objects	I, P	*
• Exercise 15.8: Classifying pictures	I, P	*
• Exercise 15.9: Comparing pictures of a glacier at different moments in time	I, P	**
Chapter 16. *Using dialectical thought patterns*		
Inquiring		
• Exercise 16.1: Using mind opening questions to explore the thoughts and feelings of a partner	P	*
• Exercise 16.2: Analysing a description of a problem	P	*
• Exercise 16.3: Formulating mind opening questions	P	**
Dialoguing		
• Exercise 16.4: Integrating arguments	P	*
• Exercise 16.5: Analysing your career description	P	*
• Exercise 16.6: Exploring a person's working life	P	**
Developing		
• Exercise 16.7: Rethinking a problem	P, G	*
• Exercise 16.8: Making an important prediction	I	*
• Exercise 16.9: Developing a career strategy	I	**

(continued)

Table 14.2 (continued)

Chapter 17. *Reflecting on dialectical thought patterns*		
Illuminating		
• Exercise 17.1: Thinking about thinking	I, P	**
• Exercise 17.2: Taking a measure of your dialectical thinking	I	*
• Exercise 17.3: Thinking in metaphors	I, P	**
Evaluating		
• Exercise 17.4: Solving an ethical dilemma	I, P	**
• Exercise 17.5: Reflecting on virtues, values and vices	I	***
Self-reflecting		
• Exercise 17.6: Analysing a description of yourself	I	*
• Exercise 17.7: Reflecting on the balance in your life	I	***
• Exercise 17.8: Exploring your personal life	P	**

Paths Through the Exercises

In order to practise Metathinking, readers are best to observe the thinking modes in their everyday lives and use them specifically to solve professional and private problems. Whilst we encourage you to try all the exercises at some stage, you may prefer to take a pick and mix approach depending on your situation and interests. For example, you may prefer to work individually or with a partner, and you may prefer to tackle a specific level of difficulty. We invite you to choose your own way to navigate through the exercises; however, we have identified three different paths that readers who fall into the following groups may find helpful.

- Organisational leaders and policy-makers:
  Start by getting a feel for the thinking modes used by managers and policy-makers using the identify exercises 15.1a and 15.3. Then, put the thinking modes and thought patterns to use by analysing and rethinking two problems (exercises 16.2 and 16.7), making a prediction (16.8) and devising a strategy (16.9). Finally, reflect on your thinking using exercise 17.2 and your thinking about your business (17.3), explore an ethical dilemma (17.4), consider your virtues and values (17.5) and reflect on your balance in life (17.7).

15.1a, 15.3, 16.2, 16.7, 16.8, 16.9, 17.2, 17.3, 17.4, 17.5, 17.7

- Mentors and coaches:
  Choose one or two exercises from the Identify category; 15.1a, 15.1b and 15.1c as they apply to you. Then, develop more experience with interviewing (exercise 15.2) and listening (exercise 15.5). Next, move on to the Use series, in particular, 16.1 and 16.3 to develop questioning techniques, followed by 16.5, 16.6 and 16.9 to explore the issues your clients may face using thought patterns. Finally, reflect on your thinking using exercise 17.2, explore an ethical dilemma (17.4), analyse a

description of yourself (17.6) which is an exercise you may wish to use with clients, and reflect on your balance in life (17.7) and non-working life (17.8).

15.1a, 15.2, 15.5, 16.1, 16.3, 16.5, 16.6, 16.9, 17.2, 17.4, 17.6, 17.7, 17.8

- Researchers and teachers:

  Begin with exercise 15.1c which explores how students feel, and then develop more experience with interviewing (exercise 15.2). Move on to more intense analysis of political speeches (15.4) and work more abstractly with pictures (15.6, 15.7, 15.8 and 15.9). Then, put the thinking modes and thought patterns to use by exploring a problem (16.2), formulating questions (16.3) and integrating opposing arguments in dialogue (16.4). Finally, hone your skills by reflecting on your thinking (17.1), your use of metaphor (17.3), ethical dilemmas (17.4) and your balance in life (17.7).

15.1c, 15.2, 15.4, 15.6, 15.7, 15.8, 15.9, 16.2, 16.3, 16.4, 17.1, 17.3, 17.4, 17.7

Becoming Practised

The biggest challenge in becoming practised as a Metathinker is that of linking different thought patterns together using a variety of thinking modes. In the first instance, we encourage you to work only with the four dialectic thinking modes, structural, process, relational and transformation. Once you have established familiarity with the four modes, we invite you to go deeper by working with the twelve individual thought patterns.

The first thought pattern of each mode is one where the thinker simply applies the mode of thought to a particular concept. We call this *differentiation* because the thinker is picking out, or pointing to, some aspect of the concept that would otherwise be ignored. For example, a thinker exploring the concept of organisational culture might state the following; “It is tempting to think about an organisation having a specific culture, but that would not do justice to the concept because culture can never be static, it is something that is constantly changing and evolving”.

The second thought pattern in each mode is one that elaborates on the theme introduced by the mode of thought. Effectively, it builds detail onto the first thought pattern. Using the example of culture, a thinker might go on to say “It is interesting to watch how an organisation’s culture develops. In some small way, it keeps changing. For example, new people leave the organisation and old people leave, and then there are shifts in roles and responsibilities, and changes to management. Each of these in some way makes a difference such that the culture is shaped and reshaped by different forces, some of which reinforce what exists whilst others cancel each other out”.

The third thought pattern is one where the thinker goes still one more step further by conceiving of the concept not just in terms of the current mode of thought, but as part of a bigger system in its entirety. What started as an abstract, isolated and independent “thing” is now thought of as integrated with other elements. So, for

Table 14.3 Breadth and depth in dialectical thinking

Depth	Breadth			
	Structural thinking	Process thinking	Relational thinking	Transformational thinking
Beginner (thought pattern 1)				
Intermediate (thought patterns 1 + 2)				
Advanced (thought patterns 1 + 2 + 3)				

example, the thinker might say of the organisational culture "I see now that it makes no sense to think of the culture as a separate thing, but instead I recognise that it is dynamically connected to organisational structure and the context in which the organisation sits. It is part and parcel of a much larger and more complex system, having an influence on that system and also being influenced by it".

In arriving at the third thought pattern, the thinker will have started to link or integrate with at least one other thinking mode. In this way, thoughts become joined up and the thinker arrives at a more complex view of reality. Each thought pattern in the sequence builds on the former and becomes more complex. Hence, we advise readers to focus at first on the four modes and then to progress to working with the set of twelve thought patterns.

Table 14.3 shows the whole spectrum of dialectical thinking. Thus, the four SPiRiT thinking modes represent the breadth, and the three thought patterns the depth, of dialectical thinking.

In passing, we will briefly mention a third level of complexity involving a larger set of twenty-eight thought patterns developed by Otto Laske from original work by Michael Basseches and Michael Bopp. The twenty-eight thought patterns (called "thought forms" by Laske) are more detailed and more specific in their application. We advise readers who wish to become fully fledged dialectical thinkers to reference Laske's "Measuring Hidden Dimensions of Human System. Vol II."[1]

Reference

Laske, O. E. (2008). *Measuring hidden dimensions of human systems: Foundations of requisite organization* (Vol. 2). Medford, MA: Interdevelopmental Institute Press.

[1]Laske, 2008.

Identifying Dialectical Thought Patterns

15

In this group of exercises, you will learn how to identify dialectical thinking modes and thought patterns from different sources of material. We begin by giving examples of different people's usage of the thinking modes for you to contrast and compare. We then present excerpts from a developmental interview that we conducted with an executive and a strategy paper on the "green economy". We continue with two speeches by political figures, Nelson Mandela and the British Prime Minister, Tony Blair, that you can listen to on-line. We follow this up with a practical listening exercise which is best done in groups of three people where you can conduct an interview and listen for dialectical thinking modes in the responses of your interviewee. We finish with four exercises involving images for you to describe what you see being represented in terms of thought patterns. You will find answers to some of the exercises in the Appendix at the end of this book.

N. Shannon and B. Frischherz, *Metathinking*, Management for Professionals,
https://doi.org/10.1007/978-3-030-41064-3_15

Reading

Exercise 15.1a: Comparing Three Managers

Purpose
This exercise teaches you to recognise the qualitative differences between descriptions of an organisation by three different people in terms of their use, or lack of use, of dialectical thinking modes.

Task
Imagine you are coaching three different managers in the same organisation, Andrew, Barbara and Clare. You ask each one (separately) to describe the biggest problem that the organisation is facing currently. Read the passages below and then identify the predominant thinking mode used by each person. Secondly, identify as many thought patterns as you can. Then answer the following questions:

1. Which manager gave the most comprehensive account of the problem that the organisation is facing?
2. Which manager displayed the broadest variety of thinking modes in their account?
3. What was missing or absent in terms of thinking modes from the accounts given by the other two managers?

Materials

Andrew—Operations Director (Oversees Products and Services)
"When we decided to buy Acme's maintenance business, we knew we would have to get greater efficiencies from the combined organisation. Efficiency involves reducing our overall costs, getting more revenue from our customer base, and less duplication of work between the two operations. We are now pricing our products more competitively, knowing that we can make up more than the loss in revenue by selling maintenance contracts. Providing a maintenance service also keeps us close to our customers so that we can get more data on the usage and lifecycle of our products. Our biggest problem is how we go about driving costs down and at the same time improving quality in both products and services".

Barbara—Sales and Marketing Director
"When we bought Acme's maintenance business, it was clear that the immediate advantage would be a broader, more efficient business. We knew we could become a more complete operation by integrating product and maintenance sales, and customers would see the benefit and buy from us as a result. However, we also knew that there would be a period of disruption while we defined the new business model and integrated our operations, retraining and re-directing our sales force. I knew we would also have to work hard to retain customers who felt our maintenance operations were weaker as a result of losing some staff during the merger. I am pushing hard to get Engineering to redesign our products so they cost less to

maintain and to get Manufacturing to drive up quality, but doing so is going to cost us in time and money. I think we will have to start offering a service to maintain our competitors' products to justify the cost of putting all this new infrastructure in place. And I am worried that some of our customers will see that as a dilution of our commitment to our own products. Our biggest problem is how we juggle so many things at once without over-extending ourselves. We have to figure out how to manage customer perceptions, achieve cost efficiencies, and improve product development all at the same time".

Clare—CEO

"When we decided to buy Acme's maintenance business, I knew that there were a lot of ramifications to consider that I could never completely foresee. I am now starting to re-evaluate everything we do in the light of this experience. In many ways we have considerably complicated not only our in-house way of working, but also the market environment in which we have to function. We are striving to become a more complete and integrated operation, but we were previously on safer ground since our business model had been thoroughly tested and validated, and we had a clear view of who our customers were and what they expected of us. Now we have to rethink almost everything that we previously took more or less for granted. I have questions about whether our workers understand and buy into the company's new mission, and whether our customers understand and want the broader offering we are now able to provide. We are also having to introduce a new accounting system, which could unsettle the parts of our operation that were already complex enough when we only sold products. So, there are now many different contexts to consider that were only partly known to us initially. Essentially, the effect of this is that I have become much more sensitive to relationships, not only between parts of our operation, but to relationships between product and services, workforce and customers, business process and financial process, and aware of new systemic interactions that may threaten the stability and harmony of our old operations. I now have to coordinate a larger number of subsystems, and these subsystems are transforming in ways that I did not initially anticipate or even could anticipate. My biggest problem is how to see and understand what is currently going on in almost every aspect of our organization from all the different possible angles".

(Adapted from Laske)[1]

[1]Laske, 2008.

Exercise 15.1b: Comparing Three Mothers

Purpose
This exercise gives you further practice in recognising the qualitative differences between three different people in terms of their use, or lack of use, of dialectical thinking modes. In this case, people are mothers discussing their relationships with their daughters.

Task
Imagine you are friends with three mothers, each of which has come to you for advice on their relationship with their grown-up daughters. You ask each one (separately) to describe how they see the problem. Read the passages below and then identify the predominant thinking mode used by each person. Then answer the following questions:

1. Which mother gave the most comprehensive account of the changes in their relationship with their daughter?
2. Which mother displayed the broadest variety of thinking modes in their account?
3. What was missing or absent in terms of thinking modes from the accounts given by the other two mothers?

Materials

Amanda
"My daughter and I don't seem able to see eye to eye on anything these days. She has a completely different view of how to conduct relationships with her partners from me. I thought I had raised her to believe in the same things that I do, but she seems to have rejected everything I tried to instil in her. I don't understand what I did wrong. She seems to have lost all respect for me and what I stand for. Maybe I don't even deserve her respect. Either I have failed as a parent to bring her up properly, or her values are right and I have based my life on a set of values that are completely wrong".

Brenda
"My daughter and I don't seem able to see eye to eye on anything these days. She has a completely different view of how to conduct relationships with her partners from me. I thought I had raised her to believe in the same things that I do, but I guess I have to accept that it is up to her to decide for herself what she believes in. Nobody has the right to tell another person how to live their lives once they are old enough to look after themselves. In any case, who is to say that one set of values is right and another is wrong? What's important is that I still respect my daughter despite our differences".

Charlotte

"My daughter and I don't seem able to see eye to eye on anything these days. She has a completely different view of how to conduct relationships with her partners from me. It's curious to me how she has developed her own set of values. Of course, I thought I had raised her to believe in the same things that I do, but now I think about it, things are very different today to how they were when I was her age. My daughter's experience of life is very different to mine, and she must have adapted the values that I tried to instil in her to fit with a new set of circumstances. It's natural that people's values change and evolve over time with changes in society. Indeed, society itself also changes as a result of changes in people's values. Instead of expecting her to behave as I would, perhaps I should try to appreciate how my daughter has transformed the beliefs that I taught her and made them her own".

(Adapted from Basseches)[2]

[2]Basseches, 1984.

Exercise 15.1c: Comparing Three Students

Purpose
This exercise gives you further practice in recognising the qualitative differences between three different people in terms of their use, or lack of use, of thought patterns. In this case, the people are university students who are struggling with their course studies.

Task
Imagine you are mentoring three students, each of which has come to you for advice on how best to continue their studies. All of them are disappointed that their degree courses have not lived up to their expectations and, instead of being inspired by their studies, they feel weighed down by the pressure of assignments, exams and by being graded. You ask each one (separately) to describe how they see the problem.

Read the passages below and then identify the predominant thinking mode used by each person. Secondly, identify as many thought patterns as you can. Then answer the following questions:

1. Which student showed the most understanding about the position of the authorities setting the coursework for students?
2. Which student displayed the broadest variety of thinking modes in their account?
3. What was missing or absent in terms of thinking modes from the accounts given by the other two students?

Materials

Arthur
"We would all learn much more if we were given some freedom to follow our interests and write about the topics that really matter to us. Instead we have endless standardized tests and boring assignments that we have to do or we don't get graded. How can the college authorities do this to us? Is this really the right way to educate and inspire a new generation of students? I just don't get it! I guess they must know best because they have been doing this for years, but to me, it still sucks!"

Barry
"We would all learn much more if we were given some freedom to follow our interests and write about the topics that really matter to us. Instead we have endless standardized tests and boring assignments that we have to do or we don't get graded. The college authorities shouldn't dictate what we can and cannot study or grade us using out-dated methods. They are just using their position of authority to impose their own personal preferences on what we think and write. We are a new generation and they are killing our creativity by passing their judgement on all our new ideas. I am getting really angry about it! But if that's the way the system

works, I'm going to be smart. I'll play along and do what they want. Once I get my degree, I'll be free of all this".

Colin

"We would all learn much more if we were given some freedom to follow our interests and write about the topics that really matter to us. Instead we have endless standardized tests and boring assignments that we have to do or we don't get graded. The college authorities are caught between a rock and a hard place. On the one hand they have to have a reliable process that can give the employers out there a sense of the calibre of graduates. On the other, they have a duty to inspire each new generation of students. Those two goals are always going to be incompatible as long as the relationship between universities and employers remains as it is. It's a really tricky problem! What's needed is some kind of development that resolves the tension of that incompatibility between institutions. While I am here I am going to make sure I do as well as I can on my grades but at the same time, I'd like to follow my interests and see if I can learn how educational establishments might be transformed to meet better the needs of both students and society".

(Adapted from Basseches)[3]

[3]Basseches, 1984.

Exercise 15.2: Analysing Interview Excerpts

Purpose

This exercise gives you practice in identifying the thought patterns used by individuals in assessment and coaching situations.

Task

1. Read the interview excerpts below.
2. Note down the thinking modes and any thought patterns that you can identify.
3. Compare your analysis results with our analysis in the Appendix.

Materials

A client talks about his professional and personal developmental potential during a session with his coach.

Number	Speaker	Interview excerpt	Thought pattern
	I:	I have a question about the overlap between the work you do for your client organisation and your private work. You are self-employed and have your own company but you do most of your work for one client. How do you see your work for that client in relation to your work for your own company?	
#01	S:	This is quite simple. Of course, I have my own objectives. I want to develop myself, and I want the tasks that I accomplish successfully to take me further financially, and the tasks that I fail to accomplish to take me further professionally. The measure for this relationship is my personal development. Now, this is a critical point. I have had lots of opportunities to realise my ideas and to gain practical experience. But I also see many situations where I can't develop any further. For example, I got an offer to be employed full-time by the company and to work as one of the permanent staff. But I haven't accepted	
	I:	Didn't you want to be employed? Did you reject the offer?	
	S:	I rejected the offer	
	I:	So, could you elaborate on your perspective regarding your own development? Firstly, regarding your own company, and secondly, regarding your own personality?	
#02	S:	Concerning my company, there are two development strands (laughs). One development strand is independent of me and the client company I am working for. It is a product that I have developed to help people learn how to sail, that I will bring to market and—if it meets my	

(continued)

(continued)

Number	Speaker	Interview excerpt	Thought pattern
		expectations—will make me independent of my work schedule The other development strand is to establish my coaching in a form that can be institutionalised. That would mean developing a standardized process (to help clients) to achieve a certain target in a fixed time frame and making it into a product that can be sold to others. The process would have to be viable for people other than me to use Well, I want to develop myself in the coaching domain and establish myself as a leadership consultant with competences that are closely linked to me as a person But, in parallel, I want to develop processes, that are not linked to me and that work perfectly, even though other individuals are performing them, because they follow a specific methodology	
	I:	Let's talk about your personal development. What are your perspectives and objectives, at the moment?	
	S:	That is a difficult topic …	
	I:	Okay	
#03	S:	Well, many things I do, I do with heart and soul. And I try to link them. This is connected to my energy management. Otherwise, I couldn't manage everything Well, the personal development is related to the spiritual. There are different aspects. I just mentioned the spiritual aspect. Often, I experience myself as someone who is ready to reinvent myself from scratch. Spiritually, this is something very precious to me, and personally, it is something very painful. Now again, I am at a point, where I realise energetically, that I must realign with where I want to go For the present my position is that I want to continue working with the company, but not in a function where I am always confronted with political opposition	
	I:	Yes	
#04	S:	Personally, … that's difficult … Well, I believe that I live in a way which is very integrated with my emotions and values. There was a situation where a potential relationship ended solely because I lived with my emotions and ideas in an integrated way I want to describe how it happened. For a long time, I was constant in my belief that this relationship could work. But many people who knew me well told me to look the facts in the face and not to pursue it. And I said	

(continued)

(continued)

Number	Speaker	Interview excerpt	Thought pattern
		to myself, I will think about what they say. So I considered the situation and I came to the conclusion that I would and must continue to believe in the relationship. And that was the right conclusion. How can I express it? It is something that you do intuitively	
	I:	But, your relationship broke apart, didn't it?	
	S:	No. It is still valid…in principle. Let me picture the situation for you. Your partner says to you, "no, I am okay, please go and leave me on my own". But deep in your heart, you feel that what she really wants is for you to break through her defensive stance by showing your love. So you take her in your arms, and this proves to be the right thing. I acted in this way, and that was how the relationship worked. But now, we have separated and I understand the reasons that led to that. I understand also where I reached my limits and where I couldn't do more to compensate and stabilise the situation	
	I:	How does this connect to your work situation? Is there a relation between the two?	
#05	S:	I can see parallels. I would say now that the kind of development I want to experience as a matter of course is something that is only possible to achieve together with other people. I think I know the extent to which I can develop on my own. Many times, I reflected and found the strength to develop myself. I left behind old things and habits. And I see that maybe this is the precondition for new possibilities. At the end, we are autonomous and alone, that is as clear as daylight. But now, I am interested in the interdependency between people, in what you can achieve together or—to say it at its most extreme—in what you can only achieve together. For example, I have to have some degree of self-belief if I want to ask someone to take dancing lessons together. Without good self-esteem in the first place, it would not work. I can't learn to dance tango by working on myself and developing myself alone. There are certain areas—I don't really know how to express this—certain aspects of life that are accessible only if you achieve them together with someone else. Often, this is more important for me than how I might profit financially, with all the consequences that this implies	

Exercise 15.3: Analysing Excerpts from Strategy Paper

Purpose

This exercise gives you practice in identifying the thought patterns used in a strategy document on green economy by United Nations Environment Programme (UNEP).

Task

1. Read the text excerpts below.
2. Note down the thinking modes and any thought patterns that you can identify.
3. Compare the results of your analysis with our analysis at the end of the exercise.

Materials

The following text excerpts describe key concepts of the "green economy". The text excerpts are cited from the following document:

United Nations Environment Programme (UNEP) (2011): Towards a green economy.[4]

Number	Text excerpt	Thought pattern
#01	"Subsidy reform is possible if done with careful attention to the poorest communities. Removing subsidies is challenging given the vested interests in their maintenance, but there are numerous examples of countries that have undertaken reform processes [...]. Subsidies are sometimes justified with the argument that they benefit low-income households, but unless the aid is targeted, the majority of the spending often flows to higher-income households. That said, subsidy reform will often lead to increases in the prices of subsidized goods. Although low-income groups typically benefit from only a small share of subsidies, they spend a larger proportion of their income on basic goods, including food, water and energy, and can be disproportionately affected if subsidies for these goods are removed. Given this, a gradual reform strategy with short-term support measures is required. Such a reform strategy could include, among other things, the use of targeted consumption subsidies to poor households or the redirection of funds into high-priority areas for public spending, such as health care or education"[a]	

(continued)

[4]United Nations Environment Programme, 2011.

(continued)

Number	Text excerpt	Thought pattern
#02	"Subsidies that have public-good characteristics or positive externalities can be a powerful enabler for a transition to a green economy. Green subsidies, such as price support measures, tax incentives, direct grants and loan support, may be used for a number of reasons: (a) to act quickly in order to avoid locking in unsustainable assets and systems, or losing valuable natural capital that people depend on for their livelihoods; (b) to ensure the realization of green infrastructure and technologies, especially those with substantial nonfinancial benefits or financial benefits that are difficult for private actors to capture; and (c) to foster green infant industries, as part of a strategy to build comparative advantage and drive long-term employment and growth"[b]	
#03	"Command and control measures may offer the lowest-cost solution in some cases. While market-based instruments have a well-deserved reputation for efficiency, in some situations command and control measures may offer the lowest-cost solution. For example, there may be no market instrument that can efficiently ensure the elimination of bottom-trawling in fisheries, and the cost-effectiveness of regulation may be preferable where there are opportunities to regulate an industry upstream—such as oil extraction and refining—that can have knock-on effects throughout the supply chain. Depending on the situation, command and control measures can be administratively easier to implement and may pose fewer political challenges. In the short term, for example, it may be easier to establish new energy-efficiency standards and remove obstacles in the planning-permission process of renewable energy projects than to establish a carbon market and eliminate fossil-fuel subsidies"[c]	
#04	"International environmental agreements can facilitate and stimulate a transition to a green economy. For instance, multilateral environmental agreements (MEAs), which establish the legal and institutional frameworks for addressing global environmental challenges, can play a significant role promoting green economic activity. The Montreal Protocol on the Substances that Deplete the Ozone Layer, which is widely considered to be one of the most successful MEAs, is a case in point. The Protocol led to the development of an entire industry focused on the replacement and phase out of ozone-depleting substances. Of course, the MEA with the most potential to influence the transition to a green economy is the United Nations Framework Convention on Climate Change (UNFCCC). The UNFCCC's Kyoto Protocol has already stimulated growth in a number of economic sectors, such as renewable energy generation and energy efficient technologies, in order to address greenhouse gas emissions. At a global level, the renewal of a post-Kyoto framework for carbon will be the single most significant factor in determining the speed and scale of the transition to a green economy"[d]	

(continued)

(continued)

Number	Text excerpt	Thought pattern
#05	"As this report has argued, a reallocation of public and private investments—spurred through appropriate policy reforms and enabling conditions—is needed to build up or enhance natural capital such as forests, water, soil and fish stocks, which are particularly important for the rural poor. These "green" investments will also enhance new sectors and technologies that will be the main sources of economic development and growth of the future: renewable energy technologies, resource and energy efficient buildings and equipment, low-carbon public transport systems, infrastructure for fuel efficient and clean energy vehicles, and waste management and recycling facilities. Complementary investments are required in human capital, including greening-related knowledge, management, and technical skills to ensure a smooth transition to a more sustainable development pathway"[e]	

[a]United Nations Environment Programme, 2011, 30
[b]United Nations Environment Programme, 2011, 28
[c]United Nations Environment Programme, 2011, 28
[d]United Nations Environment Programme, 2011, 33
[e]United Nations Environment Programme, 2011, 38

Listening

Exercise 15.4: Analysing Political Speeches

Purpose

This exercise gives you practice in identifying the thought patterns used by famous politicians giving speeches at key moments in their lives.

Task

Thought patterns can be identified in written and oral language.

1. Listen to the two speeches below which can be found on-line. We show transcripts of a selection of excerpts below.
2. Note down the thinking modes and any thought patterns that you can identify.
3. Compare your analysis results with our analysis at the end of the exercise.

Materials

(a) **Nelson Mandela—"An ideal I am prepared to die for" (1964)**[5]

This is considered to be Mandela's best known speech, that he delivered in 1964 from the dock of the Pretoria courtroom having been in jail two years already by then. The speech was made famous by its closing lines in which he speaks of democracy and free society, an ideal for which he said he was prepared to die.

Number	Interview excerpt	Thought pattern
#01	I have always regarded myself, in the first place, as an African patriot. After all, I was born in Umtata, forty-six years ago. My guardian was my cousin, who was the acting paramount chief of Thembuland, and I am related both to Sabata Dalindyebo, the present paramount chief, and to Kaiser Matanzima, the Chief Minister for the Transkei	
#02	Today I am attracted by the idea of a classless society, an attraction which springs in part from Marxist reading and, in part, from my admiration of the structure and organisation of early African societies in this country. The land, then the main means of production, belonged to the tribe. There was no rich or poor and there was no exploitation	
#03	It is true, as I have already stated that I have been influenced by Marxist thought. But this is also true of many of the leaders of the new independent states. Such widely different persons as Gandhi, Nehru, Nkrumah, and Nasser all acknowledge this fact. We all accept the need for some form of socialism to enable our people to catch up with the	

(continued)

[5]Nelson Mandela, 1964.

(continued)

Number	Interview excerpt	Thought pattern
	advanced countries of the world and to overcome their legacy of extreme poverty. But this does not mean we are Marxists….	
#04	… I have been influenced in my thinking by both West and East. All this has led me to feel that in my search for a political formula, I should be absolutely impartial and objective. I should tie myself to no particular system of society other than that of socialism. I must leave myself free to borrow the best from West and from the East	
#05	… The complaint of Africans, however, is not only that they are poor and whites are rich, but that the laws which are made by the whites are designed to preserve this situation. … There is compulsory education for all white children at virtually no cost to their parents, be they rich or poor. Similar facilities are not provided for the African children… The quality of education is also different… The Government often answers its critics by saying that Africans in South Africa are economically better off than the inhabitants of the other countries in Africa. I do not know whether this statement is true and doubt whether any comparison can be made without having regard to the cost-of-living index in such countries. But even if it is true, as far as African people are concerned, it is irrelevant. Our complaint is not that we are poor by comparison with people in other countries, but that we are poor by comparison with white people in our own country, and that we are prevented by legislation from altering this imbalance	
#06	… Above all, my Lord, we want equal political rights, because without them our disabilities will be permanent. I know this sounds revolutionary to the whites in this country, because the majority of voters will be Africans. This makes the white man fear democracy. But this fear cannot be allowed to stand in the way of the only solution which will guarantee racial harmony and freedom for all. It is not true that the enfranchisement of all will result in racial domination. Political division, based on colour, is entirely artificial and, when it disappears, so will the domination of one colour group by another. The ANC has spent half a century fighting against racialism. When it triumphs as it certainly must, it will not change that policy. This then is what the ANC is fighting. Our struggle is a truly national one. It is a struggle of the African people, inspired by our own suffering and our own experience. It is a struggle for the right to live	
#07	During my lifetime I have dedicated my life to this struggle of the African people. I have fought against white domination, and I have fought against black domination. I have cherished the ideal of a democratic and free society in which all persons will live together in harmony and with equal opportunities. It is an ideal for which I hope to live for and to see realised. But, my Lord, if it needs be, it is an ideal for which I am prepared to die	

(b) Tony Blair—Address to the Irish Parliament (1998)[6]

On Thursday, 26 November 1998, Tony Blair made history by becoming the first British Prime Minister ever to address the Irish Parliament with this speech.

Number	Speech excerpts	Thought pattern
#01	… Ireland, as you may know, is in my blood. My mother was born in the flat above her grandmother's hardware shop on the main street of Ballyshannon in Donegal. She lived there as a child, started school there and only moved when her father died; her mother remarried and they crossed the water to Glasgow. We spent virtually every childhood summer holiday up to when the troubles really took hold in Ireland, usually at Rossnowlagh, the Sands House Hotel, I think it was… Even now, in my constituency of Sedgefield, which at one time had 30 pits or more, all now gone, virtually every community remembers that its roots lie in Irish migration to the mines of Britain. So like it or not, we, the British and the Irish, are irredeemably linked	
#02	We experienced and absorbed the same waves of invasions: Celts, Vikings, Normans—all left their distinctive mark on our countries. Over a thousand years ago, the monastic traditions formed the basis for both our cultures. Sadly, the power games of medieval monarchs and feudal chiefs sowed the seeds of later trouble	
#03	Yet it has always been simplistic to portray our differences as simply Irish versus English—or British. There were, after all, many in Britain too who suffered greatly at the hands of powerful absentee landlords, who were persecuted for their religion, or who were for centuries disenfranchised. And each generation in Britain has benefited, as ours does, from the contribution of Irishmen and women. Today the links between our parliaments are continued by the British-Irish Parliamentary Body, and last month 60 of our MPs set up a new all-party "Irish in Britain Parliamentary Group." Irish parliamentarians have made a major contribution to our shared parliamentary history… So much shared history, so much shared pain. And now the shared hope of a new beginning	
#04	The peace process is at a difficult juncture. Progress is being made, but slowly. There is an impasse over the establishment of the executive; there is an impasse over decommissioning. But I have been optimistic the whole way through. And I am optimistic now. Let us not underestimate how far we have come; and let us agree that we have come too far to go back now. Politics is replacing violence as the way people do business. The Good Friday Agreement, overwhelmingly endorsed by the people on both sides of the Border, holds out the prospect of a peaceful long-term future for Northern Ireland, and the whole island of Ireland	

(continued)

[6]Tony Blair, 1998.

(continued)

Number	Speech excerpts	Thought pattern
#05	The Northern Ireland Bill provides for the new Assembly and Executive, the North-South Ministerial Council, and the British-Irish Council. It incorporates the principle of consent into British constitutional law and repeals the Government of Ireland Act of 1920. It establishes a Human Rights Commission with the power to support individual cases. We will have an Equality Commission to police a new duty on all public bodies in Northern Ireland to promote equality of opportunity. We have set up the Patten Commission to review policing. We are scaling down the military presence. Prisoners are being released. None of this is easy. I get many letters from the victims of violence asking why we are freeing terrorist prisoners. It is a tough question but my answer is clear: the agreement would never have come about if we had not tackled the issue of prisoners. That agreement heralds the prospect of an end to violence and a peaceful future for Northern Ireland…	
#06	It is time now for all the parties to live up to all their commitments. Time for North/South bodies to be established to start a new era of co-operation between you and Northern Ireland—I hope agreement on these is now close. Time to set up the institutions of the new government. Time for the gun and the threat of the gun to be taken out of politics once and for all; for decommissioning to start. I am not asking anyone to surrender. I am asking everyone to declare the victory of peace. In Belfast or Dublin, people say the same thing: make the agreement work	
#07	It is never far from my mind… I reflect on those, who though untouched directly by violence, are nonetheless victims—victims of mistrust and misunderstanding who through lack of a political settlement miss the chance of new friendships, new horizons, because of the isolation from others that the sectarian way of life brings. I reflect on the sheer waste of children taught to hate when I believe passionately children should be taught to think…	
#08	No one should ignore the injustices of the past, or the lessons of history. But too often between us, one person's history has been another person's myth. We need not be prisoners of our history. My generation in Britain sees Ireland differently today and probably the same generation here feels differently about Britain. We can understand the emotions generated by Northern Ireland's troubles, but we cannot really believe, as we approach the twenty-first century, there is not a better way forward to the future than murder, terrorism and sectarian hatred…	

Exercise 15.5: Dialectical Listening

Purpose

This exercise helps you to identify the thought patterns being used by another person as they describe a challenge they are facing at work or in their personal life.

Task

1. Work in groups of three with one person taking the role of the interviewer, another the role of the interviewee and the third acting as an observer.
2. The interviewer begins by asking the interviewee to describe a challenge that he or she is facing currently in their work or home life. As the interviewee responds, the interviewer may ask the interviewee to elaborate on any points of interest. Take about five minutes to do the interview.
3. The observer listens carefully to the interviewee's responses and makes a note of any thinking modes and thought patterns used by the interviewee (they may choose to use the Dialectical Thinking Cycle diagram as a form for the notes). The observer may make use of the thinking modes and patterns checklist to help recognise these. At the end of the interview, the observer debriefs the interviewer and interviewee of the thinking modes and thought patterns that he/she has detected and invites the interviewee to comment on any missing thought patterns.
4. Once the debrief is complete, the group changes roles and conducts another interview.

Materials

Thinking modes and thought patterns checklist (Table 15.1).

Table 15.1 Thinking modes and thought patterns checklist

	Structural Thinking
	Situates the challenge in terms of a broader context in terms of time, space, structure or scale
	Describes the challenge as being part of a stable situation or system
	Describes the system of which the challenge is a part in terms of its structure, particularly as a hierarchy
	Describes and links different perspectives on the challenge
	Process Thinking
	Describes the challenge as being in continual motion or flux
	Refers to other events going back into the past, and/or continuing into the future
	Describes how the challenge has evolved over time, changing and becoming more complex
	Embeds the challenge within a larger dynamic process of change
	Relational Thinking
	Links the challenge inextricably to some other aspects of their life or experience
	Elaborates on the nature of the relationship between the challenge and another aspect or aspects
	Describes the common ground between seemingly unrelated aspects of their situation
	Shows how different elements of the situation or challenge relate to each other and act on each other to shape themselves and make up the whole
	Transformational Thinking
	Describes conflicting elements of the challenge that are likely to lead to a substantial positive or negative change in the situation
	Elaborates on the tension between aspects of the situation and how action might be taken to resolve or reorganise these aspects at a higher level
	Describes how different systems can be brought together and coordinated to resolve the challenge
	Sets out how multiple perspectives on the challenge can be integrated to form a whole new vision or interpretation of the situation

Dialectical Thinking Cycle

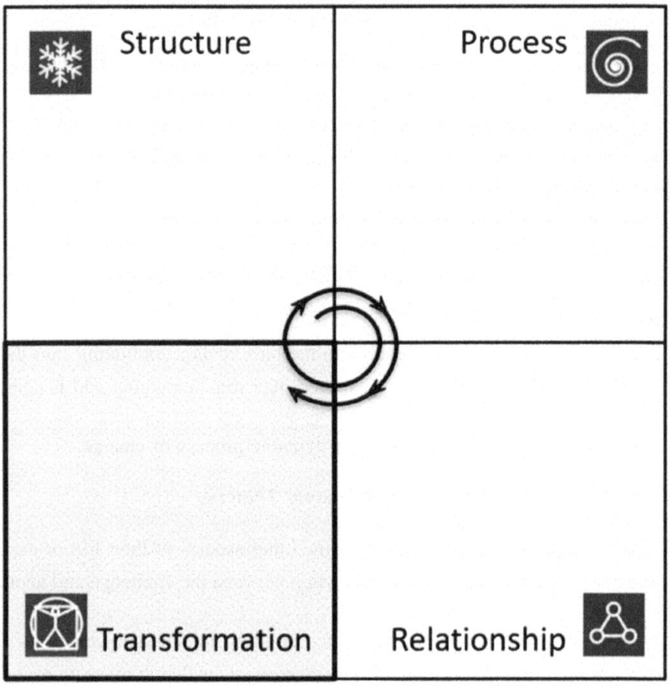

Interpreting Images

Exercise 15.6: Classifying Logos and Symbols

Purpose
This exercise stimulates you to identify thinking patterns as you look at logos and symbols that represent sustainability.

Task

1. Look at each logo or symbol in turn (Fig. 15.1).
2. Thinking about what the image represents, complete one of the sentences "Sustainablity is…." or "Sustainability is like…".
3. Note down the thinking mode that you have applied in your sentence.
4. Compare your analysis with our analysis in the Appendix.

Materials

Fig. 15.1 Symbols of sustainability (adapted from a Google images search "sustainability"). (© Nick Shannon and Bruno Frischherz 2020. All rights reserved)

Exercise 15.7: Illuminating Unusual Objects

Purpose
This exercise stimulates you to identify thinking modes as you look at an object from different perspectives.

Task

1. Study the pictures of the three unusual objects (Fig. 15.2).
2. Working with a partner, take turns for one person to ask questions to the other.
3. The first person chooses a picture and describes the object and its significance to the second person. Feel free to speculate.
4. The second person should then ask the first person questions about the object described to prompt different thought patterns (see mind opening questions below). Listen to the speaker carefully and make a note of the thought patterns used. Discuss with the speaker which thought patterns they intended.
5. Swap roles and repeat the exercise with another picture. You may also try this exercise using your own pictures.

Materials

Thinking modes

1.

2.

3.

Fig. 15.2 Unusual objects (© Bruno Frischherz)

Mind Opening Questions

	Structural Thinking
	What is this object?
	In what context(s) might this object be found?
	What is the function of the object?
	What is the object a part of?
	Process Thinking
	How did the object come into being?
	How might the object evolve over time?
	What is missing from the object that would make it more complete?
	How might the object be changing at this moment?
	Relational Thinking
	What common ground can be found between this object and other objects?
	What relationships does the object have to other objects?
	What could the object be connected to that makes it what it is?
	What might the object stand for or symbolise?
	Transformational Thinking
	How could the object be developed further?
	How might the object serve a different purpose?
	What other associations with the object come to mind?
	How might the object be absorbed or integrated within another system?

(adapted from Frischherz et al., 2016)[7]

[7]Frischherz et al. 2016

Exercise 15.8: Classifying Pictures

Purpose
This exercise stimulates a viewer to detect and suggest particular thinking modes in describing pictures.

Task

1. Study the pictures (Fig. 15.3).
2. Working with a partner, take turns to select a picture and identify the thinking mode that the picture suggests.
3. Describe the picture using a particular thinking mode that the picture brings to mind. For example, the first picture of a river suggests the notion of an entity in constant motion and is therefore an example of process thinking (P1).
4. Compare notes with your partner, explaining why you identified a particular thought pattern. Did you identify the same thought pattern? If not, explore what was the reason for the difference in your thinking.
5. Compare your descriptions of the pictures with the answers in the Appendix. Where could you find similarities in the interpretation?
   Where does the indicated thought form highlight new aspects of the picture?

Materials

Fig. 15.3 Thought patterns in images (© cf. Picture Credits)

Exercise 15.9: Comparing Pictures of a Glacier at Different Moments in Time

Purpose

In this exercise, you will learn how thinking modes and thought patterns come to mind as one observes and describes the natural world.

Task

Review the two pictures which show the retreat of the Briksdal Glacier in Norway over a period of five years (Fig. 15.4).

1. Write a brief description of what you see occurring as part of this natural phenomenon illustrated by the two photographs taken at different points in time.
2. Review your description and identify any thinking modes or thought patterns that you have applied.

Questions

(a) Did you make use of any structural thought patterns by referring to how the glacier is part of, and affected by larger systems, such as the meteorological and oceanic systems?
(b) Did you make use of any process thought patterns by referring to past current and future states of the glacier?
(c) Did you identify any relationships between the glacier and other elements in the environment?
(d) Did you specify any transformational forces at work that affect the glacier?

Materials

Fig. 15.4 Two views of the Briksdal Glacier, Norway 2003, 2008 (© Ximonic, Simo Räsänen/Wikimedia)

References

Basseches, M. (1984). *Dialectical thinking and adult development*. Norwood, N.J: Ablex Pub.

Frischherz, B., et al. (2016). *Das Reflexionsbuch. Vor- und Nachdenken über sich*. Zürich: Versus.

Laske, O. E. (2008).*Measuring hidden dimensions of human systems: Foundations of requisite organization* (Vol. 2). Medford, MA: Interdevelopmental Institute Press.

Nelson Mandela. (1964). *An Ideal I Am Prepared to Die For*, https://www.youtube.com/watch?v=-CNewYDzeDg.

Tony Blair. (1998). *Address to the Irish Parliament*, https://www.c-span.org/video/?c4289994/tony-blair-address-irish-parliament.

United Nations Environment Programme (2011). *Towards a green economy*. https://sustainabledevelopment.un.org/content/documents/126GER_synthesis_en.pdf.

16 Using Dialectical Thought Patterns

In this series of exercises you will move to the next level of skill in Metathinking by consciously applying the thinking modes and thought patterns. The exercises are designed to help you develop "rethink" a particular problem or question. The intention here is not to find the "right" answer so much as to explore issues in more depth and get a better understanding of the reality of a situation. You may already feel that you can explore the kinds of problems that we are suggesting you consider here in sufficient detail. However, the attitude of a Metathinker is that there is always something missing from one's thinking and that the systematic use of thinking modes and thought patterns is the way to gather greater insight into an issue and its solution. Although you can work on your own, most of these exercises are best done together with a partner with whom you can enter into dialogue.

N. Shannon and B. Frischherz, *Metathinking*, Management for Professionals,
https://doi.org/10.1007/978-3-030-41064-3_16

Inquiring

Exercise 16.1: Using Mind Opening Questions to Explore the Thoughts and Feelings of a Partner

Purpose

This exercise requires you to ask questions using a specific thinking mode to explore how another person feels about an aspect of their life that is particularly meaningful to them. The interviewee has the task of applying the thinking mode and using thought patterns in their response.

Task

1. Work in pairs, one person to be the interviewer and the other person, the interviewee. The interviewer invites the interviewee to choose one of the topics below to answer.
2. The interviewer listens to the interviewee answering the topic and chooses from any or all of the mind opening questions below as appropriate to get the interviewee to elaborate on their answer.
3. After a particular topic is exhausted, swap roles and repeat.
4. Debrief each other on the exercise.

Materials

Interview topics

- Describe something you find difficult at work, that you wish you could do better or more effectively.
- Describe an area of your life where you feel held back or constrained and limited in some way, or where you wish you had more control or freedom.
- Describe one of your pet hates, something that you really dislike and wish would not exist or would never happen.
- Describe what you would do to make the country, or the world, a better place if you could do anything you wanted.
- Describe a significant problem that your organisation is facing.
- Describe a recent event in your life that has a lot of meaning for you.

Mind Opening Questions

	Structural Thinking
	If you were to look at what you describe from an even higher level, what is the bigger picture that you can see here?
	What gives the picture you describe its significance and stability?
	How might what you describe change if seen in different contexts?
	Are there multiple perspectives that you can take on the picture you describe?
	Process Thinking
	How has what you describe emerged from past history?
	To what extent would you say the situation is currently shifting? How?
	What do you see emerging from the situation you describe?
	If you consider the polar opposite or antithesis of what you have described, what elements of this could be combined together with what you have described to create something new?
	Relational Thinking
	To what extent do you see what you describe as unique and unrelated to anything else that is going on?
	How might what you have described be related to something else that you see happening or that is going on in your life?
	How is what you describe shaped or influenced by some other factors or events?
	What would you say is the common ground between this and other events in your life?
	Transformational Thinking
	How might what you describe be developed further?
	Are there any conflicts that might need to be overcome in order for what you describe to be transformed?
	What is the potential for what you describe to go the other way, to fall apart or disintegrate?
	When you think about what you have described, what other thing or system might you integrate it with that would bring about its transformation?

Table of Dialectical Thought Patterns

	Structural Thinking
S1	Differentiation of elements in a whole representing a stable entity in its own right
S2	Elaboration of elements with reference to the structure, hierarchy and functionality of the elements
S3	Integration of different elements and perspectives into a structured bigger entity as a system
	Process Thinking
P1	Differentiation of a changing element, linking its current state to the past and future
P2	Elaboration of one or more elements in their developmental aspects
P3	Integration of changing and interconnected elements in an unceasing movement as a system
	Relational Thinking
R1	Differentiation of relationships between two or more separate elements
R2	Elaboration of specific relationships between interconnected elements
R3	Integration of interconnected elements and their constitutive relationships into an entity as a system
	Transformational Thinking
T1	Differentiation of conflicting elements leading to transformation or destruction of a system
T2	Elaboration of the conflicting interaction between two or more elements and their characteristics, potentially involving human agency
T3	Integration of conflicting elements into a new dynamic system, potentially involving human agency

Exercise 16.2: Analysing a Description of a Problem

Purpose

Conscious application of thought patterns can help you rethink a problem with a view to seeing new perspectives. This exercise enables you to apply different thought patterns to a specific problem in order to facilitate finding a solution.

Task

1. Write a paragraph of around 150 words to describe a particular problem that you are facing currently, either work or home related,
2. Read it to your partner and allow them to identify any of the thinking modes and thought patterns used.
3. Using the checklist of 12 thought patterns, check which ones you used and which ones are missing.
4. Reflect on your thinking about the problem you described. How might the problem change if you applied different thought patterns?

Materials

Table of dialectical thought patterns in Exercise 16.1.

Exercise 16.3: Formulating Mind Opening Questions

Purpose

The act of developing mind opening questions is itself an opportunity to practise using thinking modes and thought patterns. If you find yourself in the position of acting as a kind of coach, consultant or conversation partner to a client or friend, you may already know the value of asking the right kind of question. Here, we invite you to develop a set of questions in a structured manner using Metathinking.

Task

1. In this exercise, we ask you to consider yourself in the role of a consultant to an organisation with which you are familiar.
2. Imagine you are approached by the leader of this organisation to help solve a problem that is troubling them. For example, the leader might be concerned that the staff in the organisation are low in morale and not sufficiently engaged. Or, the leader might be worrying about how to make the organisation more efficient and competitive.
3. Now, working systematically through the dialectical thinking cycle, generate a list of mind opening questions that you could use to explore the problem in more detail with that leader using the table of dialectical thought patterns (as listed in Exercise 16.1).
4. Note down the mind opening questions in the relevant box on the dialectical thinking cycle chart. Try to identify any links between the questions in the different thinking modes.

Materials

Dialectical Thinking Cycle

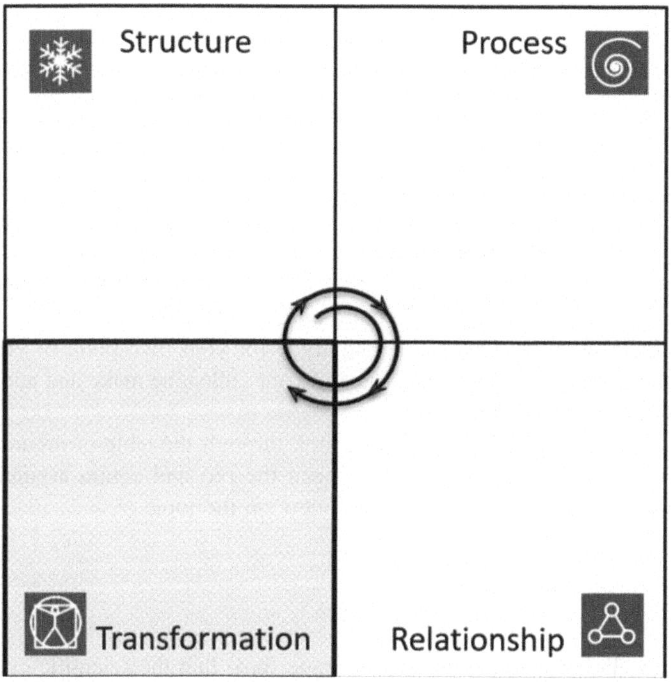

Dialoguing

Exercise 16.4: Integrating Arguments

Purpose
This exercise shows how you can integrate apparently opposing arguments to develop a richer, more elaborated solution to a particular problem.

Task

1. Choose a topic where you have a disagreement with a colleague: e.g., a person's right to choose their gender, climate change, vegetarianism, immigration, digitalisation, criminal punishment etc.
2. Prepare by listing as many arguments as you can *for* and *against* your view on the topic in the table of pro and contra arguments below.
3. Debate the topic with a colleague and argue for your own point of view.
4. Take notes of the arguments that you and your colleague make and add these to complete the table of arguments.
5. Finally, together with your colleague, look through the table of arguments and try to find some common ground between the pro and contra arguments that would enable you to synthesise a new view on the topic.

For example:

In relation to climate change, one might argue (pro) that the scientific evidence is clear that the cause is human activity. The (contra) argument is that, although the presence of greenhouse gases in the atmosphere has increased, we cannot know for sure that current climate changes are the direct effect of such increases. There may be other effects and interactions in the atmosphere that cause such changes that we have not identified yet. Correlation is not the same as causation.

A possible synthesis is as follows:

It is possible that climate change is the result of both human activity and natural causes of which we are unaware. What remains to be known is whether a reversal of the human activity that adds to greenhouse gases will impact the changes in climate. It may, for example, be too late for humans to do anything to arrest the climate change that is underway, or alternatively it may be that the planet will find a way to reach a new equilibrium without a significant change in human activities.

A further worked example can be found in the Appendix.

Materials

Complete your own example using the blank table below.

Pro/Thesis	Contra/Antithesis
Synthesis	

Exercise 16.5: Analysing your Career Description

Purpose

This exercise enables you to practise your use of thought patterns by incorporating them into a description of something that is very familiar to you—your career progression.

Task

1. Working with a partner, briefly give an account of how your career has progressed.
2. Ask your partner to identify the thinking modes and thought patterns that you use.
3. Using the checklist of 12 dialectical thought patterns in Exercise 16.1, discuss with your partner which ones you used and which ones were missing.
4. Reflect on your thinking about how you described your career progression. How might your view of your career change if you applied different thought patterns?

Materials

Table of dialectical thought patterns in Exercise 16.1.

Exercise 16.6: Exploring a Person's Working Life

Purpose

This exercise helps you to explore the professional life of a partner. By interviewing with specific questions, you can help your partner to illuminate hidden aspects of his or her working life and to initiate transformation of their situation if desired. For this exercise, we recommend that you write each question on a separate small index card and sort the cards into groups by thinking mode.

Task

1. Work in pairs, one partner to be the interviewer, the other to respond.
2. The interviewer sorts the deck of cards into the four thinking modes: structure—process—relationship—transformation (SPiRiT). The other person mentally prepares to answer questions about their career.
3. The interviewer explores the professional situation of the interviewee by asking the illuminating questions on the cards.
4. Proceeding sequentially, the interviewer starts by asking Structural questions, goes on to Process questions and then to Relational questions and finally to the Transformational questions. Take notes using the dialectical thinking cycle as a template.
5. Change roles of interviewer and interviewee and start again by asking questions.
6. Compare the two situations by discussing:
   - Where can you see similarities and where differences?
   - Where would you like to change your situation?
   - What will be the next step?
7. Reflect on the process after dialoguing.
   - Which thinking mode/s do you normally use to describe the world?
   - In which thinking mode/s do you find it easy or difficult to talk about your working life? Why?
   - Can you view aspects of your life using different thinking modes simultaneously?

Materials

Mind Opening Questions

	Structural Thinking
	How do you experience your work?
	What role models characterise the way you choose to show leadership?
	What values and motives are important in your career decisions?
	How far do you see your professional work as being successful?
	What does success mean to you?
	What developments are occurring at present in your workplace?
	In what way does your organisation typically structure people's roles?
	Which ways of working are typically characteristic in your organisation?
	Process Thinking
	Have you ever experienced some form of crisis in your professional development?
	What hopes or fears do you have for your career?
	How do you see your organisation changing and developing at the moment?
	In your organisation, are changes understood as crises to be concerned about or as innovations to be welcomed?
	What characteristics of male or female authority do you experience as being conducive and positive or disruptive and negative?
	Relational Thinking
	Does your gender matter in your working life?
	How well do your personal interests and skills fit with your work?
	To what extent do you experience support and affirmation in your work?
	In what ways do you connect the idea of power with the idea of responsibility?
	In what ways do your professional relationships support your self-esteem?
	Transformational Thinking
	How do you go about accommodating changes at work with your personal values?
	What conflicts do you experience between deciding and acting as you would like in your work and behaving as is expected of you?
	How do you influence actively the development of your organisation?
	In what ways do your experiences of authority determine your behaviour in the roles you hold within your organisation?

Dialectical Thinking Cycle as shown in in Exercise 16.3.

Developing

Exercise 16.7: Exploring a Complex Problem

Purpose

This exercise helps you to explore and solve a problem, either one of your own or that of someone else, by developing and posing questions that open up the thinking process to achieve a more complete conception of the issues.

Task

1. Work in pairs or groups of up to four people.
2. Take it turns to describe briefly a problem that you are currently experiencing in your life. At this stage, do not ask any questions.
3. If working in groups, select one person's problem for the group to work on. Nominate that person as the "problem owner", and the others as "problem explorers". If working in pairs, simply decide who wishes to go first.
4. Individually, decide and write down one or two questions from each of the four classes of dialectical thought patterns: Structural, Process, Relational and Transformational thinking (SPiRiT). You may choose questions from the generic list of mind opening questions (presented below) if you wish, or tailor these to suit the problem.
5. Using the dialectical thinking cycle, starting with the first thinking mode—Structural, and continuing in the sequence, Process, Relational, Transformational, each problem explorer in turn asks the problem holder one question. The problem holder can choose to answer that question or to pass to the next question. It is important at this stage that problem explorers do not suggest solutions.
6. Once a complete round of questions has been asked from each thinking mode, the problem owner can opt for one of the following:
    a. to have a further round of questions, or
    b. to reformulate the problem and restate it prior to having another round of questions, or
    c. to declare that she has an answer and knows what action she will take.
7. When the problem owner has an answer, and at the latest after three rounds, the problem owner should describe any insights they have gained from answering the questions. If they have not found an answer, they should say what they think is still missing for a solution.
8. Finally, all participants should discuss the process and its outcome with a focus on whether the inquiry via the dialectical modes of thinking was helpful.

(adapted from an idea by Jan DeVisch)[1]

[1]DeVisch, 2019.

Materials

Mind Opening Questions

Structural Thinking
What are the elements of the problem?
What is the structure of the problem?
Who are the involved and concerned actors?
What attitudes, interests and claims do the different actors have?
How can the situation be seen from different perspectives?
Which cultural or ethical values are touched?
Process Thinking
Which processes do not work?
What is the history of the problem?
What could be the consequence of the problem?
How do the participants interact?
How might the participants develop the situation?
What events could change the situation?
Relationship Thinking
What elements of the problem are inseparable?
What values underlie the problem?
What kinds of relationships are there?
What kinds of interactions are there?
What are the preconditions for a solution?
What are the evaluation criteria for a decision?
Transformational Thinking
What would your decision be to resolve the problem?
What reasons do you give for the decision?
What measures follow from the decision?
What are the advantages and disadvantages, and for whom?
How would the various measures be coordinated?

Dialectical Thinking Cycle as shown in in Exercise 16.3.

Exercise 16.8: Making an Important Prediction

Purpose

The decisions that people make in life are based typically on certain assumptions or predictions about the future that are often taken for granted but which are rarely one hundred percent certain. This exercise helps you to improve the quality of your thinking when trying to make predictions and hence aids your decision making. You can improve the accuracy of your predictions if you think systematically using the thinking modes.

Task

1. Imagine you had to make a prediction about the probability of an important upcoming event. For example, how likely is it that your preferred politician or political party will win the next election?
2. Have a guess right now giving your answer as a percentage probability (between 0%—impossible, and 100%—certain).
   - What information did you use to make your prediction?
   - How could you improve the accuracy of your prediction? Consider for a moment, what information might be useful to you in making such a prediction, then work through the mind opening questions below.
   - How would you adjust your prediction in the light of working through the questions?

Materials

Mind Opening Questions

Structural Thinking
What are the economic issues, such as how do people feel about the strength of the economy?
What are the social issues, such as who is most likely to vote, and who is not—young versus old, females versus males etc.?
What are the environmental issues, such as how might the weather on polling day affect the voter turn out?
What are the media issues, such as how are certain commentators and journalists predicting the vote will go?
Process Thinking
What have been the trends in voting intentions to date?
What new factors might emerge that could change voting intentions?
How have voters behaved in similar situations in the past?
What if the vote was in the opposite direction—who should not be elected as opposed to who should be elected?
Relational Thinking
How are the policies offered by your preferred politician or political party related to the concerns of other voters?
How are the things that your preferred politician or political party stands for related to the wishes of other influential groups in society, such as trade unions, party sponsors, major corporations?
What concerns do people on opposite sides have in common?
How is one side affecting the views of the other, and vice versa, in this debate?
Transformational Thinking
What is the potential for a dramatic shift in voting intentions, for example triggered by a specific event such as a terrorist attack, political scandal or natural disaster?
How might the conflict between people and politicians on opposites sides of the debate play out and what effect might that have?
How might the issues that your preferred politician or political party are promoting be integrated with a bigger and more fundamental problem, such as global climate change or growing imbalances between the wealthy and the poor?
What new vision for your region or your country could emerge as a result of the election of your preferred politician or political party? How might this differ from that offered by the other candidates?

Exercise 16.9: Developing a Career Strategy

Purpose

One means to generate a strategy is to imagine the achievement of a particular objective and to work backwards, thinking of all the things necessary for it to have been achieved.[2] In this exercise, you will apply the thinking modes and thought patterns to generate a rich picture of what might need to occur in order for a particular career goal to be reached.

Task

1. Think of a particular goal that you have for your career. Describe the goal in terms of achieving a specific outcome (the WHAT) by a certain time (the WHEN).

   For example:

   To reach a certain position of authority by the time you are aged 40.

   To generate a specific increase in your earnings in two to three years.

   To achieve a certain professional status and level of recognition within five years.

2. Now, imagine that the goal you have chosen has been achieved by the time you specified, and that you are standing at that point in the future looking back to the present. The task is to think of all the conditions that would have led to the successful achievement of your goal. What would have had to have been TRUE in order for the goal to be achieved? At this stage, you do not need to think about whether those conditions would in fact be true, only that it would be necessary for them to be so. Many of them may lie outside of your control.

   For example, if you had achieved your goal of reaching certain position in your career, what are all the conditions that would have had to have been true for that to happen? In order to generate a set of conditions, think in terms of the questions presented below.

[2]Lafley and Martin, 2013.

Materials

Mind Opening Questions

	Structural Thinking
	What would have to be true about your colleagues in the organisation and their aspirations and ambitions?
	What would have to be true about the internal structure of the organisation?
	What would have to be true about the senior management in the organisation and their attitudes to promotion, development and compensation systems within the organisation?
	What aspects of the organisation and its environment would have, at the very least, remained stable to create opportunities for you?
	Process Thinking
	What knowledge, skills and abilities would you have had to acquire?
	What was missing previously in your repertoire of skills and knowledge that would have appeared?
	In what new ways would you be behaving, and how would these behaviours have emerged from your old ways?
	What new interactions between you and different people and different parts of the organisation would you have engaged in?
	Relational Thinking
	What new relationships would you have developed with different people?
	What common ground would it have been necessary for you to find with other people in different parts of the organisation?
	In what new ways would your relationships with certain people operate?
	What other relationships within the organisation and between the organisation and its environment might you have developed?
	Transformational Thinking
	In what ways might you have transformed the way you work?
	What conflicts might have you managed successfully, and how?
	What different systems or patterns of behaviour would you have integrated into your current way of working?
	How would your personal professional capability have become, at the same time, more inclusive, integrated and differentiated?

References

DeVisch, J. *Re-Thinking game*. Accessed 6 January 2019. https://connecttransform.be/re-thinking-game/.

Lafley, A. G., & Martin, R. L. (2013). *Playing to win: How strategy really works.* Boston, Massachusetts: Harvard Business Review Press.

17 Reflecting on Dialectical Thought Patterns

Our final set of exercises invite you to turn the spotlight on yourself and how you see your life using Metathinking. We hope that you will now find it beneficial to explore your identity in a deeper and more nuanced manner.

N. Shannon and B. Frischherz, *Metathinking*, Management for Professionals,
https://doi.org/10.1007/978-3-030-41064-3_17

Illuminating

Exercise 17.1: Thinking about Thinking

Purpose

This exercise helps you to systematically reflect and expand your thinking about an axiom that you might hold as part of your view of the way the world works or should work. An axiom is a statement that one regards as self-evidently true. For example, the United States Declaration of Independence famously states "We hold these truths to be self-evident, that all men are created equal, that they are endowed by their Creator with certain unalienable rights, that among these are life, liberty and the pursuit of happiness". The statement "All men are created equal" is an axiom.

Task

1. Identify an axiom from your personal view of the world related to your professional or private life. For example:
   "The goal of a business is to make money".
   "The most important thing in life is to be happy".
2. Think about your axiom in logical thinking mode.
   Ask yourself:
   - What makes your axiom true?
   - Is the negation of your axiom obviously false?
   - Why is it that the axiom cannot sometimes be both true and false at the same time?
   - If the axiom was false, what would the consequences be?
3. Now think about your axiom using the four modes of dialectical thinking.
   Ask yourself the following in:
   - Structural mode: Might the truth of the axiom depend on the context?
   - Process mode: Might the truth of the axiom change from time to time?
   - Relational mode: Might the truth of the axiom depend on the meaning of specific ideas and how these relate to each other. (For example, if your axiom is that the most important thing in life is to be happy, what does the word "happy" mean to you?)
   - Transformational mode: How might you develop the axiom into a more complex and complete statement about the world, given the answers you gave in the structural, process and relational modes?

4. Invite a dialogue partner to say what they think about the axiom and what it means to them.
   Ask yourself
   - Does your partner share your view of the truth of the axiom?
   - In what ways does your partner interpret the axiom differently to you?
   - What are the areas of common ground between you and your partner in your understanding of the axiom?
5. Now move into Metathinking mode.
   Ask yourself
   - How has this process transformed your view of the initial axiom?
   - Is it possible for you to hold different perspectives of the axiom simultaneously?
   - Can the axiom be both true and not true, depending on your perspective?
   - What has been helpful in examining one of your axioms in this way?

Exercise 17.2: Taking a Measure of your Dialectical Thinking

Purpose

How are you progressing with becoming a Metathinker? This exercise will provide you with an opportunity to check on your use of the thinking modes in relation to a number of statements which typically provoke a strong response from people. Answers are given in the Appendix. Please note that this questionnaire is not intended as a psychometrically valid tool, but we have included it for your reflection and for you to see where you apply dialectical thinking and where not.

Task

The following questionnaire presents you with a series of statements in groups of three. You are asked to read the statement in each group and indicate which statement comes closest to your view. Record your answers by putting a circle around the letter corresponding to the appropriate statement.

1a. In the final analysis, what is morally right or wrong is in flux and subject to constant re-evaluation.
1b. In the final analysis, there are things that we can be certain are morally right or wrong.
1c. In the final analysis, what is morally right or wrong will always depend on the circumstances.

2a. Advances in science mean that we are able to make predictions about things but only with relative certainty.
2b. Advances in science mean that we are able to make predictions about things but these have to be constantly revised and updated.
2c. Advances in science mean that we are able to make predictions about things with 100% certainty.

3a. A person's personality is determined by their genes and does not change throughout their life.
3b. A person's personality is fluid and subject to variations that are unexpected and, sometimes quite substantial.
3c. A person's personality is dependent on how they are seen by other people and will vary in relation to the society and culture in which they live.

4a. Happiness in life can never be completely achieved because it is always dependent in some way on experiencing unhappiness.
4b. Happiness in life depends on many things, but finding the right partner is one of the most significant.
4c. Happiness is life can be achieved if one finds the right partner.

5a. Conflicts between people can always be resolved if people follow the right kind of process.
5b. Conflicts between people can only ever be resolved partially because some degree of conflict remains in people's minds.
5c. Conflicts between people ebb and flow unpredictably. Sometimes they resolve of their own accord and at other times they escalate uncontrollably.

6a. You will always remain uncertain as to who has the most potential for success in life because success and failure are inextricably linked.
6b. You can tell that some people have lot more potential to be successful in life than others.
6c. You can only judge partially whether some people will be more successful in life than others because success is not something that is possible to measure objectively.

7a. A leader is someone who is intellectually, emotionally or physically superior to others.
7b. A leader is defined by the extent to which others, for whatever reason, are willing to follow him or her.
7c. A leader cannot be defined by specific characteristics, it is only after the event that one may know whether someone was a leader.

8a. A good person is someone who behaves better than those around him.
8b. A good person is someone who has vices as well virtues,. and who is more aware of the former.
8c. A good person is someone who follows the law.

9a. Beauty and ugliness are intertwined and interchangeable.
9b. What is beautiful and what is ugly can be objectively determined.
9c. Beauty and ugliness are in the eyes of the beholder.cv

10a. A system is something that can be identified by clear boundaries and precise causal links.
10b. A system is not something that can be clearly defined because everything is interlinked with everything, even with what we think of as being nothing.
10c. A system is defined by looking at some aspect of reality in a particular way.

11a. In an organisation, some changes can be managed but others cannot, one has to manage as much as one can.
11b. In an organisation, change has to be managed in order for the organisation to thrive.
11c. In an organisation, change is not something that one can manage, since it is ever present whether or not people want things to change.

12a. Democracy, capitalism and the rule of law are ideals that contain their own contradictions, and which can lead both to the success and to the death of a society.
12b. Democracy, capitalism and the rule of law are the best way we have of creating a successful society.
12c. Democracy, capitalism and the rule of law are the cornerstones of a successful society.

13a. Society should abandon hope of ever achieving equality of opportunity, because the degree of control that would be necessary to achieve it would deprive people of certain freedoms, and therefore create other inequalities.
13b. Society should strive for equality of opportunity. Everyone should have an equal chance in life.
13c. Society should hold equality of opportunity as an ideal, whilst realising that equality can only ever be relative to whatever inequality was felt before.

14a. A person's sense of their gender is almost entirely fixed because it is strongly related to their biological makeup and reinforced by social factors early in life.
14b. A person's sense of their gender is changeable and varies according to the norms prevalent in the society in which they live.
14c. A person's sense of their gender is the result of an interplay between biological, mental and social factors, carrying with it the potential for dramatic change or tremendous stability.

A scoring key and instructions can be found in Appendix A4. Total your scores and identify the extent to which you used different types of thinking. Reviewing your scores for the three different dimensions of the questionnaire, consider the following questions:

(a) How do your scores vary across the three different types of thinking?
(b) If you had a score in the dialectical category, to what extent were you aware that you are already a dialectical thinker?
(c) How has the way you think about the world changed, over your lifespan?
(d) In what areas, and under what circumstances, does your thinking become more relativistic, or absolute?
(e) How do you view other people who think very differently to you?

Exercise 17.3: Thinking in Metaphors

Purpose

This exercise helps you to see a business in a new light. You will map features systematically between a source domain and a target domain of a metaphor. You may also find and develop a unique metaphor for your own business.

Task

1. Think about your own business in metaphors:
   BUSINESS as a MACHINE;
   BUSINESS as a PLANT;
   BUSINESS as a FAMILY;
   BUSINESS as an ORCHESTRA.

2. Identify features in the source domain of the metaphor that can be mapped onto the target domain BUSINESS. In the table below you will find the source domain of the metaphor in the right-hand column and the target domain in the left-hand column. We have completed the first example with Structural thinking. There, you will see BUSINESS as a MACHINE, its employees as parts of the machine, its processes as movements of the machine, and management mistakes as malfunctioning of the machine. Now complete the mappings using the three other metaphors.

3. Reflect on the metaphor:
   Apply process thinking, relational thinking, and transformational thinking to the relevant metaphors in the table.
   What are the implications of a certain metaphor using that thinking mode?
   Which features are highlighted by the metaphor?
   Which features are concealed by the metaphor?

4. Look for a unique metaphor for your business.

Materials

	Structural Thinking	
Business	AS	Machine
Employees	AS	Parts
Defined processes	AS	Movements of the machine
Management mistakes	AS	Malfunctions of the machine
	Process Thinking	
Business	AS	Plant
Employees	AS	…
Increase in sales	AS	…
Profit, gain	AS	…
	Relational Thinking	
Business	AS	Family
Employees	AS	…
Network of people	AS	…
Founder	AS	…
	Transformational Thinking	
Business	AS	Orchestra
Employees	AS	…
Entrepreneur, manager	AS	…
Performance	AS	…
	Metaphor for My Business	
Business	AS	…
	AS	
	AS	
	AS	

Note:

Interesting theoretical basics on metaphors can be found in the books of Kövecses "Metaphor: a practical introduction"[1] and Lakoff and Johnson "Metaphors we live by".[2]

[1]Kövecses, 2002.
[2]Lakoff and Johnson, 1985.

Evaluating

Exercise 17.4: Solving an Ethical Dilemma

Purpose
This exercise helps you to reflect on an ethical dilemma. Using the three cases below, you will identify stakeholders and their interests and rights, evaluate them and take a decision. Your decision will be the basis for further action.

Task

1. Think through the ethical dilemma using the dialectical thinking cycle framework and take notes.
2. Structural thinking: Analyse the structure of the ethical dilemma.
3. Process thinking: Reconstruct the development of the ethical dilemma.
4. Relational thinking: Evaluate the ethical dilemma by balancing different values and potential conflicts.
5. Transformational thinking: Plan actions to implement the decision.
6. Reflect on the process.

Materials

Case 1
After lunch, Stephan's telephone is ringing. It's Michael, a supplier, with whom Stephan has been working for many years. Michael wants to thank Stephan for the excellent cooperation during the last five years and he invites Stephan for a skiing weekend in the Swiss mountains free of charge. Stephan loves skiing but since he has a family he can't afford to spend holidays in the mountains. Switzerland is really an expensive place! But the compliance regulations of his company do not allow its employees to accept gifts from customers and suppliers. Stephan also knows that his manager accepted a similar invitation for a sailing trip last year. Additionally, Stephan doesn't want to upset someone who he sees as an important partner doing good business with his organisation by turning down the invitation.

What should he do?

Case 2
Julie is working as an external coach to a senior executive within a large corporation. Her brief is to help the executive become more effective as a leader of a particular division going through a significant transformation. During the course of the coaching, the executive shares with Julie certain aspects of his private life that leads Julie to doubt whether the executive has the capability and resilience required to perform effectively in what is a highly demanding role. The director of human resources for the company invites Julie to a meeting with the CEO where the CEO expresses concern about the executive's performance and asks Julie for her view on

the likely success of the coaching programme, suggesting that if the executive does not improve he will have to be replaced.

Should Julie share what she knows about the executive?

Case 3

You work for an organisation as its director of procurement. The organisation has been struggling because it has not been winning sufficient work for some time. Its customers appear to like its products but frequently say it prices them too high. As it turns out, one of your suppliers is owned by a relative of your spouse. You are on good terms with the owner and have been open with him about some of the difficulties your company has been experiencing. He has offered to give you a significant reduction on some key components he supplies in return for an exclusive contract and a substantial donation to a second company that he owns, headquartered overseas in a tax haven, but he has asked you to keep such details confidential. The reduction in price that he is offering would greatly increase the chances of your organisation winning the work it needs going forward.

How should you respond?

(Adapted from Renz et al., 2015)

Mind Opening Questions

	Structural Thinking
	What exactly is the ethical issue?
	Who are the key stakeholders on the individual, organisational and societal levels?
	What are the interests and rights of the stakeholders?
	What additional background information do you need?
	Process Thinking
	How has this ethical dilemma emerged from the past?
	What actions have the stakeholders already taken?
	What options do the stakeholders have to influence the situation?
	How will the ethical dilemma develop in future?
	Relational Thinking
	Where are the interests and rights of some stakeholders in conflict with the interests and rights of others?
	Is there any common ground between the stakeholders in terms of what they want to achieve?
	How do the ethics of the situation relate to the legal position and/or common-sense values?
	How might the position of one stakeholder affect the positions of any others?
	Transformational Thinking
	What is your decision and what are the reasons for it?
	What are the consequences of the decision for the stakeholders?
	What measures are to be taken on the individual, organisational and societal level?
	How would you schedule the actions?
	What resources do you need to implement the actions?

Exercise 17.5: Reflecting on Virtues, Values and Vices

Purpose
This exercise helps you to see the hidden aspects of your own virtues and values.

Task

1. Choose a personal virtue or value that is very important to you and that you try to live up to (e.g. to be goal oriented)
   What characteristics and behaviours do you identify associated with this value? Can you give an example? Write the value and the behaviours you associate with it in box 1 in Fig. 17.1.
2. Now think of the opposite of this value, something that you try *not* to exemplify (e.g. to be indifferent, relaxed or easy come/easy go). What is the problem for you of having such a value? Write this value and the behaviours that you associate with it in box 2.
3. Now think of someone different who would exemplify the negative value and behaviours that you described in box 2. What is the positive value that they associate with their behaviour—the "virtue in the vice" of the other person? Write the positive value that they feel that they are living up to in box 3. Why do you consider the view that person holds of their behaviour to be completely wrong?
4. Now think how the other person might see you and the positive value that you first identified (in box 1). What would they accuse you of? What negatives might they associate with your virtue (e.g. to be single-minded, blinkered or dogmatic). Write the value that they think your virtuous behaviour represents in box 4.
5. Notice how what you have written in boxes 2 and 3 are opposite perspectives of the same behaviour and attitude. Notice how what you have written in boxes 1 and 4 are also opposites of the same behaviour and attitude. Which perspective is correct and why? Is there any way that you can integrate the opposite perspectives?

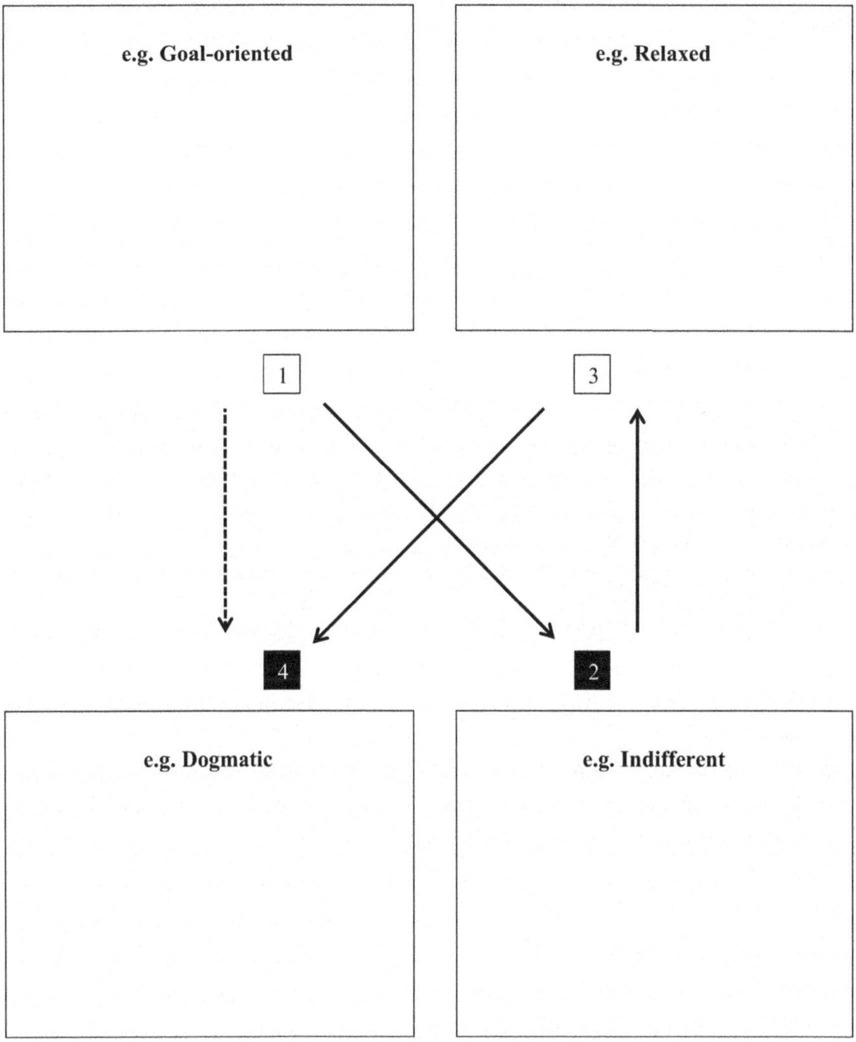

Fig. 17.1 Value square (own representation based on Schulz von Thun et al., 2003, 53)

Self-reflecting

Exercise 17.6: Analysing a Description of Yourself

Purpose
This exercise gives you practice at using the thought patterns whilst at the same time exploring your personal sense of identity and how you locate yourself in the world

Task

1. Write a short article describing yourself in the third person (typically 500 to 1000 words is sufficient) starting with the words "[Insert your name] is …".
2. In the piece, reflect on any key moments in your past that you think have contributed to who you are currently, for example, successes that you have had or times that you were up "against it".
3. Also include a paragraph about how you see your future, what sort of person you would like to be come, or what you plan to do.
4. Once you have written your piece, put it aside for a day or two, and then review it by analysing the thinking modes and thought patterns that you used.
   - What were the predominant thinking modes and thought patterns that you used?
   - What were the thinking modes and thought patterns that you did not use?
   - Make some alterations to your article using any thinking modes and thought patterns that you previously left out.

Exercise 17.7: Reflecting on the Balance in your Life

Purpose

Reflecting on what makes for a good life, the German philosopher Martin Seel distinguishes four dimensions: work, play, interaction and contemplation.[3] This exercise helps you to evaluate the importance of these different dimensions in your life.

Task

1. Think about the four dimensions in your life:
   - Work: career, job, studies …
   - Play: leisure time, hobbies, relaxation …
   - Interaction: relationships, conversation. dialogue …
   - Contemplation: reflection, meditation and spiritual practices …
   - Using the chart in Fig. 17.2, allocate 10 points on the axis of work–play and 10 points on the axis of interaction–contemplation for the actual *time* you spend on these different dimensions. For example, if you spend 80% of your time working and 20% playing, write "A" at 8 along the work axis and at 2 along the play axis. Connect the letters with lines.
2. Now, allocate 10 points on the axis of work–play and 10 points on the axis of interaction–contemplation for how you would like it to be *ideally* in terms of the relative time you spend on these dimensions. For example, if you would like to be spending 60% of your time on work and 40% on play, write an "I" at 6 along the work axis and at 4 along the play axis. Connect the letters with lines.
3. Note down some keywords on the diagram for the activities in your life that contribute to the dimensions.
4. Notice any tensions between how things are and how you would like things to be. Explain your diagram to a partner, and answer the following questions:
   - How do you feel about the differences between how you live your life now and how you would like to live your life?
   - Do you see the dimensions as true opposites?
   - How might you integrate better the different dimensions so that the time you spend on different activities is closer to how you would like to live?
   - What action will you take?

   Revisit the diagram periodically and notice how things are changing for you.

(adapted from Frischherz et al., 2016)[4]

[3]Seel, 1999, 138.
[4]Frischherz et al., 2016.

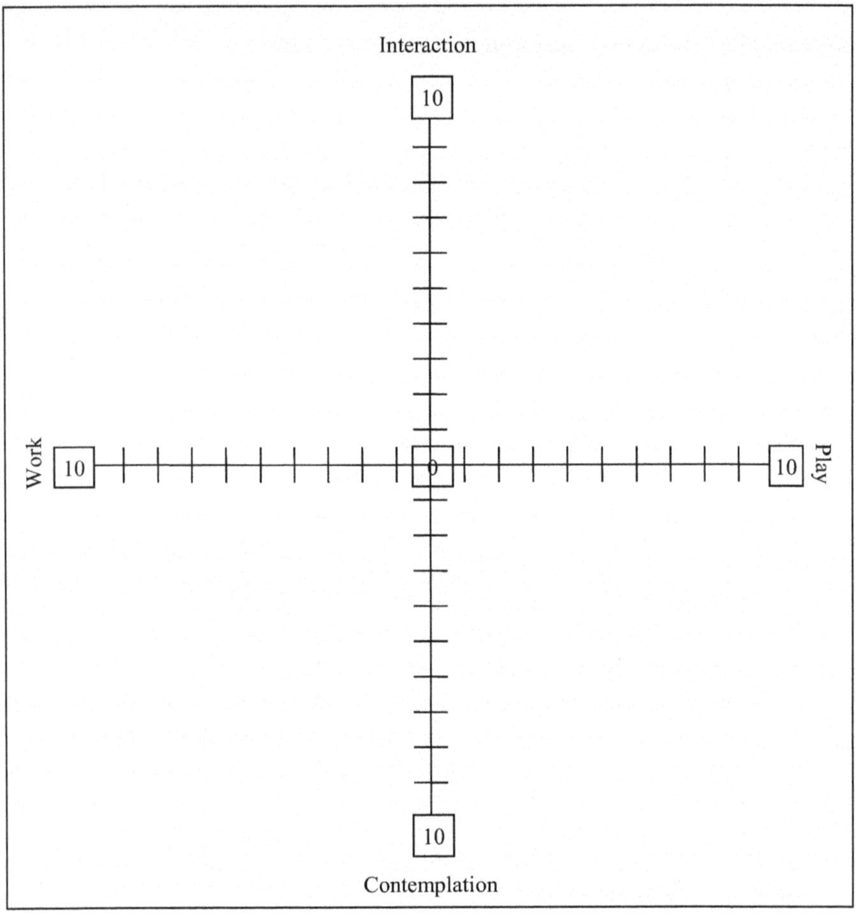

Fig. 17.2 Four dimensions of good life (own representation based on Seel, 1999)

Exercise 17.7: Reflecting on the Balance in your Life

Purpose
This exercise helps you to explore your personal life.
By asking yourself and reflecting on specific questions you can illuminate hidden aspects of your personal life and initiate transformation of your situation if you so wish.

Task

1. Review the mind opening questions listed in the materials. Place a tick by the questions that you feel most drawn to answer, or find easiest to answer, and a cross by the questions that you find difficult or would prefer to leave aside.
2. Count up the ticks and crosses in each of the four sections. Where do you have the most ticks? Where do you have the most crosses? Which thinking mode (if any) comes the easiest for you and which the hardest when you contemplate your personal life?
3. Write answers to the questions that you have placed a tick against.
4. Contemplate some of the questions that you have placed a cross against. What is missing that prevents you from, or makes it difficult for you, to answer those questions?
5. Working through the first three thinking modes in the dialectical thinking cycle, write the change you would most like to occur in your personal life in terms of structure, process and relationship.
6. Thinking in terms of transformation, write down your vision of how you would like your life to be, ideally. What would be most important for you to happen? What actions can you take to bring about that transformation?
7. Finally, notice and write down the thoughts and feelings that come up for you when you contemplate such actions which might prevent you taking such action. Imagine yourself taking action despite having such negative thoughts and feelings. Accept that such thoughts and feelings are likely to arise and notice that they can also disappear again. What steps can you take to transform yourself?

Materials

Mind Opening Questions

	Structural Thinking
	How would you describe the main characteristics of your personal life?
	Which role models do you find yourself following in the way you conduct your personal life?
	What values and motives drive you in your personal life?
	To what extent do you see your personal life as successful?
	What developments are occurring currently in your personal life?
	Which kind of lifestyle typifies your personal life?
	Which role patterns are typical of your personal life?
	Process Thinking
	What path has your personal development taken? Have you experienced any personal crises? How have you emerged from these?
	How are you coming to terms with the fact that you are getting older?
	What is the balance between stability and change in your life?
	What was your experience of authority like when you were a child?
	Which significant experiences have shaped your values ?
	What kind of social changes have you noticed? How do you find yourself reacting to them?
	Relational Thinking
	How well do the various roles that you play in life fit together?
	To what extent do you feel you share things in common with the people you are close to in life?
	How do your private relationships contribute to your personal sense of self-esteem?
	How good are you at coping with the different requirements that people place on you?
	What is the ideal balance between the different domains of your life for you?
	Transformational Thinking
	What is your concept of the best life you could lead?
	What can you do now that you could not do five or ten years ago?
	To what extent do you see yourself as the same person as you were earlier in your life?
	What has been the most challenging decade of your life? What did you learn from it?
	What effect have your personal experiences had on your personal relationships and vice versa?
	What conflicts have you have to manage, or are managing in your private life?
	How effectively do you find yourself coping with losses in your personal life?

Dialectical Thinking Cycle

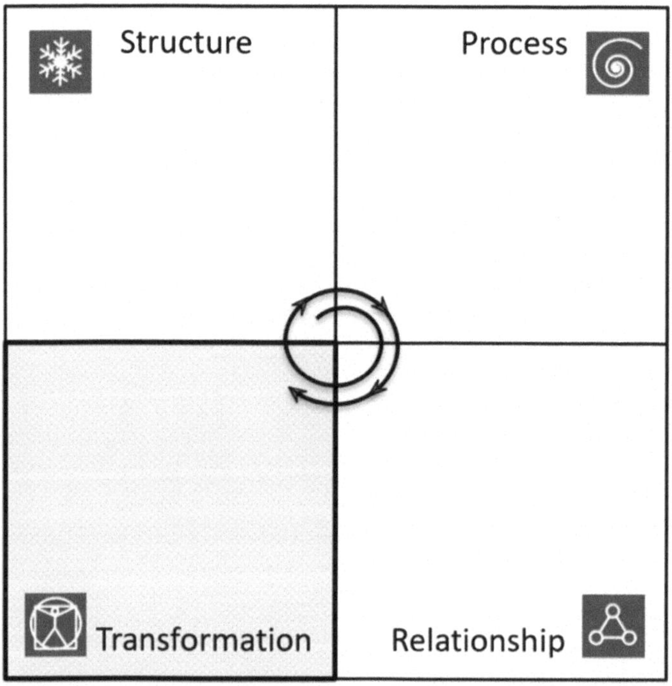

References

Frischherz, B., et al. (2016). *Das Reflexionsbuch. Vor- und Nachdenken über sich*. Zürich: Versus.
Kövecses, Z. (2002). *Metaphor: A practical introduction*. New York: Oxford University Press.
Lakoff, G., & Johnson, M. (1985). *Metaphors we live by* (5th ed.). Chicago: University of Chicago press.
Renz, P. S., Frischherz, B., & Wettstein, I. (2015). *Integrität im Managementalltag: ethische Dilemmas im Managementalltag erfassen und lösen*. Berlin and Heidelberg: Springer Gabler.
Schulz von Thun, F., Ruppel, J., & Stratmann, R. (2003). *Miteinander reden: Kommunikationspsychologie für Führungskräfte*. Reinbek bei Hamburg: Rowohlt-Taschenbuch-Verl.
Seel, M. (1999). *Versuch über die Form des Glücks: Studien zur Ethik*. Frankfurt am Main: Suhrkamp.

Part IV
Conclusion

Conclusion

18

In 2015, the United Nations General Assembly set out a total of seventeen sustainable development goals.[1] These challenges include items such as no poverty, zero hunger, gender equality, climate action, and peace, justice and strong institutions and are to be achieved by 2030. With nearly eight billion people living on our planet, there is a sense that despite the progress the human race has made, the problems that future generations face are significant and mounting. Scientists are declaring that the current epoch, the Holocene, which is characterised by 12,000 years of stable climate since the last Ice Age, is being superseded by a new epoch—the Anthropocene.[2] What defines this new epoch of geological change is that its primary cause is human activity. Whilst it can be argued that humans are not the only influence at work, whether we like it or not, human agency has become a force for transformational change in the very planet on which we live. If the destiny of the Earth is in our hands, how we think about sustainable development and the goals we set ourselves are of paramount importance, since thought leads to action. We believe that the human capacity to reflect on the content of our minds, to think about thinking, in short, to be a *Metathinker* is a reason to be optimistic about our futures and that of the world. If humans are serious about creating a sustainable future for themselves and their environment, they must be prepared to delve deep into their own understanding of the reality in which they live, explore the limits of their knowledge and challenge their assumptions. We cannot pretend that this is an easy task, but we believe it is possible and that what we have set out in this book creates a starting point to become better, more complete thinkers.

[1]United Nations, 2019.
[2]Working Group on the Anthropocene, 2019.

N. Shannon and B. Frischherz, *Metathinking*, Management for Professionals,
https://doi.org/10.1007/978-3-030-41064-3_18

Revitalising Thinking by Applying Dialectical Thinking

Metathinking begins with the understanding that our minds are designed to make models of our environmental reality and that such models can be partial or deep depending on the extent to which we use all the thinking processes available to us. To that end, we have four thinking *modes* of dialectical thinking that transcend what passes for formal logical thinking. The first of these, *structural thinking*, invites us to consider that the things we can conceptualise are never isolated entities but are always parts of a bigger whole that, whether we can discern it or not, has a particular structure. The second, *process thinking*, invites us to consider that what we might assume is static, is in fact in some kind of motion, and changing moment by moment. Hence, change is a constant, not something that happens periodically or that can be "managed". The third, *relational thinking*, invites us to consider how what we presume are separate entities, are in reality, related. The cup is related to the saucer, and the saucer is related to the cup. It is in this relation that the cup is truly a cup, and the saucer truly a saucer. Hence, it makes little sense to make assertions like "masculinity is toxic" (as some would have it currently) since without femininity there can be no masculinity. If one of these is toxic, what does that make the other? Our fourth thinking mode is one of *transformational thinking*. This is our sense that things can and do indeed transform whilst retaining their identity. The caterpillar becomes a butterfly, the state becomes an empire, and in our imagination, the frog becomes a prince. When we ignore these thinking modes, our conception of reality becomes impoverished and we are vulnerable to errors. We fail to see that actions have consequences and that those consequences have other consequences.

Our exercises have been designed to enable you, as an individual, and with partners and colleagues to think more holistically and hence to develop a deeper and more nuanced perception of the reality in which you find yourself. This does not mean putting aside logical analytic thinking, rather it means supplementing it with a more fluid, dynamic form of thought that sees logic as one set of rules for thinking among many. Dialectical thinking modes and thought forms allow for the creative combination of ideas that may appear to contradict each other in a way that logical rules do not permit. There is evidence to suggest that the dialectic structures of thinking that we have been describing are present in children at the early ages of five to seven but disappear as children go through formal schooling and do not re-appear until adulthood.[3] Somehow the emphasis on formal logic instilled by our educational systems curtails the greater fluidity of thinking that is present in young children's minds. Other research suggests that this is largely a European and American phenomenon. In an interesting study, Kaiping Peng and Richard Nisbett analysed the reactions of Chinese and Americans to apparent contradictions and found that the Chinese preferred dialectical resolutions whilst Americans tended to polarise their views.[4] The important point, however, is not that dialectical

[3]Veraksa et al., 2013.
[4]Peng and Nisbett, 1999.

thinking is necessarily better than logical thinking, but that different modes of thinking have their different uses and it behoves us to use as many different ways as we can. After all Western scientific thought following the laws of formal logic has been highly effective in driving the technological developments of the last two centuries. We believe that learning to become a Metathinker may take time but can be achieved by anyone through repetition and practice, much as any other form of learning as thinking structures that are latent in the human brain are re-awakened. In an increasingly complex world, we owe it to ourselves to think in a more complex way if we are to avoid catastrophic error in our decision-making.

Metathinking and Leadership

If we wish to transform some aspect of our world, we must first "re-imagine" it by thinking about it in a new way. We can do this one quadrant at a time by mentally transforming a single quadrant. Doing so then provides the starting point for transformation in the other quadrants since it requires us to re-align them with the new conception that we have developed of the quadrant in which we started. Let us look again at the diagram that we described in Chap. 13, the summary to the case studies section (Fig. 18.1). This diagram summarises the process of *rethinking* any particular concept representing an aspect of reality. We invite you to work through the process in order to get a deeper appreciation of the true essence of your chosen concept. Take, for example, the concept of "staff engagement" which is a popular topic in current organisational discourse. By using the four quadrants as four different perspectives, one can examine staff engagement from the upper left, personal

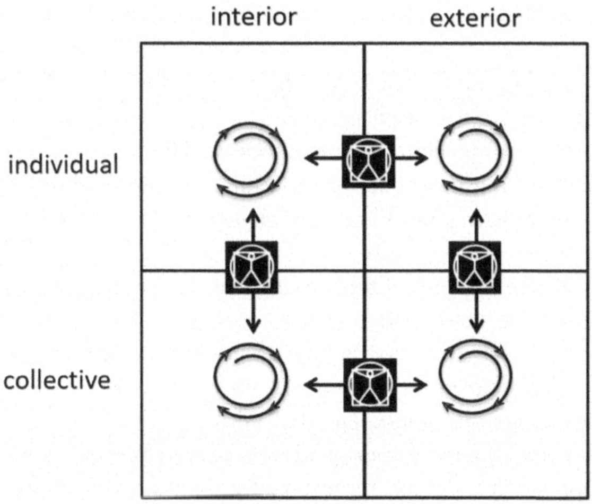

Fig. 18.1 Transformation in and across integral quadrants (own representation)

perspective, the lower left, team perspective, the upper right, organisational process perspective, and finally the lower right whole organisation (or societal) perspective. Within each quadrant's perspective, one can identify themes and aspects and subject them to further analysis using the four thinking modes. Rethinking the quadrants in this systematic manner raises potential possibilities for re-alignment between the quadrants, which itself is transformation. Perhaps you were thinking about staff engagement in terms of the attitudes and values of particular individuals. Metathinking invites you to go deeper into how those attitudes and values are structured, how they are changing, what they are related to and how they might transform. It also invites you to consider the impact of the team and its culture on staff engagement, the effect of organisational tasks and roles, and the broader organisational and societal context. You now have a tool with which to critique models that are claimed to foster staff engagement. You can see what such models might be missing and hence avoid the errors that might arise from taking only a partial, reductionist view of what staff engagement means.

In our case studies, we have shown how people can think differently and how such thinking can change the impact that they have on the environment around them. Firstly, with the example of Sonja, we have shown at an individual level how Sonja's thinking developed over a period of four years, and how her focus changed from a relatively narrow view of how she herself was changing and might transform, to how she could transform the team over which she had responsibility. We also saw in the second case study how an executive team might start to think differently about their individual resilience, and how that was connected to the way they worked with each other and the way they managed their organisation. In our third case study we looked at organisation-wide digital transformation and examined a case where "silo-ed" thinking had led to the failure of an entire digital transformation programme. We also compared the thinking of five different CEOs each of whom were engaged in transforming their organisations digitally. And in our final case study we took a look at three different national health systems through the lens provided by press reports on those systems and identified how the public discourse about creating more viable health systems appears to be missing a focus on the individual, their values, their perception of their needs from a health system, and their ability to manage their own well-being. The evidence is clear—there is always something missing from people's thinking, and we believe that it is through structured dialogue and Metathinking that such gaps can be filled.

Metathinking is an activity with which people who embrace it will inevitably take on a kind of leadership role. Questioning one's own thinking and that of other people is not always an activity that people welcome. Yet it is through dialogue, both with oneself, and with other people that we can develop and expand our thinking. When we transform the contents of our minds, we create the potential for transforming the minds of others and by taking action we can transform our environment. Consider again the four quadrants of Ken Wilber's structural model in Fig. 18.2. The upper left quadrant represents the individual contents of your mind. As you intentionally develop a new vision for the future by questioning your current view of reality, so you can start to make that vision become a reality by

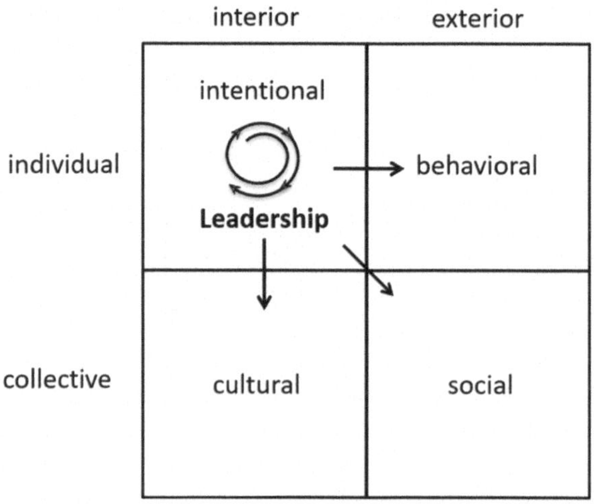

Fig. 18.2 Role of leadership in organisational transformation (own representation)

taking action to align the other quadrants in accordance with your vision. Then, by entering into dialogue with colleagues you can begin to transform the lower left quadrant, generating interest and enthusiasm for your ideas, and building the social will to make the necessary changes in the right (external) quadrants. As you and others take action, so you start to transform your environment, perhaps first in terms of specific things and then, finally, collectively in terms of complete social systems.

If human activity has been, to date, unintentionally transforming our planet to the detriment of the balance of its ecosystem, the potential must still exist to transform the planet to the benefit of the ecosystem and hence to reverse at least some of the damage and create a more sustainable future for all species. Such intentional transformation can occur if humans are able and willing to begin by transforming their own thinking and taking action to align their environment with a new vision of a sustainable planet. There is therefore a moral imperative for working on ourselves to become better thinkers. Anyone who wishes to take up a leadership role and have responsibility for proposing and enabling a transformation, be it on a small or large scale (e.g. by means of governmental policy proposals, corporate reports and strategic reviews) can benefit by using Metathinking in order to generate a more complete account of the complexity inherent in the realities that they wish to transform. We can all change the world.

Developing the Metathinking Framework

Our Metathinking Framework combines Wilber's integral quadrants to generate four different perspectives on content with dialectical thinking modes to apply four different ways of thinking about that content. From our point of view, the framework is an initial systematic application of dialectical thinking modes and a helpful tool with which to analyse diverse case studies and plan one's own transformational initiatives. However, it is far from the last word in thinking, numerous other applications and extensions of the Metathinking Framework are conceivable. To conclude this book, we would like to briefly outline how the Metathinking Framework could be developed further. To do so we will apply the four modes of dialectical thinking to think about the Metathinking Framework itself.

Structural Thinking

We have made use of Wilber's integral quadrants to delineate four different prototypical perspectives on a particular subject matter. Wilber himself has differentiated the integral quadrants further into eight "primordial" perspectives and developed these into a methodology for investigating the nature of reality—what he terms "integral methodological pluralism". Applying this distinction to the upper left interior individual quadrant for example, the contents of a person's mind (or consciousness) can and should be viewed from both inside and the outside perspectives. The inside perspective is one where I observe and talk about my own consciousness, and the outside perspective is taken when another person talks about what they consider to be my consciousness. In the lower left interior collective quadrant, when we as members of a group speak about our culture we are using the internal perspective. When a foreign observer describes our culture, they are examining it from an outside perspective. Structural thinking involves building a multiplicity of perspectives. Besides the quadrants, Wilber also distinguishes stages, states and types,[5] repeatedly applying structural thinking in building up his concept of an integral worldview. In a similar manner, our Metathinking Framework could be extended to encompass other types of thinking, for example intuitive thinking and imaginative thinking. Similarly, one can consider that thinking occurs at different levels in the mind. Whilst we have focused on thought in language, some thinking can be considered to take place at an unconscious level and a preconscious level.

[5]Wilber, 2008.

Process Thinking

Process thinking focuses on movement and emergence. A person's thinking changes and develops continuously. One way in which a person's thought moves is to build on previously held ideas by making new distinctions or, to put it another way, differentiating a concept and then re-integrating it by establishing how the new idea relates to the old one. Identifying and assembling different ideas can be described as a form of convergent thinking process. This can be contrasted with a divergent thinking process where one idea leads to another seemingly unrelated idea. The connection of the two ideas is unexpected and often obscure. Such moves in thought can often be taken as humorous or simply bizarre. As people practise Metathinking, they may find new and different uses for it. For us, it serves as a means to conduct dialogue, to assess complexity of thinking and to identify what might be missing from a piece of analysis. In the future, more thinking modes and more thought patterns may be found so increasing the power of the process. Those who study adult development may be able to make cross-comparisons with other dimensions of human experience such as the social–emotional, moral, aesthetic and religious lines of development.

Relational Thinking

We have described the four modes of dialectical thinking and the corresponding patterns of thinking as separate modes. But we have also hinted at how they can be linked, most specifically in terms of the way transformational thinking contains elements of structural, process and relational thinking modes. Of course, there are other relationships between the thinking modes and other kinds of thought. For example, analogous and metaphorical thinking can be understood as a combination of structural and relational thinking. Terms and words from one domain are transferred to a new domain in order to make the new domain cognitively available. Such cognitive metaphors shape large parts of our everyday thinking.[6]

The examples and case studies in our book come from everyday experience and scientific discourse. An interesting research question now would be to examine to what extent the framework is also useful for the analysis of aesthetic, ethical and religious thought. One might also investigate the extent to which thought in language relates to thought in images and other forms of perceptual experience such as dreams.

[6]Lakoff and Johnson, 1985.

Transformational Thinking

Transformation of the Metathinking Framework involves its integration with another model of human experience with which it is in apparent conflict. Since we have focused primarily on thinking logically or dialectically in language, our model is in tension, if not in conflict, with models that see transformation occurring through some form of spiritual or transcendental force or experience. Since such experiences are by definition, ineffable, we can only hint in language how Metathinking could be transformed. However, humans have long tried to describe forms of ecstatic mystical experience that somehow conferred great knowledge and meaning to them. It seems as though such experiences are rarely part of everyday living, indeed one interpretation of them would be to say that they are psychotic, but they are nevertheless much sought after. For instance, they are the target of a variety of religious and meditative practices as well as the aim of experimentation with psychedelic drugs such as LSD and MDMA.

In his later works, the philosopher Roy Bhaskar (on whose early work we have drawn for this book) speculated that reality contains a spiritual aspect just as much as a material one.[7,8] He argued that reality itself contains spiritual values and has a kind of unity that is not apparent in the way we see the world in our everyday experience. Such awareness strikes us a transformation of the Metathinking concept. What makes it so fascinating is that it is not really possible to explain and justify in language terms alone, which is most likely why philosophers are continuing to argue over what is described as Bhaskar's "spiritual turn". The underlying idea of a transformed Metathinking Framework would be to take the position that thinking is so much more than using language and that making sense of reality and extracting meaning can sometimes reach levels at which they coalesce and transcend our power to describe them. For the present, however, such experiences are rare and occur only at the fringes of everyday life, potentially placing some limits on our ability to transform our world. The future holds out the possibility that people will find new ways to capture and control the brain's extraordinary creative thinking processes.

Metathinking in Everyday Life

We live in an age where it is commonplace to experience the impact of disruptive innovations which have the capacity to transform established industries, creating powerful new businesses and sweeping aside some traditional businesses. The Internet, with its precursor the personal computer and its offspring the smartphone,

[7]Bhaskar, 2002a.
[8]Bhaskar, 2002b.

has changed so much in terms of shopping, entertainment, travel, publishing and advertising. Artificial intelligence technologies (AI) and robotics threaten to transform the world of work, whilst medical technologies ranging from gene therapy to micro-devices that monitor a person's physiology have the potential to transform health care.

At one level, such changes seem to promise better, richer lives for people freed from mundane work with longer healthier lifespans and greater freedom to communicate, access information and education. At another level, they also herald significant social and political changes, amplified by uncertain environmental and ecological impacts. For people to thrive in this age of disruption, they need to be able to supplement fixed, linear ways of thinking and envisage reality at a deeper, more complex level. We submit that Metathinking is one way to start such a process.

To conclude on an altogether lighter note, we recall the words of the now deceased Canadian poet and singer-song-writer Leonard Cohen in the song he wrote "Anthem":

"Forget your perfect offering. There is a crack in everything. That's how the light gets in."

There is little question in our minds that Cohen was a dialectical thinker, even if it was rare for him to talk about or interpret his work for others. His first sentence reminds us that we must expect our work to fall short in some ways, whilst his second sentence consoles us with the idea that nothing is perfect. But then he offers us hope again by saying "that's how the light gets in". Cracks allow the light in with which we can then illuminate our work and remediate its deficiencies. We hope our readers will forgive the omissions in what we have presented here in this book and, by thinking dialectically, illuminate the dark spots and remediate the absences that we have left behind.

References

Bhaskar, R. (2002a). *Meta-reality. The philosphy of meta-reality. Creativity, love and freedom.* New Delhi; Thousand Oaks, CA: Sage Publications.

Bhaskar, R. (2002b). Reflections on meta-reality: Transcendence, emancipation, and everyday Life. In *The Bhaskar Series*. New Delhi ; Thousand Oaks, Calif: Sage Publications..

Lakoff, G., & Johnson, M. (1985). *Metaphors we live by* (5th ed.). Chicago: University of Chicago Press.

Peng, K., & Nisbett, R. (1999). Culture, dialectics, and reasoning about contradiction. *American Psychologist 54*(9), 741–754.

United Nations. *Sustainable Development Goals. United Nations Sustainable Development (blog).* https://www.un.org/sustainabledevelopment/sustainable-development-goals/. Accessed January 8, 2019.

Veraksa, N. E., Belolutskaya, A. K., Vorobyeva, I. I., Krasheninnikov, E. E., Rachkova, E. V., Shiyan, I. B., & Shiyan, O. A. (2013). Structural dialectical approach in psychology: problems and research results. *Psychology in Russia: State of the Art, 6*(2), 65–77. https://doi.org/10.11621/pir.2013.0206.

Wilber, K. (2007). *Integral spirituality: A startling new role for religion in the modern and postmodern world.* Boston, MA: Integral Books.

Working Group on the Anthropocene. *Subcommission on Quaternary Stratigraphy.* http://quaternary.stratigraphy.org/working-groups/anthropocene/. Accessed January 8, 2019.

Appendix

A1: Table of Dialectical Thought Patterns

	***Structural Thinking***
S1	Differentiation of elements in a whole representing a stable entity in its own right
S2	Elaboration of elements with reference to the structure, hierarchy and functionality of the elements
S3	Integration of different elements and perspectives into a structured bigger entity as a system
	***Process Thinking***
P1	Differentiation of a changing element, linking its current state to the past and future
P2	Elaboration of one or more elements in their developmental aspects
P3	Integration of changing and interconnected elements in an unceasing movement as a system
	***Relational Thinking***
R1	Differentiation of relationships between two or more separate elements
R2	Elaboration of specific relationships between interconnected elements
R3	Integration of interconnected elements and their constitutive relationships into an entity as a system
	***Transformational Thinking***
T1	Differentiation of conflicting elements leading to transformation or destruction of a system
T2	Elaboration of the conflicting interaction between two or more elements and their characteristics, potentially involving human agency
T3	Integration of conflicting elements into a new dynamic system, potentially involving human agency

N. Shannon and B. Frischherz, *Metathinking*, Management for Professionals,
https://doi.org/10.1007/978-3-030-41064-3

A2: Dialectical Thinking Cycle

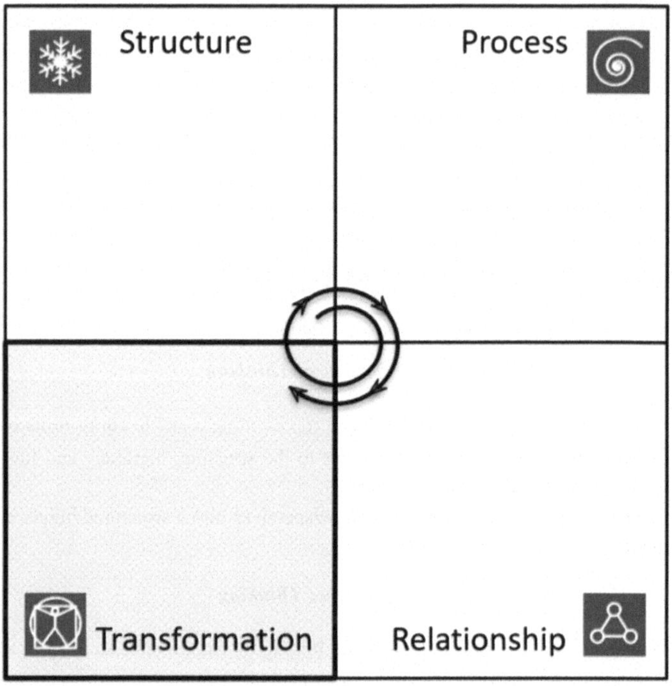

A3: Table of Exercises

Chapter 15. Identifying Dialectical Thought Patterns		
Reading		
• Exercise 15.1a: Comparing three Managers	I, P	*
• Exercise 15.1b: Comparing three Mothers	I, P	*
• Exercise 15.1c: Comparing three Students	I, P	*
• Exercise 15.2: Analysing Interview Excerpts	I, P	**
• Exercise 15.3: Analysing Excerpts from Strategy paper	I, P	***
Listening		
• Exercise 15.4: Analysing Political Speeches	I, P	**
• Exercise 15.5: Dialectical Listening	G	**
Interpreting Images		
• Exercise 15.6: Classifying Logos and Symbols	I, P	*
• Exercise 15.7: Illuminating Unusual Objects	I, P	*
• Exercise 15.8: Classifying Pictures	I, P	*
• Exercise 15.9: Comparing Pictures of a Glacier at Different Moments in Time	I, P	**
Chapter 16. Using Dialectical Thought Patterns		
Inquiring		
• Exercise 16.1: Using Mind Opening Questions to Explore the Thoughts and Feelings of a Partner	P	*
• Exercise 16.2: Analysing a Description of a Problem	P	*
• Exercise 16.3: Formulating Mind Opening Questions	P	**
Dialoguing		
• Exercise 16.4: Integrating Arguments	P	*
• Exercise 16.5: Analysing your Career Description	P	*
• Exercise 16.6: Exploring a Person's Working Life	P	**
Developing		
• Exercise 16.7: Rethinking a Problem	P, G	*
• Exercise 16.8: Making an Important Prediction	I	*
• Exercise 16.9: Developing a Career Strategy	I	**
Chapter 17. Reflecting on Dialectical Thought Patterns		
Illuminating		
• Exercise 17.1: Thinking about Thinking	I, P	**
• Exercise 17.2: Taking a Measure of your Dialectical Thinking	I	*
• Exercise 17.3: Thinking in Metaphors	I, P	**
Evaluating		
• Exercise 17.4: Solving an Ethical Dilemma	I, P	**
• Exercise 17.5: Reflecting on Virtues, Values and Vices	I	***
Self-reflecting		
• Exercise 17.6: Analysing a Description of Yourself	I	*
• Exercise 17.7: Reflecting on the Balance in your Life	I	***
• Exercise 17.8: Exploring your Personal Life	P	**

A4: Proposed Solutions for the Exercises

Exercise 15.1a: Comparing three Managers

1. *Which manager gave the most comprehensive account of the problem that the organisation is facing?*

   Andrew's account focuses on an extension of services (by including maintenance) and the positive impact this may have on reducing prices. He sees greater efficiency as a valuable goal but concludes that it will still be a problem to cut costs and improve quality simultaneously to which he offers no solution.

   Barbara's account also focuses on efficiency but she sees more clearly the upsides and downsides of being a broader "make and maintain" business. She can see the effect of this going two ways, some customers will be attracted but others may be switched off. She then worries about the impact in terms of money and time of improving quality and reducing production costs and wonders whether the organisation can manage all of the initiatives simultaneously.

   Clare, the CEO, notes that complexity has been increased both internally and externally. Internally, workers will have to change their ways of working and a new financial system will be required. Externally, new approaches may need to be taken to ensure customers understand the value of the company's products and services. She conceptualises the challenge as one of coordinating a large number of interrelated subsystems and wonders whether she has the resource to see and understand all of these simultaneously.

   It can be seen from the above that Clare sees the greatest level of complexity in the challenges facing the company. She alone conceptualises the problem in terms of interacting dynamic systems. Andrew takes the positive impact on customers for granted. He can see the tension between cutting costs and improving quality but does not go any deeper than simply stating the problem. Barbara has a more sophisticated view of the impact on customers and can see how management resources may be stretched but, again, stops short of defining the task facing management.
2. *Which manager displayed the broadest variety of thinking modes in their account?*

   When we look at what Andrew said, we find it hard to see him describing parts of a systemic whole, movements and changes within a system, relationships between different parts of the system or potential transformations. At best, he notices a bigger picture in terms of how increasing services may impact prices and picks up on the relationship between the provision of a maintenance service and knowledge about the usage and lifecycle of their products.

   Barbara, however, is able to see the bigger picture of a make and maintain business with its upsides and downsides. She speaks about juggling many things at once, as though there were many changing and interconnected elements moving together. And she sees a tension between the positive view that customers have of a combined manufacturing and maintenance business with the negative view that they might take of the act of maintaining competitors' products. These points, although not fully articulated, are suggestive that she sees the potential for form of transformation.

Clare immediately takes a systemic and structural view by identifying many uncertain ramifications as a result of the merger. Assumptions that previously could be taken for granted were now up for question, highlighting the movement inherent in the organisation's systems. And she has started to see that there are many complex relationships which she has to take into account. Finally, she also explicitly references the unpredictable nature of the transformation of subsystems.

Therefore, overall Clare displays all four thinking modes in contrast to Barbara, who manages to think in terms the structural and process thinking modes, with a partial nod towards transformation, whilst Andrew is focused solely on structural thinking.

3. *What was missing or absent in terms of thinking modes from the accounts given by the other two managers?*

   Andrew's brief description of the problem facing the organisation is missing the process thinking mode because he fails to highlight the dynamic nature of the changes being made. He also fails to demonstrate transformational thinking because his account stops short of identifying how the tension between driving costs down and improving quality could result in, on the one hand, collapse of the previous system, or on the other a developmental advance.

   Whilst Barbara hints at potential transformation, she fails to highlight the complex interrelationships between different functions in the organisation or between internal and external aspects such as retraining the sales force to deal more effectively with customers and engendering improvements in the engineering and production functions.

Exercise 15.1b: Comparing Three Mothers

1. *Which mother gave the most coherent account of the changes in their relationship with their daughter?*

   Amanda complains that her daughter has rejected everything she taught her. She considers the problem in binary fashion. Either she is at fault as a parent, or her own value system is faulty and therefore her daughter is right to reject it and Amanda is not worthy of her respect. Amanda's thinking locates herself as the unique source of the problem.

   Brenda starts from the same position as Amanda, but instead of blaming herself, finds a way to accept that she and her daughter have different value systems. Brenda follows a "live and let live" philosophy and adheres to the value that the most important thing is to respect her daughter despite their differences, not realising that this too could be source of difference.

   Charlotte also starts from the same position as Amanda and Brenda, but she situates values within a particular social context. Moreover, she recognises as the social context changes there is an evolution in people's values, which reciprocally impacts the evolution of the social context. Rather than seeing the situation as a problem of either her or her daughter's making, she finds a way to accept the situation and to see what she can learn as a result.

   It may strike you that Charlotte's response is somewhat more satisfactory than those of Amanda and Brenda. Amanda ends up feeling guilty and inadequate, whilst Brenda (who like Charlotte finds a way to accept the situation) just gives up on trying to understand or reconcile the differences between her daughter and herself.

2. *Which mother displayed the broadest variety of thinking modes in their account?*

   Charlotte quickly notices that things are very different for her daughter to when she was at her daughter's age. There has been a movement in the social context, and she can appreciate that different contexts give rise to different values. Consequently, she has engaged both the structural and the process thinking modes. However, she does not stop there, she notices that her daughter's values must have evolved from her own, and that her daughter has transformed these to fit better with the times she lives in. Hence, she has applied transformational thinking. Evidence of relational thinking is, perhaps, less obvious. She might have used this mode to elaborate on how society and individual values are linked and reciprocally influence each other.

3. *What was missing or absent in terms of thinking modes from the accounts given by the other two mothers?*

   Neither Amanda nor Brenda managed to apply any of the thinking modes. Amanda's thinking was stuck in a logical "either/or" dichotomy, whilst Brenda simply sees values as arbitrary and neither related to specific contexts nor linked to a particular pattern of change.

Exercise 15.1c: Comparing Three Students

(a) *Which student showed the most understanding about the position of the authorities setting the coursework for students?*

Arthur locates the authorities as the source of the problem and tries to rationalise their action in terms of their having sufficient and knowledge and experience to know best. However, he cannot reconcile their perspective with his own and the two perspectives are incompatible to him. If one is right, the other must be wrong.

Barry takes the line that the college authorities are approaching the issue from their own idiosyncratic perspective and are out of touch with what is best for his generation of students. He sees the standardised assessment and grading system as incompatible with him being creative.

Colin sees the incompatibility as lying in the dual goals of the college authorities, on the one hand to grade students for the benefit of future employers, and on the other to inspire learning. However, he is able to situate that incompatibility within a context of the relationship between employers and college authorities. Unlike his fellow students, he does not see that incompatibility as irreconcilable, but instead believes that he might be able to do something about it.

We can see that Colin has the most nuanced view of the authorities' position. For him, it is not simply a matter of right or wrong, nor is it just a question of intergenerational differences, as Barry suggests. He sees the issue arising out of different relationships which lead to different goals for the authorities. Moreover, he believes that if one of the relationships is changed, then the problem might be solved.

(b) *Which student displayed the broadest variety of thinking modes in their account?*

Arthur takes a very limited perspective based on the formal logic of the incompatibility of "right" and "wrong". Barry goes a bit further by recognising that the college authorities and students have differing perspectives, but he is not up to seeing how these perspectives might evolve, nor how they might be in relationship to the needs of the different stakeholders. Colin is able to see transformational possibilities relating to potential shifts in the relationship between the authorities and employers. He makes use of all the thinking modes, noticing how the situation contains opposites in tension (process), different perspective (structure), and is constituted by relationships. This enables him to realise the possibility of transformation. He might, however, have elaborated on the evolving nature of student and employers' needs by way of giving a more complete account in the process thinking mode.

(c) *What was missing or absent in terms of thinking modes from the accounts given by the other two students?*

Being apparently locked into logical thinking, Arthur's account seems to lack all of the thinking modes. Barry is able to muster the structural thinking mode in terms of the different perspectives, but does not engage either process, relationship or transformational thinking.

Exercise 15.2: Analysing Interview Excerpts

Number	Comment	Thought pattern
#01	There are three predominant thinking modes here. The speaker starts of by noting that his personal development is the link between the work he does for his client and for himself privately—a relationship thought pattern. He then anticipates how he wishes to change financially and professionally—a process thought pattern. Finally, he notes that there are limits to the extent of his development in his work with his client—a structural thought pattern indicating system stability	R1 P1 S1
#02	Principally structural thinking. The speaker describes three different aspects of his professional development, developing a new training product, developing a coaching methodology and developing his competence as a leadership coach and consultant. Structurally, these are elements of his "development system"	S3
#03	There is evidence of transformational thinking here. The speaker discusses the tension between his spiritual desire to renew himself and the painful emotions that such an idea invokes for him, saying—"personally it is something very painful". He then talks about wanting to re-align with where he wants to go which means that, for the present, he must find a role with his client where he is not facing political opposition and can also pursue his personal projects	T2
#04	There is a great deal of ambiguity in what the speaker says in these two excerpts. On the one hand, the relationship with a partner appears to be over, and on the other the speaker appears to believe that the relationship continues. The speaker also refers to the ambiguity inherent in his partner's request to be left alone, a request that is ignored for a while. The sense of the ebb and flow of the relationship is typical of the process thinking mode, where the interaction between the speaker and his partner as two changing and interconnected elements is typical of the third process thought pattern	P3
#05	The speaker begins by immediately acknowledging the common ground between his development in a personal relationship and his development at work. This is the relational thinking mode. He then goes on to distinguish the development that an individual can achieve on his or her own, from development that can occur within an interaction with another person. This is structural thinking—that of different contexts for development. He then relates personal development (in terms of developing self-esteem) to development that occurs in concert with another person (using the metaphor of learning to dance). This is a transformational thought pattern because the speaker is talking about the integration of two different systems of development	R1 S3 T3

Exercise 15.3: Analysing Excerpts from Strategy Paper

Number	Text excerpt	Thought pattern
#01	The text is relational thinking. It elaborates on the relationship between subsidy reform and the economic well-being of poor communities. The removal of subsidies is thought to disproportionally hurt low income groups because of related price increases in basic goods, which make up a large part of spending for such groups	R2
#02	The text describes three different ways in which certain types of subsidies (green subsidies) could support a shift from a brown economy to a green economy. This is logical thinking because it implies direct causal links without specifying other potential relationship and knock-on consequences or defining the contexts in which these subsidies would have the desired effect	logic
#03	The text compares two methods of government intervention to bring a shift towards a green economy, regulation or market-based instruments (creating incentives for polluters to reduce their negative impact). It points out the limitations of the latter and the advantages of the former. The advantages of the former are viewed as being context-dependent, a structural thinking pattern	S2
#04	The text describes two multilateral environmental agreements (MEAs) that have led to the development of green economy industries that are working to create a more sustainable environment and highlights the renewal of a post-Kyoto framework for carbon as the most important factor influencing the scale and speed of the change—the process thinking mode	P1
#05	The text summarises conditions for a transformation to a green economy by pointing to an implicit tension or conflict between historical investment in non-sustainable activities on the one hand and green investment on the other. The author suggests that policy reform can create the incentive for a re-allocation of investment by disadvantaging the former in favour of the latter. In addition, the text suggests that investment in (hitherto neglected) natural resources and technologies should be integrated with investments in human capital and greening-related knowledge. Although the text is not strongly explicit, it is an example of transformational thinking because it highlights the tension between one system and another (T1), and suggests integrating systems to achieve the transformation (T3)	T1, T3

Exercise 15.4a: Analysing Political Speeches—Nelson Mandela

Number	Comment	Thought pattern
#01	Mandela comments that he has always regarded himself as an African patriot. Here he is making a claim regarding the stability of the system that relates him to his country. In addition, he cites his relationship to certain prominent citizens as evidence. This is therefore a structural thought pattern	S1
#02	In this passage about his attraction to a classless society, Mandela links the past, in terms of how early African societies were organised, with the present, his assessment of the current inequality of South African society, and a future that he is fighting for, a return to classlessness. He is implicitly recognising the changing nature of society, a process thought pattern. However, he is also referencing the structure of society—land belongs to a tribe, and there are no rich or poor. Hence, there is also an element of structural thinking involved here	P1, S1
#03	Here Mandela draws a parallel between himself and famous leaders such as Gandhi in terms of the influence that Marx has had on them. Hence, he identifies a relationship, a form of common ground between them and him	R1
#04	Having set out his fundamental belief in a socialist ideal, Mandela seeks to integrate political thinking from both East and West. His political philosophy is a stable system integrating different perspectives. Structural thinking	S3
#05	He then describes and critiques the stability of the current political system that keeps whites rich and Africans poor—more evidence of structural thinking. He also draws our attention to relationships—the relationship between whites and Africans, the relationship between rich and poor, and the relationship between these categories, which are united by the common ground of living in South Africa	S1, R1
#06	Mandela argues that political division based on colour can give way to a society that is more inclusive since racial domination will no longer exist. He sees a conflict in terms of the fear that whites have for democracy on the one hand, and the establishment of racial harmony and freedom on the other. He sees the fight against racial discrimination succeeding, ultimately resulting in a transformation of the social system. Here he identifies the conflicting elements and how they will lead to social transformation. The justification for the ANC's fight is to have the same rights as whites—the right to live	T1
#7	Finally, Mandela re-iterates his dedication to the fight against any kind of racial domination in the pursuit of the ideal of a more developed society where people live in harmony with equal opportunities. He elaborates on the conflict as one where he is prepared to sacrifice his life	T2

Exercise 15.4b: Analysing Political Speeches—Tony Blair

Number	Comment	Thought pattern
#01	Blair begins by identifying common ground with his audience "Ireland is in my blood". He and the Irish people might see themselves as different, but they share a common ground. Relational thinking	R1
#02	He goes on to elaborate the relationship in more detail. It exists because of common invasions leading to monastic divisions. He then points out that these monastic divisions led to later trouble. Here Blair develops the relationship thought pattern in the previous excerpt and then adds a process thought pattern by noting how monastic divisions changed from being a solution to being a problem	R2, P1
#03	Blair continues to elaborate on the common ground between Irish and British—both suffered, were persecuted and disenfranchised. But a system has arisen of institutional links between the two parliaments, i.e. interconnected elements now make up a system with "shared history, shared pain and shared hope"	R3
#04	Blair now shifts back to the process thinking mode. He talks about slow change "progress is being made, but slowly". However, a significant change has occurred, he says "politics is replacing violence as the way people do business" and there is now the prospect of long-term peace. Hence, he sees the political and social systems changing and developing	P2
#05	Now Blair outlines a number of new political structures that are aimed at transforming Irish and British relations. One of these involves the release of prisoners which is still an issue of conflict. He argues that the Good Friday agreement would not have come about unless the release of prisoners had been allowed. By combining the conflicting elements into a new system, Blair believes that the Irish situation is being transformed	T3
#06	In this passage, Blair calls for integrated action to transform Ireland —a "new era of cooperation" between Northern Ireland and the Irish Republic. This call to action involves living up to commitments and the creation of new structures between the conflicting elements of North and South, with guns and the threat of guns put aside. He then points again to common ground—"In Belfast or Dublin, people say the same thing"	T3, R3
#07	Blair continues to draw out relationships. This time he identifies children, who although untouched by violence, are also victims	R1
#08	Structural thinking and process thinking are linked together in this passage where Blair identifies the different perspectives of the different parties, and how these have changed over time. Perspectives are influenced by the shifting context, hence he says "we need not be prisoners of our history"	S3, P1

Exercise 15.6: Classifying Logos and Symbols

1.	R	Sustainability is dependent on people working together in relationship
2.	P	Sustainability is like a continuous circle of recycling materials
3.	T	Sustainability is about transforming our sources of energy
4.	S	Sustainability is founded on the three pillars of social, environmental and economic considerations
5.	P	Sustainability is like a process combining social and environmental elements
6.	S	Sustainability is like an ever growing spiral
7.	R	Sustainability is dependent on the relationship with water, without which there could be no life on the planet
8.	T	Sustainability is a function of how humans cultivate the earth
9.	S	Sustainability is a matter of seeing the economy in the context of society, which itself must be seen in the context of the environment
10.	T	Sustainability is a question of how humans make their mark on the planet
11.	P	Sustainability is a continuous cycle between social, environmental, and economic elements
12.	R	Sustainability is like balancing the relationship between different countries and parts of the earth
13.	T	Sustainability is like positively managing the impact of the waste that humans produce
14.	R	Sustainability is a function of multiple interactive relationships
15.	S	Sustainability is at the intersection between economy, environment and society
16.	T	Sustainability is dependent on how wisely money is spent to manage the impact of humans on the planet

Exercise 15.7: Illuminating Unusual Objects

1. The object in the photograph is the lens of a lighthouse light, a so called "Fresnel" lens after the name of its inventor. It is made from a series of glass prisms in a brass framework. This particular lens was found in the Museum of the History of Riga and Navigation, in Latvia. Structurally speaking, the context for such an object is that of lighthouses, or more generally, locations where very powerful lights are needed. In terms of process thinking, one might say that this kind of light has evolved from the early use of torches and fires on hills over-looking the sea, and developed with the inventions, first of gas lights, and then electric lights. For the future, such lights might be superseded by the use of GPS systems with warnings. One can draw relationships between this kind of light and other warning systems, such as fog horns for example. Thinking transformationally, one might consider other uses for such light technology extending towards things like optic fibres, or architectural lighting in buildings, or alternatively the design of glass jewellery.
2. The suitcase, made out of concrete, is part of an art installation at the Museum of Occupations in Tallinn, Estonia. It conjures up ideas of travel, immigration and emigration, and movement but at the same time its concrete weight and solidity give it a feeling of permanence. Thinking structurally, one can position the suitcase in a social and political context where people had either the freedom to travel, or were prevented from doing so, and to a period historically before suitcases had wheels. Such thoughts take us into the process thinking mode where we can consider how suitcases have evolved over the years, and the relational thinking mode where we think of other forms of luggage such as rucksacks or baskets. Thinking transformationally, one might consider the tension between travelling and staying in the same place which raises ideas about "virtual" travel, partly experienced by reading or watching films about travel.
3. This sign was photographed at the river Pärnu in Latvia. It is an astonishingly simple graphic that conveys a strong message prohibiting the drinking of alcohol and swimming. We can speculate on the social structures that give rise to the demand for such a sign, and also on the different kind of locations where it might be found, most commonly rivers and public swimming pools. We can also think in terms of process about the historical antecedents of such signs, perhaps a high incidence of anti-social or dangerous behaviour, and also about other possible signs to prohibit other kinds of unsafe behaviour. We can relate this kind of sign to other types of symbolic messaging from verbal warnings to informational videos or the presence of life-guards preventing access to people carrying alcohol. Transformationally, we might think about the role such signs have in controlling and developing social behaviour, how drinking has been restricted at certain times and in certain places, and how "free" people are in society to behave as they wish if it brings disapproval from others.

Exercise 15.8: Classifying Pictures

1.	Process	The river is changing all the time but retains its identity as a unique river in itself
2.	Relationship	The picture highlights family relationships. These may be of many different kinds: parents, grandparents, siblings; relations of love and hate, etc.
3.	Structural	The functionality of a watch is signified by reference to parts within the whole, its mechanism
4.	Transformation	The dynamic interaction of the sun, the earth's movement and the ecosystem creates the transformative phenomenon of weather
5.	Relationship	The forest is formed by interrelationships between soil, air, rain, plants and animals, which form together the ecosystem
6.	Process	The magnolia tree undergoes constant change, flowering in spring and fading in summer
7.	Structural	The rocky outgroup has a well-defined structure with constituent parts
8.	Process	The baby desert tortoise emerges from its past on its way to becoming an adult
9.	Transformation	A football game is an elaborated form of a conflict with both planned strategies and spontaneous interactions
10.	Relationship	The pyramid juxtaposed against the Louvre museum points to the relationship between monumental architectures from different eras
11.	Structural	The anatomic model of a human body shows the form and position of the organs that make up the whole
12.	Transformation	People protest in opposition to a government. The conflict may or may not result in transformation to a new political system

Exercise 16.4: Integrating Arguments

Here, we present a worked example as a guide for you to follow on the topic: It is right that people should be able to choose their gender, male, female or something in between?

Pro/Thesis	Contra/Antithesis
Social conditions (such as patriarchy and commercial pressures) are responsible for forcing people to adopt a particular gender, sometimes against their personal sense of identity Many people do not identify with the gender aligned to their biological sex, but instead identify with their opposite sex Some people are born with mixed sex organs, whilst others experience a change in sex during their early life. Hence gender is not fixed Many other species exhibit the capacity to change biological sex, nature does not establish sex at birth exclusively as either male or female	The vast majority of people identify with the gender aligned with their biological sex. Those that do not are the minority exception, as are those that experience ambiguity or change of sex Identity, whether gender or not, is not solely a matter for individuals. It is determined through agreement with others in the community Research shows that sex differences result in consistent differences in interests (males in things, females in people) which transcend social influences. Other research shows that infants younger than 1 year show different interests related to their sex
Synthesis	
There are a variety of influences on people's sense of gender, some biological some social. As the human species evolves, one may expect variations in the relative contributions that each of these factors makes to how people construct their identity. Ultimately, such changes will stand or fail due to the test of time. Hence, natural processes will eventually determine whether a shift towards a more fluid sense of human gender identity becomes established. For the present, we may expect a degree of conflict between people holding opposing views with the final outcome indeterminate.	

Exercise 17.2: Taking a Measure of your Dialectical Thinking

Score Sheet

Transfer your circles from the questionnaire itself onto the score sheet below and total the scores in each column. Notice how your scores for the three categories of response vary.

Question	Absolute	Relative	Dialectical
1	b	c	a
2	c	a	b
3	a	c	b
4	c	b	a
5	a	b	c
6	b	a	c
7	a	b	c
8	c	a	b
9	b	c	a
10	a	c	b
11	b	a	c
12	c	b	a
13	b	c	a
14	a	b	c
Total			

The responses have been categorised according to three different types of thinking:

Absolute—which is to say that the response indicates your thinking that there is a single, correct point of view on the issue.

Relative—which is to say that the response indicates your thinking that there may be more than one correct point of view and the issue will depend on certain circumstances.

Dialectical—which is to say that the response indicates your thinking that the issue has a dynamic and potentially contradictory character, with the capacity for transformation in a positive or negative direction.

Exercise 17.3: Thinking in Metaphors

	Structural Thinking	
BUSINESS	AS	MACHINE
Employees	AS	Parts
Defined processes	AS	Movements of the machine
Management mistake	AS	Malfunctions of the machine

The metaphor BUSINESS as MACHINE implies that you can design and run a company according to a blueprint. Structures and processes are defined, planned and then implemented. Management is a scientific discipline. A good machine works smoothly. The employees are functioning parts of the system. Management mistakes lead to machine failure and must be prevented if possible.

The metaphor BUSINESS as MACHINE emphasizes that companies are planned and managed according to scientific criteria and should function smoothly. The metaphor obscures the fact that people with different knowledge and interests must work together in the company.

	Process Thinking	
BUSINESS	AS	PLANT
Employees	AS	Stem, branches, leaves
Increase in sales	AS	Natural growth
Profit, gain	AS	Fruits

The metaphor BUSINESS as PLANT implies that companies emerge, blossom and perish like a plant. The employees are organic parts of a larger entity. Healthy companies grow. There are seasons, i.e. good and bad phases for a company. After the phase of growth and ripeness comes the harvest, when the ripe fruits are picked. The market is the natural environment of a company. Adaptation to the environment is necessary, because only the strongest survive.

The metaphor BUSINESS as PLANT emphasizes that business is a natural process. There is growth, maturity and harvest. Adaptation to the environment is necessary. The metaphor obscures the fact that the development of a company also depends on personal decisions, internal power relations and the legal framework.

	Relational Thinking	
BUSINESS	AS	FAMILY
Employees	AS	Parents, children, siblings
Network of people	AS	Relatives, genealogy
Founder	AS	Father, Mother

The metaphor BUSINESS as FAMILY implies that a company needs founding figures like a father or mother. Companies have a family tree. The family is a community of destiny whose members support each other even in bad times. The company never lets its employees down and offers its employees a warm, human culture in which they can feel comfortable.

The metaphor BUSINESS as FAMILY emphasizes mutual support among employees and human warmth. The metaphor hides the fact that there is often a strict hierarchy in the family and that children sometimes remain dependent on their parents even in adulthood.

	Transformational Thinking	
BUSINESS	AS	ORCHESTRA
Employees	AS	Musicians
Entrepreneur, manager	AS	Conductor
Performance	AS	Concert

The metaphor BUSINESS as ORCHESTRA implies that the interaction of employees is crucial for success. Although there are soloists and first, second and third voices, the decisive factor is the perfect interaction of all participants under the direction of the conductor. The conductor orchestrates, coordinates, and acts as a role model for the music. Competence is more important than hierarchy. There are classical orchestras, but also jazz combos and amateur bands. The decisive factor is the joint performance and the joy of music.

The metaphor BUSINESS as ORCHESTRA emphasizes that all employees in different roles work towards the common performance. The metaphor hides the fact that behind the creative, artistic product there are often clear hierarchies and a lot of hard work.

Exercise 17.5: Reflection on Virtues, Values, and Vices

1. Goal-oriented I know exactly what I want. In groups, normally, I push through my ideas	**3. Relaxed** These indifferent people seem to be quite relaxed. When they just chat together, sometimes they develop new ideas

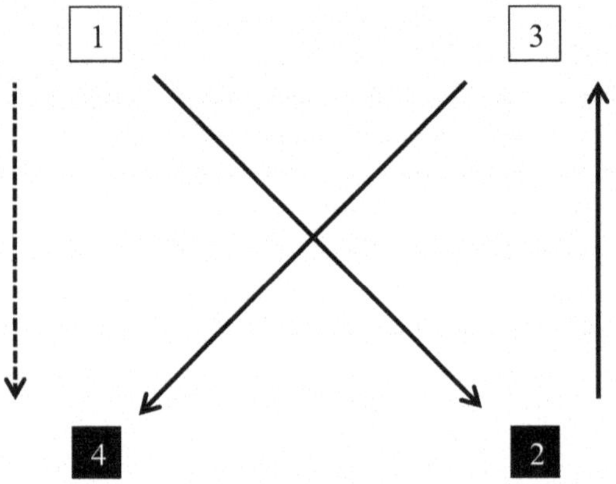

4. Dogmatic The downside of a goal-oriented person such as myself is that sometimes I am dogmatic and do not see new aspects of a topic	**2. Indifferent** I often have conflicts with indifferent and unmotivated, indifferent people. They are not reliable as partners in projects

A5: Picture Credits

Figure 2.1	Yin-Yang symbol (© Wikipedia) https://en.wikipedia.org/wiki/Yin_and_yang
Figure 2.2	Types of thinking (own representation based on Laske, 2008, 179)
Figure 3.1	Snowflake (© Alexey Kljatov/Wikimedia) https://commons.wikimedia.org/w/index.php?curid=39993014 All quadrants, all levels AQAL (own representation based on Wilber, 2005, 26)
Figure 4.1	Cyclone Catarina (© Pixabay) https://pixabay.com/en/tropical-cyclone-catarina-1167137/ Evolving Self (own representation based on Kegan, 2001, 109)
Figure 5.1	Paramecium (© Wikimedia) https://commons.wikimedia.org/wiki/Category:Paramecium?uselang=de-ch#/media/File:Mikrofoto.de-Gruenes_Pantoffeltier_2.jpg Perspectives in Dialog (own representation based on McNab, 2005, 127)
Figure 6.1	Geyser (© Wikipedia) https://en.wikipedia.org/wiki/Geyser#/media/File:Strokkur_geyser_eruption,_close-up_view.jpg Complete U (own representation based on Scharmer, 2009, 38)
Figure 7.1	Necker cube (own representation)
Figure 7.2	How Metathinking can transform thought (own representation)
Figure 7.3	Dialectical thinking cycle (own representation) (© Nick Shannon & Bruno Frischherz 2020. All rights reserved)
Figure 8.1	Integral quadrants (own representation based on Wilber, 2005, 26)
Figure 8.2	Integral quadrants and thinking modes combined (own representation)
Figure 8.3	Holarchy: individual—team—organisation—society (own representation)
Figure 9.1	Topics of the cognitive interview (own representation based on Laske, 2008, 277)
Figure 9.2	Sonja's cognitive footprints I and II (own representation)
Figure 10.1	Teambuilding topics mapped against quadrants (own representation)
Figure 11.1	Digital transformation: structure (© Altimeter) https://www.flickr.com/photos/altimetergroup/13716509913
Figure 11.2	Digital transformation: process (adapted from © Wikipedia) https://de.wikipedia.org/wiki/Datei:Die_digitale_Transformation_in_Unternehmen.png
Figure 11.3	Digital transformation: relationship (adapted from © Wikimedia) https://commons.wikimedia.org/wiki/File:Digitale_Transformation.png
Figure 11.4	Digital transformation: transformation (© Gerd Leonhard) https://www.flickr.com/photos/gleonhard/16474476590
Figure 11.5	Thinking profile: The nine elements of digital transformation (own representation)
Figure 11.6	Thinking profile: Why so many high-profile digital transformations fail (own representation)
Figure 11.7	Thinking profile: The onlife manifesto (own representation)
Figure 11.8	Davos panel discussion 2016: Thinking profile (own representation)
Figure 11.9	Thinking profile of each participant of the panel discussion (own representation)
Figure 12.1	Life expectancy (own representation based on OECD 2018)
Figure 12.2	Infant mortality (own representation based on OECD 2018)

(continued)

(continued)

Figure 12.3	Absence from work due to illness (days) (own representation based on OECD 2018)
Figure 12.4	Share of gross domestic product (own representation based on OECD 2018)
Figure 12.5	Perceived health status, females aged 15+ (own representation based on OECD 2018)
Figure 12.6	Perceived health status, males aged 15+ (own representation based on OECD 2018)
Figure 12.7	Thinking modes in lead texts on health care (NZZ 2017, n = 104) (own representation)
Figure 13.1	Metathinking: all quadrants, all thinking modes (AQAT) (own representation)
Figure 15.1	Symbols of sustainability (adapted from Google Search "Sustainability") (© Nick Shannon and Bruno Frischherz 2020. All rights reserved)
Figure 15.2	Unusual objects (© Bruno Frischherz)
Figure 15.3	Thought patterns in images 1: Aldeyjarfoss (© LalouBLue) https://pixabay.com/en/aldeyjarfoss-iceland-cascade-roche-2676792/ 2: The Big Family Portrait (© sflovestory) https://www.flickr.com/photos/sflovestory/3138083817 3: Clockwork (© ephotographythemes) https://pixabay.com/en/clockwork-movement-watch-mechanic-471760/ 4: Sky (© Tama66) https://pixabay.com/en/sky-clouds-rays-sun-hope-sunbeam-1107952/ 5: Forest (© MemoryCatcher) https://pixabay.com/en/forest-trees-ecology-environment-272595/ 6: Magnolia (© javallma) https://pixabay.com/en/magnolia-blossom-bloom-spring-pink-2218165/ 7: Rock (© 3282700) https://pixabay.com/en/rock-nature-landscape-structure-1674188/ 8: Baby Desert Tortoise (© U.S. Geological Survey/Wikimedia) https://upload.wikimedia.org/wikipedia/commons/1/1e/Baby_Desert_Tortoise_%2816490346262%29.jpg 9: Football (© KeithJJ) https://pixabay.com/en/football-line-of-scrimmage-linemen-1531667/ 10: Louvre (© EdiNugraha) https://pixabay.com/en/louvre-pyramid-paris-architecture-102840/ 11: Anatomical (© www_slon_pics) https://pixabay.com/en/anatomical-anatomy-body-gut-health-2261006/ 12: Protest (© niekverlaan) https://pixabay.com/en/protest-protest-action-464616/
Figure 15.4	Two views of the Briksdal Glacier, Norway 2003 and 2008 (© Ximonic, Simo Räsänen/Wikimedia) https://de.wikipedia.org/wiki/Datei:Briksdalsbreen_Norway_2003_%26_2008.JPG
Figure 17.1	Value square (own representation based on Schulz von Thun et al., 2003, 53)
Figure 17.2	Four dimensions of good life (own representation based on Seel, 1999)
Figure 18.1	Transformation in and across integral quadrants (own representation) (© Nick Shannon and Bruno Frischherz 2020. All rights reserved)
Figure 18.2	Role of leadership in organisational transformation (own representation)

Glossary

Abductive Thinking Abductive thinking is the process of deriving a possible conclusion from a set of individual cases. Abductive conclusions are potentially but not necessarily true.

Deductive Thinking Deductive thinking is the process of deriving a particular conclusion from a set of general premises or rules. Deductive conclusions are always true.

Dialectical Thinking Dialectical thinking is the generic term for structural, process, relational and transformative thinking (SPiRiT). The use of the four thinking modes can be conscious or not.

Dialectical Thinking Cycle The dialectical thinking cycle is the thinking process that systematically and repeatedly applies the four thinking modes—SPiRiT.

Dialogue Dialogue is a verbal interaction between people in which the thinking of two or more participants develops through questions and answers.

Inductive Thinking Inductive thinking is the process of deriving a general conclusion or rule from a set of particular cases. Inductive conclusions are considered always true until otherwise discovered.

Logical Thinking We use logical thinking as the generic term for inductive, deductive and abductive thinking.

Metathinking Metathinking is the deliberate use of different thinking modes (logical and—of course—dialectical thinking modes).

Metathinking Framework The Metathinking Framework is our combination of Wilber's integral quadrants for the structure of content and dialectical thinking modes for the thinking process.

Mind Opening Questions Mind opening questions are questions that develop a person's thinking.

Process Thinking Process thinking is based on the principle of dynamism and describes how reality changes continuously.

N. Shannon and B. Frischherz, *Metathinking*, Management for Professionals,
https://doi.org/10.1007/978-3-030-41064-3

Relational Thinking Relational thinking is based on the principle of common ground and describes how everything is connected.

SPiRiT SPiRiT is the abbreviation for the four thinking modes: **S**tructural thinking, **P**rocess thinking, **R**elational thinking and **T**ransformational thinking.

Structural Thinking Structural thinking is based on the principle of holism and describes how the whole is created through the interplay of its parts.

System A set of things that are connected together to make up a whole with properties that are greater than the sum of its parts.

Thinking Mode A thinking mode is a subclass of logical thinking or dialectical thinking. We distinguish four modes of dialectical thinking: structural thinking, process thinking, relational thinking and transformational thinking.

Thought Pattern Thought patterns are typical forms of thinking. For each of the four modes of dialectical thinking, we distinguish three thought patterns: differentiation, elaboration and integration.

Transformational Thinking Transformational thinking is based on the principle of development and describes reality as change through forms.

Index

N. Shannon and B. Frischherz, *Metathinking*, Management for Professionals,
https://doi.org/10.1007/978-3-030-41064-3

About the Authors

Nick Shannon is a chartered psychologist who works with organisations to help them select and develop high-performance senior managers and senior management teams. He provides coaching, mentoring, facilitation and talent management services as a consultant. He has a particular interest in adult developmental psychology and the cognitive and emotional transitions that managers must make in order to work successfully at higher levels of complexity and hierarchy.

He has broad-based business experience having started his career in 1979 as precious metals and soft commodities physical and futures dealer. He subsequently went on to be a trader in financial futures and other derivatives. Later, he moved into management and for 7 years led the growth of a highly successful London-based foreign exchange business. Convinced that the most fascinating and challenging issues in business were those arising from the selection, development and management of people, he subsequently moved into consultancy and has spent the last 21 years working with a broad portfolio of clients.

He has an MA in Psychology and Philosophy from the Oxford University, an M. Sc. in Organisational Psychology from the Birkbeck University and an MBA from the Open University. e-mail: nick.shannon@metathinking.org

Bruno Frischherz is a senior lecturer at the Lucerne University of Applied Sciences and Arts for almost 20 years. He teaches modules in communication, ethics and science theory. His special interests are in digital ethics, adult development and discourse and text analysis.

He studied German language and literature, philosophy and education and has a doctorate in Linguistics from the University of Freiburg (Switzerland). After completing his studies, he worked as a lecturer at the university's language centre for about 10 years, leading language courses and teacher trainings. In 2000, he moved to the Lucerne School of Business, where he still works today. He is also a master certified developmental consultant at the Interdevelopmental Institute, Gloucester, MA, founded by Otto Laske.

He founded his own consulting company in 1999, which offers coaching and further education. His specialities are philosophy courses and reading groups for lay people.

N. Shannon and B. Frischherz, *Metathinking*, Management for Professionals,
https://doi.org/10.1007/978-3-030-41064-3

He has published numerous books and articles on rhetoric, conversation, image and text communication, business ethics, integrity management and personal self-reflection. e-mail: bruno.frischherz@metathinking.org

Additional information about Metathinking and the work of Nick Shannon and Bruno Frischherz can be found at https://metathinking.org

The manufacturer's authorised representative in the EU is Springer Nature Customer Service Centre GmbH, Europaplatz 3, 69115 Heidelberg, Germany. If you have any concerns regarding our products, please contact ProductSafety@springernature.com

Printed and bound by CPI Group (UK) Ltd, Croydon, CR0 4YY
30/09/2026
02225452-0007